Learning jQuery

Better Interaction Design and Web Development with Simple JavaScript Techniques

Jonathan Chaffer

Karl Swedberg

BIRMINGHAM - MUMBAI

Learning jQuery

Better Interaction Design and Web Development with Simple JavaScript Techniques

Copyright © 2007 Packt Publishing

All rights reserved. No part of this book may be reproduced, stored in a retrieval system, or transmitted in any form or by any means, without the prior written permission of the publisher, except in the case of brief quotations embedded in critical articles or reviews.

Every effort has been made in the preparation of this book to ensure the accuracy of the information presented. However, the information contained in this book is sold without warranty, either express or implied. Neither the authors, Packt Publishing, nor its dealers or distributors will be held liable for any damages caused or alleged to be caused directly or indirectly by this book.

Packt Publishing has endeavored to provide trademark information about all the companies and products mentioned in this book by the appropriate use of capitals. However, Packt Publishing cannot guarantee the accuracy of this information.

First published: June 2007

Production Reference: 1220607

Published by Packt Publishing Ltd.
32 Lincoln Road
Olton
Birmingham, B27 6PA, UK.

ISBN 978-1-847192-50-9

www.packtpub.com

Cover Image by Karl Swedberg (karl@learningjquery.com)

Credits

Authors

Jonathan Chaffer

Karl Swedberg

Reviewers

Jörn Zaefferer

Dave Methvin

Paul Bakaus

Dan Bravender

Mike Alsup

Senior Acquisition Editor

Douglas Paterson

Assistant Development Editor

Nikhil Bangera

Technical Editor

Bansari Barot

Editorial Manager

Dipali Chittar

Project Manager

Patricia Weir

Project Coordinator

Abhijeet Deobhakta

Indexer

Bhushan Pangaonkar

Proofreader

Chris Smith

Production Coordinator

Shantanu Zagade

Cover Designer

Shantanu Zagade

About the Authors

Jonathan Chaffer is the Chief Technology Officer of Structure Interactive, an interactive agency located in Grand Rapids, Michigan. There he oversees web development projects using a wide range of technologies, and continues to collaborate on day-to-day programming tasks as well.

In the open-source community, Jonathan has been very active in the Drupal CMS project, which has adopted jQuery as its JavaScript framework of choice. He is the creator of the Content Construction Kit, a popular module for managing structured content on Drupal sites. He is responsible for major overhauls of Drupal's menu system and developer API reference.

Jonathan lives in Grand Rapids with his wife, Jennifer.

I would like to thank Jenny, who thinks this is wonderful even if it bores her to tears. I'd also like to thank Karl for sharing my love for linguistics, producing a book that hopefully is grammatically immaculate enough to cover up any technical sins.

Karl Swedberg is a web developer at Structure Interactive in Grand Rapids, Michigan, where he spends much of his time implementing design with a focus on web standards—semantic HTML, well-mannered CSS, and unobtrusive JavaScript.

Before his current love affair with web development, Karl worked as a copy editor, a high-school English teacher, and a coffee house owner. His fascination with technology began in the early 1990s when he worked at Microsoft in Redmond, Washington, and it has continued unabated ever since.

Karl's other obsessions include photography, karate, English grammar, and fatherhood. He lives in Grand Rapids with his wife, Sara, and his two children, Benjamin and Lucia.

I wish to thank my wife, Sara, for her steadfast love and support during my far-flung adventures into esoteric nonsense. Thanks also to my two delightful children, Benjamin and Lucia. Jonathan Chaffer has my deepest respect and gratitude for his willingness to write this book with me and to explain the really difficult aspects of programming in a gentle manner when I just don't get it. Finally, I wish to thank John Resig for his brilliant JavaScript library and his ongoing encouragement for the book, as well as Rey Bango, Brandon Aaron, Klaus Hartl, Jörn Zaefferer, Dave Methvin, Mike Alsup, Yehuda Katz, Stefan Petre, Paul Bakaus, Michael Geary, Glen Lipka and the many others who have provided help and inspiration along the way.

About the Reviewers

Jörn Zaefferer is a software developer and a consultant from Köln, Germany. He is currently working at Maxence Integration Technologies GmbH. His work is centered on developing web-based applications as JSR-168 portlets in JEE environments, mostly Websphere Portal 5.1 based. He is currently working on a project based on JSF and Spring.

Dave Methvin has more than 25 years of software development experience in both the Windows and UNIX environments. His early career focused on embedded software in the fields of robotics, telecommunications, and medicine. Later, he moved to PC-based software projects using C/C++ and web technologies.

Dave also has more than 20 years of experience in computer journalism. He was Executive Editor at *PC Tech Journal* and *Windows Magazine*, covering PC and Internet issues; his how-to columns on JavaScript offered some of the first cut-and-paste solutions to common web page problems. He was also a co-author of the book *Networking Windows NT* (John Wiley & Sons, 1997).

Currently, Dave is Chief Technology Officer at PC Pitstop, a website that helps users fix and optimize the performance of their computers. He is also active in the jQuery community.

Paul Bakaus is a programmer and core developer living in Germany. His work with jQuery has been focused on transforming jQuery into a high-speed library capable of handling difficult large-scale rich interface operations. He was largely responsible for creating the jQuery Dimensions plug-in and he now works together with Stefan Petre on the rich effects and components library Interface. Paul is currently involved in creating a JavaScript multiplayer game featuring jQuery.

Dan Bravender has been working with open-source software for over 10 years. His fondest memories are of staying up all night to install and compile Linux in college with his roommate. He has collected a massive collection of German board games. When not playing board games, he enjoys playing soccer and hockey and studying Korean and Chinese etymology. He misses working with Karl and Jon and is very proud of all the hard work that they put into this book.

Mike Alsup is a Senior Software Developer at ePlus where he works on J2EE and web development projects. He is a graduate from Potsdam College and has been serving the software industry since 1989. Mike lives in Palmyra, NY with his wife, Diane, and their three sons.

His jQuery plug-ins can be found at `http://malsup.com/jquery/`.

Table of Contents

Preface

jQuery is a powerful JavaScript library that can enhance your websites regardless of your background.

Created by *John Resig*, jQuery is an open-source project with a dedicated core team of top-notch JavaScript developers. It provides a wide range of features, an easy-to-learn syntax, and robust cross-platform compatibility in a single compact file. What's more, over a hundred plug-ins have been developed to extend jQuery's functionality, making it an essential tool for nearly every client-side scripting occasion.

Learning jQuery provides a gentle introduction to jQuery concepts, allowing you to add interactions and animations to your pages—even if previous attempts at writing JavaScript have left you baffled. This book guides you past the pitfalls associated with AJAX, events, effects, and advanced JavaScript language features.

A working demo of the examples in this book is available at:
`http://book.learningjquery.com`

What This Book Covers

The first part of the book introduces jQuery and helps you to understand what the fuss is all about. *Chapter 1* covers downloading and setting up the jQuery library, as well as writing your first script.

The second part of the book steps you through each of the major aspects of the jQuery library. In *Chapter 2*, you'll learn how to get anything you want. The selector expressions in jQuery allow you to find elements on the page, wherever they may be. You'll work with these selector expressions to apply styling to a diverse set of page elements, sometimes in a way that pure CSS cannot.

In *Chapter 3*, you'll learn how to pull the trigger. You will use jQuery's event-handling mechanism to fire off behaviors when browser events occur. You'll also get the inside scoop on jQuery's secret sauce: attaching events unobtrusively, even before the page finishes loading.

In *Chapter 4*, you'll learn how to add flair to your actions. You'll be introduced to jQuery's animation techniques and see how to hide, show, and move page elements with the greatest of ease.

In *Chapter 5*, you'll learn how to change your page on command. This chapter will teach you how to alter the very structure an HTML document on the fly.

In *Chapter 6*, you'll learn how to make your site buzzword compliant. After reading this chapter, you, too, will be able to access server-side functionality without resorting to clunky page refreshes.

The third part of the book takes a different approach. Here you'll work through several real-world examples, pulling together what you've learned in previous chapters and creating robust jQuery solutions to common problems. In *Chapter 7*, you'll sort, sift, and style information to create beautiful and functional data layouts.

In *Chapter 8*, you'll master the finer points of client-side validation, design an adaptive form layout, and implement interactive client-server form features such as auto-completion.

In *Chapter 9*, you'll enhance the beauty and utility of page elements by showing them in bite-size morsels. You'll make information fly in and out of view both on its own and under user control.

In *Chapter 10* you'll learn about jQuery's impressive extension capabilities. You'll examine three prominent jQuery plug-ins and how to use them, and proceed to develop your own from the ground up.

Appendix A provides a handful of informative websites on a wide range of topics related to jQuery, JavaScript, and web development in general.

Appendix B recommends a number of useful third-party programs and utilities for editing and debugging jQuery code within your personal development environment.

Appendix C discusses one of the common stumbling blocks with the JavaScript language. You'll come to rely on the power of closures, rather than fear their side effects.

Who This Book Is for

This book is for web designers who want to create interactive elements for their designs, and for developers who want to create the best user interface for their web applications.

The reader will need the basics of HTML and CSS, and should be comfortable with the syntax of JavaScript. No knowledge of jQuery is assumed, nor is experience with any other JavaScript libraries required.

Conventions

In this book, you will find a number of styles of text that distinguish between different kinds of information. Here are some examples of these styles, and an explanation of their meaning.

There are three styles for code. Code words in text are shown as follows: "Taken together, $() and .addClass() are enough for us to accomplish our goal of changing the appearance of the poem text."

A block of code will be set as follows:

```
$(document).ready(function() {
  $('span:contains(language)').addClass('emphasized');
});
```

When we wish to draw your attention to a particular part of a code block, the relevant lines or items will be made bold:

```
$(document).ready(function() {
  $('a[@href$=".pdf"]').addClass('pdflink');
});
```

New terms and **important words** are introduced in a bold-type font. Words that you see on the screen, in menus or dialog boxes for example, appear in our text like this: "The next step is to run those tests by clicking the **All** button."

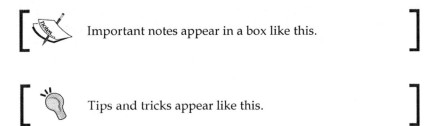

Important notes appear in a box like this.

Tips and tricks appear like this.

Reader Feedback

Feedback from our readers is always welcome. Let us know what you think about this book, what you liked or may have disliked. Reader feedback is important for us to develop titles that you really get the most out of.

To send us general feedback, simply drop an email to feedback@packtpub.com, making sure to mention the book title in the subject of your message.

If there is a book that you need and would like to see us publish, please send us a note in the **SUGGEST A TITLE** form on www.packtpub.com or email suggest@packtpub.com.

If there is a topic that you have expertise in and you are interested in either writing or contributing to a book, see our author guide on www.packtpub.com/authors.

Customer Support

Now that you are the proud owner of a Packt book, we have a number of things to help you to get the most from your purchase.

Downloading the Example Code for the Book

Visit http://www.packtpub.com/support, and select this book from the list of titles to download any example code or extra resources for this book. The files available for download will then be displayed.

The downloadable files contain instructions on how to use them.

Errata

Although we have taken every care to ensure the accuracy of our contents, mistakes do happen. If you find a mistake in one of our books—maybe a mistake in text or code—we would be grateful if you would report this to us. By doing this you can save other readers from frustration, and help to improve subsequent versions of this book. If you find any errata, report them by visiting http://www.packtpub.com/support, selecting your book, clicking on the **Submit Errata** link, and entering the details of your errata. Once your errata are verified, your submission will be accepted and the errata added to the list of existing errata. The existing errata can be viewed by selecting your title from http://www.packtpub.com/support.

Questions

You can contact us at questions@packtpub.com if you are having a problem with some aspect of the book, and we will do our best to address it.

1
Getting Started

Up on the buzzer
Quick on the start
Let's go! Let's go! Let's go!
                    — Devo,
            "Let's Go"

Today's World Wide Web is a dynamic environment, and its users set a high bar for both style and function of sites. To build interesting, interactive sites, developers are turning to JavaScript libraries such as jQuery to automate common tasks and simplify complicated ones. One reason the jQuery library is a popular choice is its ability to assist in a wide range of tasks.

Because jQuery does perform so many different functions, it can seem challenging to know where to begin. Yet, there is a coherence and symmetry to the design of the library; most of its concepts are borrowed from the structure of HTML and **Cascading Style Sheets (CSS)**. Because many web developers have more experience with these technologies than with JavaScript, the library's design lends itself to a quick start for designers with little programming experience. In fact, in this opening chapter we'll write a functioning jQuery program in just three lines of code. On the other hand, experienced programmers will also be aided by this conceptual consistency, as we'll see in the later, more advanced chapters.

But before we illustrate the operation of the library with an example, we should discuss why we might need it in the first place.

What jQuery Does

The jQuery library provides a general-purpose abstraction layer for common web scripting, and is therefore useful in almost every scripting situation. Its extensible nature means that we could never cover all possible uses and functions in a single book, as plug-ins are constantly being developed to add new abilities. The core features, though, address the following needs:

- **Access parts of a page.** Without a JavaScript library, many lines of code must be written to traverse the **Document Object Model (DOM)** tree, and locate specific portions of an HTML document's structure. jQuery offers a robust and efficient selector mechanism for retrieving exactly the piece of the document that is to be inspected or manipulated.

- **Modify the appearance of a page.** CSS offers a powerful method of influencing the way a document is rendered; but it falls short when web browsers do not all support the same standards. jQuery can bridge this gap, providing the same standards support across all browsers. In addition, jQuery can change the classes or individual style properties applied to a portion of the document even after the page has been rendered.

- **Alter the content of a page.** Not limited to mere cosmetic changes, jQuery can modify the content of a document itself with a few keystrokes. Text can be changed, images can be inserted or swapped, lists can be reordered, or the entire structure of the HTML can be rewritten and extended—all with a single easy-to-use API.

- **Respond to a user's interaction with a page.** Even the most elaborate and powerful behaviors are not useful if we can't control when they take place. The jQuery library offers an elegant way to intercept a wide variety of events, such as a user clicking on a link, without the need to clutter the HTML code itself with event handlers. At the same time, its event-handling API removes browser inconsistencies that often plague web developers.

- **Add animation to a page.** To effectively implement such interactive behaviors, a designer must also provide visual feedback to the user. The jQuery library facilitates this by providing an array of effects such as fades and wipes, as well as a toolkit for crafting new ones.

- **Retrieve information from a server without refreshing a page.** This code pattern has become known as **Asynchronous JavaScript and XML (AJAX)**, and assists web developers in crafting a responsive, feature-rich site. The jQuery library removes the browser-specific complexity from this process, allowing developers to focus on the server-end functionality.

- **Simplify common JavaScript tasks.** In addition to all of the document-specific features of jQuery, the library provides enhancements to basic JavaScript constructs such as iteration and array manipulation.

Why jQuery Works Well

With the recent resurgence of interest in dynamic HTML comes a proliferation of JavaScript frameworks. Some are specialized, focusing on just one or two of the above tasks. Others attempt to catalog every possible behavior and animation, and serve these all up pre-packaged. To maintain the wide range of features outlined above while remaining compact, jQuery employs several strategies:

- **Leverage knowledge of CSS.** By basing the mechanism for locating page elements on CSS selectors, jQuery inherits a terse yet legible way of expressing a document's structure. Because a prerequisite for doing professional web development is knowledge of CSS syntax, jQuery becomes an entry point for designers who want to add behavior to their pages.

- **Support extensions.** In order to avoid *feature creep*, jQuery relegates special-case uses to plug-ins. The method for creating new plug-ins is simple and well-documented, which has spurred the development of a wide variety of inventive and useful modules. Even most of the features in the basic jQuery download are internally realized through the plug-in architecture, and can be removed if desired, yielding an even smaller library.

- **Abstract away browser quirks.** An unfortunate reality of web development is that each browser has its own set of deviations from published standards. A significant portion of any web application can be relegated to handling features differently on each platform. While the ever-evolving browser landscape makes a perfectly browser-neutral code base impossible for some advanced features, jQuery adds an abstraction layer that normalizes the common tasks, reducing the size of code, and tremendously simplifying it.

- **Always work with sets.** When we instruct jQuery, *Find all elements with the class 'collapsible' and hide them*, there is no need to loop through each returned element. Instead, methods such as `.hide()` are designed to automatically work on sets of objects instead of individual ones. This technique, called **implicit iteration**, means that many looping constructs become unnecessary, shortening code considerably.

- **Allow multiple actions in one line.** To avoid overuse of temporary variables or wasteful repetition, jQuery employs a programming pattern called **chaining** for the majority of its methods. This means that the result of most operations on an object is the object itself, ready for the next action to be applied to it.

These strategies have kept the jQuery package slim—roughly 20KB compressed—while at the same time providing techniques for keeping our custom code that uses the library compact, as well.

The elegance of the library comes about partly by design, and partly due to the evolutionary process spurred by the vibrant community that has sprung up around the project. Users of jQuery gather to discuss not only the development of plug-ins, but also enhancements to the core library. Appendix A details many of the community resources available to jQuery developers.

Despite all of the efforts required to engineer such a flexible and robust system, the end product is free for all to use. This open-source project is dually licensed under the **GNU Public License** (appropriate for inclusion in many other open-source projects) and the **MIT License** (to facilitate use of jQuery within proprietary software).

Our First jQuery Document

Now that we have covered the range of features available to us with jQuery, we can examine how to put the library into action.

Downloading jQuery

The official jQuery website (`http://jquery.com/`) is always the most up-to-date resource for code and news related to the library. To get started, we need a copy of jQuery, which can be downloaded right from the home page of the site. Several versions of jQuery may be available at any given moment; the most appropriate for us will be the latest uncompressed version of the library.

No installation is required. To use jQuery, we just need to place it on our site in a public location. Since JavaScript is an interpreted language, there is no compilation or build phase to worry about. Whenever we need a page to have jQuery available, we will simply refer to the file's location from the HTML document.

Setting Up the HTML Document

There are three pieces to most examples of jQuery usage: the HTML document itself, CSS files to style it, and JavaScript files to act on it. For our first example, we'll use a page with a book excerpt that has a number of classes applied to portions of it.

```
<?xml version="1.0" encoding="UTF-8" ?>
<!DOCTYPE html PUBLIC "-//W3C//DTD XHTML 1.0 Transitional//EN"
          "http://www.w3.org/TR/xhtml1/DTD/xhtml1-transitional.dtd">
<html xmlns="http://www.w3.org/1999/xhtml" xml:lang="en" lang="en">
  <head>
    <meta http-equiv="Content-Type" content="text/html;
                                              charset=utf-8"/>
    <title>Through the Looking-Glass</title>
```

```
    <link rel="stylesheet" href="alice.css" type="text/css"
                                        media="screen" />
    <script src="jquery.js" type="text/javascript"></script>
    <script src="alice.js" type="text/javascript"></script>
  </head>
  <body>
    <div id="container">
      <h1>Through the Looking-Glass</h1>
      <div class="author">by Lewis Carroll</div>
      <div class="chapter" id="chapter-1">
        <h2 class="chapter-title">1. Looking-Glass House</h2>
        <p>There was a book lying near Alice on the table, and while
           she sat watching the White King (for she was still a
           little anxious about him, and had the ink all ready to
           throw over him, in case he fainted again), she turned over
           the leaves, to find some part that she could read, <span
           class="spoken">"&mdash;for it's all in some language I
           don't know,"</span> she said to herself.</p>
        <p>It was like this.</p>
        <div class="poem">
          <h3 class="poem-title">YKCOWREBBAJ</h3>
          <div class="poem-stanza">
            <div>sevot yhtils eht dna ,gillirb sawT'</div>
            <div>;ebaw eht ni elbmig dna eryg diD</div>
            <div>,sevogorob eht erew ysmim llA</div>
            <div>.ebargtuo shtar emom eht dnA</div>
          </div>
        </div>
        <p>She puzzled over this for some time, but at last a bright
        thought struck her. <span class="spoken">"Why, it's a
        Looking-glass book, of course! And if I hold it up to a
        glass, the words will all go the right way again."</span></p>
        <p>This was the poem that Alice read.</p>
        <div class="poem">
          <h3 class="poem-title">JABBERWOCKY</h3>
          <div class="poem-stanza">
            <div>'Twas brillig, and the slithy toves</div>
            <div>Did gyre and gimble in the wabe;</div>
            <div>All mimsy were the borogoves,</div>
            <div>And the mome raths outgrabe.</div>
          </div>
        </div>
      </div>
    </div>
  </body>
</html>
```

The actual layout of files on the server does not matter. References from one file to another just need to be adjusted to match the organization we choose. In most examples in this book, we will use relative paths to reference files (`../images/foo.png`) rather than absolute paths (`/images/foo.png`). This will allow the code to run locally without the need for a web server.

Immediately following the normal HTML preamble, the stylesheet is loaded. For this example, we'll use a spartan one.

```css
body {
  font: 62.5% Arial, Verdana, sans-serif;
}
h1 {
  font-size: 2.5em;
  margin-bottom: 0;
}
h2 {
  font-size: 1.3em;
  margin-bottom: .5em;
}
h3 {
  font-size: 1.1em;
  margin-bottom: 0;
}
.poem {
  margin: 0 2em;
}
.emphasized {
  font-style: italic;
  border: 1px solid #888;
  padding: 0.5em;
}
```

After the stylesheet is referenced, the JavaScript files are included. It is important that the script tag for the jQuery library be placed *before* the tag for our custom scripts; otherwise, the jQuery framework will not be available when our code attempts to reference it.

Throughout the rest of this book, only the relevant portions of HTML and CSS files will be printed. The files in their entirety are available from the book's companion website `http://book.learningjquery.com` or from the publisher's website `http://www.packtpub.com/support`.

Now we have a page that looks like this:

Through the Looking-Glass
by Lewis Carroll

1. Looking-Glass House

There was a book lying near Alice on the table, and while she sat watching the White King (for she was still a little anxious about him, and had the ink all ready to throw over him, in case he fainted again), she turned over the leaves, to find some part that she could read, "—for it's all in some language I don't know," she said to herself.

It was like this.

> **YKCOWREBBAJ**
> sevot yhtils eht dna ,gillirb sawT'
> ;ebaw eht ni elbmig dna eryg diD
> ,sevogorob eht erew ysmim llA
> .ebargtuo shtar emom eht dnA

She puzzled over this for some time, but at last a bright thought struck her. "Why, it's a Looking-glass book, of course! And if I hold it up to a glass, the words will all go the right way again."

This was the poem that Alice read.

> **JABBERWOCKY**
> 'Twas brillig, and the slithy toves
> Did gyre and gimble in the wabe;
> All mimsy were the borogoves,
> And the mome raths outgrabe.

We will use jQuery to apply a new style to the poem text.

 This example is contrived, just to show a simple use of jQuery. In real-world situations, styling such as this could be performed purely with CSS.

Writing the jQuery Code

Our custom code will go in the second, currently empty, JavaScript file, which we included from the HTML using `<script src="alice.js" type="text/javascript"></script>`. For this example, we only need three lines of code:

```
$(document).ready(function() {
  $('.poem-stanza').addClass('emphasized');
});
```

Finding the Poem Text

The fundamental operation in jQuery is selecting a part of the document. This is done with the `$()` construct. Typically, it takes a string as a parameter, which can contain any CSS selector expression. In this case, we wish to find all parts of the document that have the `poem-stanza` class applied to them; so the selector is very simple, but we will cover much more sophisticated options through the course of the book. We will step through the different ways of locating parts of a document in Chapter 2.

The `$()` function is actually a factory for the jQuery object, which is the basic building block we will be working with from now on. The jQuery object encapsulates zero or more DOM elements, and allows us to interact with them in many different ways. In this case, we wish to modify the appearance of these parts of the page, and we will accomplish this by changing the classes applied to the poem text.

Injecting the New Class

The `.addClass()` method is fairly self-explanatory; it applies a CSS class to the part of the page that we have selected. Its only parameter is the name of the class to add. This method, and its counterpart, `.removeClass()`, will allow us to easily observe jQuery in action as we explore the different selector expressions available to us. For now, our example simply adds the `emphasized` class, which our stylesheet has defined as italicized text with a border.

Note that no iteration is necessary to add the class to all the poem stanzas. As we discussed, jQuery uses implicit iteration within methods such as `.addClass()`, so a single function call is all it takes to alter all of the selected parts of the document.

Executing the Code

Taken together, `$()` and `.addClass()` are enough for us to accomplish our goal of changing the appearance of the poem text. However, if this line of code is inserted alone in the document header, it will have no effect. JavaScript code is generally run as soon as it is encountered in the browser, and at the time the header is being processed, no HTML is yet present to style. We need to delay the execution of the code until after the DOM is available for our use.

The traditional mechanism for controlling when JavaScript code is run is to call the code from within **event handlers**. Many handlers are available for user-initiated events, such as mouse clicks and key presses. If we did not have jQuery available for our use, we would need to rely on the `onload` handler, which fires after the page (along with all of its images) has been rendered. To trigger our code from the `onload` event, we would place the code inside a function:

```
function emphasizePoemStanzas() {
  $('.poem-stanza').addClass('emphasized');
}
```

Then we would attach the function to the event by modifying the HTML `<body>` tag to reference it:

```
<body onload="emphasizePoemStanzas();">
```

This causes our code to run after the page is completely loaded.

There are drawbacks to this approach, though. We altered the HTML itself to effect this behavior change. This tight coupling of structure and function clutters the code, possibly requiring the same function calls to be repeated over many different pages, or in the case of other events such as mouse clicks, over every instance of an element on a page. Adding new behaviors would then require alterations in two different places, increasing the opportunity for error and complicating parallel workflows for designers and programmers.

To avoid this pitfall, jQuery allows us to schedule function calls for firing once the DOM is loaded — without waiting for images — with the `$(document).ready()` construct. With our function defined as above, we can write:

```
$(document).ready(emphasizePoemStanzas);
```

This technique does not require any HTML modifications. Instead, the behavior is attached entirely from within the JavaScript file. We will learn how to respond to other types of user actions, divorcing their effects from the HTML structure as well, in Chapter 3.

This incarnation is still slightly wasteful, though, because the function `emphasizePoemStanzas()` is defined only to be used immediately, and exactly once. This means that we have used an identifier in the global namespace of functions that we have to remember not to use again, and for little gain. JavaScript, like some other programming languages, has a way around this inefficiency called **anonymous functions** (sometimes also called **lambda functions**). We arrive back at the code as originally presented:

```
$(document).ready(function() {
  $('.poem-stanza').addClass('emphasized');
});
```

By using the `function` keyword without a function name, we define a function exactly where it is needed, and not before. This removes clutter and brings us back down to three lines of JavaScript. This idiom is extremely convenient in jQuery code, as many methods take a function as an argument and such functions are rarely reusable.

When this syntax is used to define an anonymous function within the body of another function, a **closure** can be created. This is an advanced and powerful concept, but should be understood when making extensive use of nested function definitions as it can have unintended consequences and ramifications on memory use. This topic is discussed fully in Appendix C.

The Finished Product

Now that our JavaScript is in place, the page looks like this:

Through the Looking-Glass
by Lewis Carroll

1. Looking-Glass House

There was a book lying near Alice on the table, and while she sat watching the White King (for she was still a little anxious about him, and had the ink all ready to throw over him, in case he fainted again), she turned over the leaves, to find some part that she could read, "—for it's all in some language I don't know," she said to herself.

It was like this.

YKCOWREBBAJ

sevot yhtils eht dna ,gillirb sawT'
;ebaw eht ni elbmig dna eryg diD
,sevogorob eht erew ysmim llA
.ebargtuo shtar emom eht dnA

She puzzled over this for some time, but at last a bright thought struck her. "Why, it's a Looking-glass book, of course! And if I hold it up to a glass, the words will all go the right way again."

This was the poem that Alice read.

JABBERWOCKY

'Twas brillig, and the slithy toves
Did gyre and gimble in the wabe;
All mimsy were the borogoves,
And the mome raths outgrabe.

The poem stanzas are now italicized and enclosed in boxes, due to the insertion of the emphasized class by the JavaScript code.

Summary

We now have an idea of why a developer would choose to use a JavaScript framework rather than writing all code from scratch, even for the most basic tasks. We also have seen some of the ways in which jQuery excels as a framework, and why we might choose it over other options. We also know in general which tasks jQuery makes easier.

In this chapter, we have learned how to make jQuery available to JavaScript code on our web page, use the `$()` factory function to locate a part of the page that has a given class, call `.addClass()` to apply additional styling to this part of the page, and invoke `$(document).ready()` to cause this code to execute upon the loading of the page.

The simple example we have been using demonstrates how jQuery works, but is not very useful in real-world situations. In the next chapter, we will expand on the code hereby exploring jQuery's sophisticated selector language, finding practical uses for this technique.

2
Selectors—How to Get Anything You Want

She's just the girl
She's just the girl
The girl you want
— Devo,
"Girl U Want"

jQuery harnesses the power of **Cascading Style Sheets (CSS)** and **XPath selectors** to let us quickly and easily access elements or groups of elements in the Document Object Model (DOM). In this chapter, we will explore a few of these CSS and XPath selectors, as well as jQuery's own **custom selectors**. We'll also look at jQuery's **DOM traversal methods** that provide even greater flexibility for getting what we want.

The Document Object Model

One of the most powerful aspects of jQuery is its ability to make DOM traversal easy. The Document Object Model is a family-tree structure of sorts. HTML, like other markup languages, uses this model to describe the relationships of things on a page. When we refer to these relationships, we use the same terminology that we use when referring to family relationships—parents, children, and so on. A simple example can help us understand how the family tree metaphor applies to a document:

```
<html>
  <head>
    <title>the title</title>
  </head>
  <body>
    <div>
      <p>This is a paragraph.</p>
      <p>This is another paragraph.</p>
      <p>This is yet another paragraph.</p>
```

```
        </div>
      </body>
    </html>
```

Here, `<html>` is the **ancestor** of all the other elements; in other words, all the other elements are **descendants** of `<html>`. The `<head>` and `<body>` elements are **children** of `<html>`. Therefore, in addition to being the ancestor of `<head>` and `<body>`, `<html>` is also their **parent**. The `<p>` elements are children (and descendants) of `<div>`, descendants of `<body>` and `<html>`, and **siblings** of each other. For information on how to visualize the family-tree structure of the DOM using third-party software, see Appendix B.

An important point to note before we begin is that the resulting set of items from our various selectors and methods is actually a jQuery object. jQuery objects are very easy to work with when we want to actually do something with the things that we find on a page. We can easily bind events to these objects and add slick effects to them, as well as *chain* multiple modifications or effects together. Nevertheless, jQuery objects are different from regular DOM elements, and as such do not necessarily provide the same methods and properties as plain DOM elements for some tasks. In the final part of this chapter, therefore, we will look at ways to access the DOM elements that are wrapped in a jQuery object.

The $() Factory Function

No matter which type of selector we want to use in jQuery—be it CSS, XPath, or custom—we always start with the dollar sign and parentheses: `$()`

As mentioned in Chapter 1, the `$()` function removes the need to do a `for` loop to access a group of elements since whatever we put inside the parentheses will be looped through automatically and stored as a jQuery object. We can put just about anything inside the parentheses of the `$()` function. A few of the more common examples include:

- **A tag name**: `$('p')` gets all paragraphs in the document.
- **An ID**: `$('#some-id')` gets the single element in the document that has the corresponding `some-id` ID.
- **A class**: `$('.some-class')` gets all elements in the document that have a class of `some-class`.

Making jQuery Play Well with Other JavaScript Libraries

In jQuery, the dollar sign $ is simply shorthand for `jQuery`. Because a `$()` function is very common in JavaScript libraries, conflicts could arise if more than one of these libraries is being used in a given page. We can avoid such conflicts by replacing every instance of $ with `jQuery` in our custom jQuery code. Additional solutions to this problem are addressed in Chapter 10.

Now that we have covered the basics, we're ready to start exploring some more powerful uses of selectors.

CSS Selectors

jQuery supports most of the selectors included in CSS specifications 1 through 3, as outlined on the *World Wide Web Consortium*'s site: http://www.w3.org/Style/CSS/#specs. This support allows developers to enhance their websites without worrying about which browsers (particularly Internet Explorer 6 and below) might not understand advanced selectors, as long as the browsers have JavaScript enabled.

 Responsible jQuery developers should always apply the concepts of **progressive enhancement** and **graceful degradation** to their code, ensuring that a page will render as accurately, even if not as beautifully, with JavaScript disabled as it does with JavaScript turned on. We will continue to explore these concepts throughout the book.

To begin learning how jQuery works with CSS selectors, we'll use a structure that appears on many websites, often for navigation—the nested, unordered list.

```
<ul id="selected-plays">
  <li>Comedies
    <ul>
      <li><a href="http://www.mysite.com/asyoulikeit/">
                                        As You Like It</a></li>
      <li>All's Well That Ends Well</li>
      <li>A Midsummer Night's Dream</li>
      <li>Twelfth Night</li>
    </ul>
  </li>
  <li>Tragedies
    <ul>
      <li><a href="hamlet.pdf">Hamlet</a></li>
      <li>Macbeth</li>
      <li>Romeo and Juliet</li>
    </ul>
  </li>
  <li>Histories
    <ul>
      <li>Henry IV (<a href="mailto:henryiv@king.co.uk">email</a>)
        <ul>
          <li>Part I</li>
          <li>Part II</li>
```

```
      </ul>
    <li><a href="http://www.shakespeare.co.uk/henryv.htm">
                                      Henry V</a></li>
      <li>Richard II</li>
    </ul>
  </li>
</ul>
```

Notice that the first `<ul>` has an ID of `selected-plays`, but none of the `<li>` tags have a class associated with them. Without any styles applied, the list looks like this:

- Comedies
  - As You Like It
  - All's Well That Ends Well
  - A Midsummer Night's Dream
  - Twelfth Night
- Tragedies
  - Hamlet
  - Macbeth
  - Romeo and Juliet
- Histories
  - Henry IV (email)
    - Part I
    - Part II
  - Henry V
  - Richard II

The nested list appears as we would expect it to — a set of bulleted items arranged vertically and indented according to their level.

Styling List-Item Levels

Let's suppose that we want the top-level items, and *only* the top-level items, to be arranged horizontally. We can start by defining a `horizontal` class in the stylesheet:

```
.horizontal {
  float: left;
  list-style: none;
  margin: 10px;
}
```

The `horizontal` class floats the element to the left of the one following it, removes the bullet from it if it's a list item, and adds a 10 pixel margin on all sides of it.

Rather than attaching the `horizontal` class directly in our HTML, we'll add it dynamically to the top-level list items only — **Comedies**, **Tragedies**, and **Histories** — to demonstrate jQuery's use of selectors:

```
$(document).ready(function() {
  $('#selected-plays > li').addClass('horizontal');
});
```

As discussed in Chapter 1, we begin the jQuery code with the `$(document).ready()` wrapper, which makes everything inside of it available as soon as the DOM has loaded.

The second line uses the child combinator (>) to add the `horizontal` class to all top-level items only. In effect, the selector inside the `$()` function is saying, *find each list item (`li`) that is a child (>) of an element with an ID of* selected-plays (`#selected-plays`).

With the class now applied, our nested list looks like this:

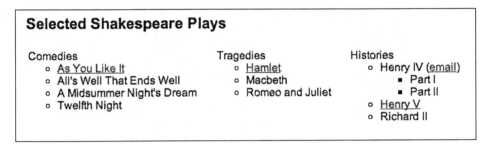

Styling all of the other items—those that are *not* in the top level—can be done in a number of ways. Since we have already applied the `horizontal` class to the top-level items, one way to get all sub-level items is to use a **negation pseudo-class** to identify all list items that do *not* have a class of `horizontal`. Note the addition of the third line of code:

```
$(document).ready(function() {
  $('#selected-plays > li').addClass('horizontal');
  $('#selected-plays li:not(.horizontal)').addClass('sub-level');
});
```

This time we are getting every list item (`li`) that:

1. Is a descendant of an element with an ID of `selected-plays` (`#selected-plays`), and
2. Does not have a class of `horizontal` (`:not(.horizontal)`).

When we add the `sub-level` class to these items, they receive the pale yellow background color defined in the stylesheet: `.sub-level {background-color: #ffc;}`. Now the nested list looks like this:

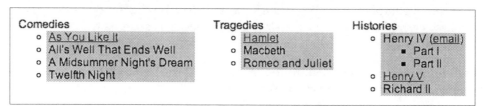

XPath Selectors

XML Path Language (XPath) is a type of language for identifying different elements or their values within XML documents, similar to the way CSS identifies elements in HTML documents. The jQuery library supports a basic set of XPath selectors that we can use alongside CSS selectors, if we so desire. And with jQuery, both XPath and CSS selectors can be used regardless of the document type.

When it comes to **attribute selectors**, jQuery uses the XPath convention of identifying attributes by prefixing them with the @ symbol inside square brackets, rather than the less-flexible CSS equivalent. For example, to select all links that have a `title` attribute, we would write the following:

```
$('a[@title]')
```

This XPath syntax allows for another use of square brackets, without the @, to designate an element that is contained within another element. We can, for example, get all `div` elements that contain an `ol` element with the following selector expression:

```
$('div[ol]')
```

Styling Links

Attribute selectors accept regular-expression-like syntax for identifying the beginning (^) or ending ($) of a string. They also take an asterisk (*) to indicate an arbitrary position within a string.

Let's say we wanted to display different types of links with different text colors. We would first define the styles in our stylesheet:

```
a {
  color: #00f; /* make plain links blue */
a.mailto {
  color: #f00; /* make email links red */
```

```
}
a.pdflink {
  color: #090; /* make PDF links green */
}
a.mysite {
  text-decoration: none; /* remove internal link underline */
  border-bottom: 1px dotted #00f;
}
```

Then, we would add the three classes—mailto, pdflink, and mysite—to the appropriate links using jQuery.

To get all email links, we would construct a selector that looks for all anchor elements (a) with an href attribute ([@href]) that begins with mailto (^="mailto:"); as follows:

```
$(document).ready(function() {
  $('a[@href^="mailto:"]').addClass('mailto');
});
```

To get all links to PDF files, we would use the dollar sign rather than the caret symbol; to get all links with an href attribute that ends with .pdf, the code would look as follows:

```
$(document).ready(function() {
  $('a[@href^="mailto:"]').addClass('mailto');
  $('a[@href$=".pdf"]').addClass('pdflink');
});
```

Finally, to get all internal links—i.e., links to other pages on mysite.com—we would use the asterisk:

```
$(document).ready(function() {
  $('a[@href^="mailto:"]').addClass('mailto');
  $('a[@href$=".pdf"]').addClass('pdflink');
  $('a[@href*="mysite.com"]').addClass('mysite');
});
```

Here, mysite.com can appear anywhere within the href value. This is especially important if we want to include links to any sub-domain within mysite.com as well.

With the three classes applied to the three types of links, we should see the following styles applied:

- Blue text with dotted underline:

  ```
  <a href="http://www.mysite.com/asyoulikeit/">As You Like It</a>
  ```

- Green text: `<a href="hamlet.pdf">Hamlet</a>`
- Red text: `<a href="mailto:henryiv@king.co.uk">email</a>`

Following is a screenshot of the styled links:

Selected Shakespeare Plays

Comedies
- As You Like It
- All's Well That Ends Well
- A Midsummer Night's Dream
- Twelfth Night

Tragedies
- Hamlet
- Macbeth
- Romeo and Juliet

Histories
- Henry IV (email)
  - Part I
  - Part II
- Henry V
- Richard II

Custom Selectors

To the wide variety of CSS and XPath selectors, jQuery adds its own custom selectors. Most of the custom selectors allow us to pick certain elements out of a line-up, so to speak. The syntax is the same as the CSS pseudo-class syntax, where the selector starts with a colon (:). For example, if we wanted to select the second item from a matched set of `div`s with a class of `horizontal`, we would write it like this:

```
$('div.horizontal:eq(1)')
```

Note that the `eq(1)` gets the second item from the set because JavaScript array numbering is **zero-based**, meaning that it starts with 0. In contrast, CSS is **one-based**, so a CSS selector such as `$('div:nth-child(1)')` gets any `div` that is the first child of its parent.

Styling Alternate Rows

Two very useful custom selectors in the jQuery library are `:odd` and `:even`. Let's take a look at how we can use these selectors for basic table striping, given the following table:

```
<table>
<tr>
  <td>As You Like It</td>
  <td>Comedy</td>
</tr>
<tr>
  <td>All's Well that Ends Well</td>
  <td>Comedy</td>
```

```
  </tr>
  <tr>
    <td>Hamlet</td>
    <td>Tragedy</td>
  </tr>
  <tr>
    <td>Macbeth</td>
    <td>Tragedy</td>
  </tr>
  <tr>
    <td>Romeo and Juliet</td>
    <td>Tragedy</td>
  </tr>
  <tr>
    <td>Henry IV, Part I</td>
    <td>History</td>
  </tr>
  <tr>
    <td>Henry V</td>
    <td>History</td>
  </tr>
  </table>
```

Now we can add two classes to the stylesheet—one for the odd rows and one for the even:

```
.odd {
  background-color: #ffc; /* pale yellow for odd rows */
}
.even {
  background-color: #cef; /* pale blue for even rows */
}
```

Finally, we write our jQuery code, attaching the classes to the table rows (<tr> tags):

```
$(document).ready(function() {
  $('tr:odd').addClass('odd');
  $('tr:even').addClass('even');
});
```

That simple bit of code should produce a table that looks like this:

As You Like It	Comedy
All's Well that Ends Well	Comedy
Hamlet	Tragedy
Macbeth	Tragedy
Romeo and Juliet	Tragedy
Henry IV, Part I	History
Henry V	History

At first glance, the row coloring might appear the opposite of what it should be. However, just as with the :eq() selector, the :odd() and :even() selectors use JavaScript's native zero-based numbering. Therefore, the first row counts as 0 (even) and the second row counts as 1 (odd), and so on.

Note that we may see unintended results if there is more than one table on a page. For example, since the last row in this table has a pale-blue background, the first row in the next table would have the pale-yellow background. We will examine ways to avoid this type of problem in Chapter 7.

For one final custom-selector touch, let's suppose for some reason we wanted to highlight any table cell that referred to one of the **Henry** plays. All we'd have to do is add a class to the stylesheet to make the text bold and red (.highlight {font-weight:bold; color: #f00;}) and add a line to our jQuery code, using the :contains() selector.

```
$(document).ready(function() {
  $('tr:odd').addClass('odd');
  $('tr:even').addClass('even');
  $('td:contains("Henry")').addClass('highlight');
});
```

So, now we can see our lovely striped table with the **Henry** plays prominently featured:

As You Like It	Comedy
All's Well that Ends Well	Comedy
Hamlet	Tragedy
Macbeth	Tragedy
Romeo and Juliet	Tragedy
Henry IV, Part I	History
Henry V	History

Admittedly, there are ways to achieve the highlighting without jQuery — or any client-side programming, for that matter. Nevertheless, jQuery, along with CSS, is a great alternative for this type of styling, in cases when the content is generated dynamically and we don't have access to either the HTML or server-side code.

DOM Traversal Methods

The jQuery selectors that we have explored so far allow us to get a set of elements as we navigate *across* and *down* the DOM tree and filter the results. If this were the only way to get elements, our options would be quite limited (although, frankly, the selector expressions on their own are robust in their own right, especially when compared to the regular DOM scripting). There are many occasions on which getting a **parent** or **ancestor** element is essential. And that is where jQuery's DOM traversal methods come to play. With these methods at our disposal, we can go up, down, and all around the DOM tree with ease.

Some of the methods have a nearly identical counterpart among the selector expressions. For example, the line we used to add the odd class, `$('tr:odd').addClass('odd');`, could be rewritten with the `.filter()` method as follows:

```
$('tr').filter(':odd').addClass('odd');
```

For the most part, however, the two ways of getting elements complement each other. Let's take a look at the striped table again, to see what is possible with these methods.

First, the table could use a heading row, so we'll add another `<tr>` element with two `<th>` elements inside it, rather than the `<td>` elements:

```
[...]
  <tr>
    <th>Title</th>
    <th>Category</th>
  </tr>
[...]
```

 This could also be done more semantically by wrapping the heading row in `<thead></thead>` and wrapping the rest of the rows in `<tbody></tbody>`, but for the sake of this example we'll just go along without the extra explicit markup.

We'll style that heading row differently from the rest, giving it a bold yellow background color instead of the pale blue that it would get with the code the way we left it.

Second, our client has just looked at the site and loves the stripes, but wants the bold red text to appear in the category cells of the **Henry** rows, and not in the title cells.

Styling the Header Row

The task of styling the header row differently can be achieved by hooking into the `<th>` tags and getting their parent. The other rows can be selected for styling by combining CSS, XPath, and custom selectors to filter the `<tr>` elements as follows:

```
$(document).ready(function() {
  $('th').parent().addClass('table-heading');
  $('tr:not([th]):even').addClass('even');
  $('tr:not([th]):odd').addClass('odd');
  $('td:contains("Henry")').addClass('highlight');
});
```

With the heading row, we get a generic parent without anything in the parentheses — `parent()` — because we know that it is a `<tr>` and that there is only one of them. Although we might expect this `<tr>` to have the `table-heading` class added to it twice because there are two `<th>` elements within it, jQuery intelligently avoids adding a class name to an element if the class is already there.

For the body rows, we begin by excluding any `<tr>` element that has a `<th>` as a descendant, after which we apply the `:odd` or `:even` filter. Note that the order of selectors is important. Our table would look quite different if we used, for example, `$('tr:odd:not([th])')` rather than `$('tr:not([th]):odd')`.

Styling Category Cells

To style the cell next to each cell containing **Henry**, we can start with the selector that we have already written, and simply add the `next()` method to it:

```
$(document).ready(function() {
  $('the').parent().addClass('table-heading');
  $('tr:not([th]):even').addClass('even');
  $('tr:not([th]):odd').addClass('odd');
  $('td:contains("Henry")').next().addClass('highlight');
});
```

With the added `table-heading` class and the `highlight` class now applied to cells in the category column, the table should look like this:

Title	Category
As You Like It	Comedy
All's Well that Ends Well	Comedy
Hamlet	Tragedy
Macbeth	Tragedy
Romeo and Juliet	Tragedy
Henry IV, Part I	History
Henry V	History

The `.next()` method gets only the very next sibling element. What would we do if there were more columns? If there were a **Year Published** column, for example, we might want the text in that column to be highlighted too, when its row contains **Henry** in the **Title** column. In other words, for each row in which a cell contains **Henry**, we want to get all of the other cells in that row. We can do this in a number of ways, using a combination of selector expressions and jQuery methods:

1. Get the cell containing **Henry** and then get its siblings (not just the next sibling). Add the class:

    ```
    $('td:contains("Henry")').siblings().addClass('highlight');
    ```

2. Get the cell containing **Henry**, get its parent, and then find all cells inside it that are greater than 0 (where 0 is the first cell). Add the class:

    ```
    $('td:contains("Henry")').parent().find('td:gt(0)')
                                     .addClass('highlight');
    ```

3. Get the cell containing **Henry**, get its parent, find all cells inside it, and then filter those to exclude the one containing **Henry**. Add the class:

    ```
    $('td:contains("Henry")').parent().find('td').not(':
                     contains("Henry")') ).addClass('highlight');
    ```

4. Get the cell containing **Henry**, get its parent, find the second cell among the children, add the class, cancel the last `.find()`, find the third cell among the children, and add the class:

    ```
    $('td:contains("Henry")').parent().find('td:eq(1)').addClass(
          'highlight').end().find('td:eq(2)').addClass('highlight');
    ```

All of these options will produce the same result:

Title	Category	Year Published
As You Like It	Comedy	
All's Well that Ends Well	Comedy	1601
Hamlet	Tragedy	1604
Macbeth	Tragedy	1606
Romeo and Juliet	Tragedy	1595
Henry IV, Part I	History	1596
Henry V	History	1599

Just to be clear, not all of these ways of combining selector expressions and methods are recommended. In fact, the fourth way is circuitous to the point of absurdity. They should, however, illustrate the incredible flexibility of jQuery's DOM traversal options.

Chaining

All four of those options also illustrate jQuery's **chaining** capability. It is possible with jQuery to get multiple sets of elements and do multiple things with them, all within a single line of code. And it is possible to break a single line of code into multiple lines for greater readability. For example, option 4 in the preceeding section can be rewritten in seven lines, with each line having its own comment, even though they are acting as a single line:

```
$('td:contains("Henry")')          //get every cell containing "Henry"
.parent()                                    //get its parent
.find('td:eq(1)')                  //find inside the parent the 2nd cell
.addClass(highlight')              //add the "highlight" class to that cell
.end()         //revert back to the parent of the cell containing "Henry"
.find('td:eq(2)')                  //find inside the parent the 3rd cell
.addClass('highlight');            //add the "highlight" class to that cell
```

Chaining can be like speaking a whole paragraph's worth of words in a single breath—it gets the job done quickly, but it can be hard for someone else to understand. Breaking it up into multiple lines and adding judicious comments can save more time in the long run.

Accessing DOM Elements

Every selector expression and most jQuery methods return a jQuery object, which is almost always what we want, because of the implicit iteration and chaining capabilities that it affords.

Still, there may be points in our code when we need to access a DOM element directly. For example, we may need to make a resulting set of elements available to another JavaScript library. Or we might need to access an element's tag name. For these admittedly rare situations, jQuery provides the `.get()` method. To access the first DOM element referred to by a jQuery object, we would use `.get(0)`. If the DOM element is needed within a loop, we would use `.get(index)`. So, if we want to know the tag name of an element with `id="my-element"`, we would write:

```
var myTag = $('#my-element').get(0).tagName;
```

For even greater convenience, jQuery provides a shorthand for `.get()`. Instead of writing `$('#my-element').get(0)`, for example, we can use square brackets immediately following the selector: `$('#my-element')[0]`. It's no accident that this syntax looks like an array of DOM elements; using the square brackets is like peeling away the jQuery wrapper to get at these elements.

Summary

With the techniques that we have covered in this chapter, we should now be able to style top-level and sub-level items in a nested list by using CSS selectors, apply different styles to different types of links by using XPath attribute selectors, add rudimentary striping to a table by using the custom jQuery selectors `:odd` and `:even`, and highlight text within certain table cells by chaining jQuery methods.

So far, we have been using the `$(document).ready()` event to add a class to a matched set of elements. In the next chapter, we'll explore ways in which to add a class in response to a variety of user-initiated events.

3

Events—How to Pull the Trigger

Getting bigger, pull the trigger
— Devo,
"Puppet Boy"

JavaScript has several built-in ways of reacting to user interaction and other events. To make a page dynamic and responsive, we need to harness this capability so that we can, at the appropriate times, use the jQuery techniques we have learned so far. While we could do this with vanilla JavaScript, jQuery enhances and extends the basic event handling mechanisms to give them a more elegant syntax while at the same time making them more powerful.

Performing Tasks on Page Load

We have already seen how to make jQuery react to the loading of a web page. The `$(document).ready()` event handler can be used to fire off a function's worth of code, but there's a bit more to be said about it.

Timing of Code Execution

In Chapter 1, we noted that `$(document).ready()` was jQuery's way to perform tasks that were typically triggered by JavaScript's built-in `onload` event. While the two have a similar effect, however, they trigger actions at subtly different times.

The `window.onload` event fires when a document is completely downloaded to the browser. This means that every element on the page is accessible to JavaScript, which is a boon for writing featureful code without worrying about load order.

On the other hand, a handler registered using $(document).ready() is invoked when the DOM is completely ready for use. This also means that all elements are accessible by our scripts, but does not mean that every associated file has been downloaded. As soon as the HTML has been downloaded and parsed into a DOM tree, the code can run.

Consider, for example, a page that presents an image gallery; such a page may have many large images on it, which we can hide, show, move, and otherwise manipulate with jQuery. If we set up our interface using the onload event, user will have to wait until each and every image is completely downloaded before they can use the page. Or worse, if behaviors are not yet attached to elements that have default behaviors (such as links), user interactions could produce unintended outcomes. However, when we use $(document).ready() for the setup, the interface gets ready to use much earlier with the correct behavior.

> Using $(document).ready() is almost always preferable to using an onload handler, but we need to keep in mind that because supporting files may not have loaded, attributes such as image height and width are not necessarily available at this time. If these are needed, we may at times also choose to implement an onload handler (or more likely, jQuery's .load() equivalent); the two mechanisms can coexist peacefully.

Multiple Scripts on One Page

The traditional mechanism for registering event handlers through JavaScript (rather than adding handler attributes right in the HTML) is to assign a function to the DOM element's corresponding attribute. For example, suppose we had defined the function:

```
function doStuff() {
  // Perform a task...
}
```

We could then either assign it within our HTML markup:

```
<body onload="doStuff();">
```

Or, we could assign it from within JavaScript code:

```
window.onload = doStuff;
```

Both of these approaches will cause the function to execute when the page is loaded. The advantage of the second is that the behavior is more cleanly separated from the markup. However, suppose we have a second function:

```
function doOtherStuff() {
  // Perform another task...
}
```

We could then attempt to assign this function to run on page load:

```
window.onload = doOtherStuff;
```

However, this assignment trumps the first one. The `.onload` attribute can only store one function reference at a time, so we can't add to the existing behavior.

The `$(document).ready()` mechanism handles this situation gracefully. Each call to the method adds the new function to an internal queue of behaviors; when the page is loaded all of the functions will execute. The functions will run in the order in which they were registered.

 To be fair, jQuery doesn't have a monopoly on workarounds to this issue. We can write a JavaScript function that forms a new function that calls the existing `onload` handler, then calls a passed-in handler. This approach, used for example by Simon Willison's `addLoadEvent()`, avoids conflicts between rival handlers like `$(document).ready()` does, but lacks some of the other benefits we have discussed.

Shortcuts for Code Brevity

The `$(document).ready()` construct is actually calling the `.ready()` method on a jQuery object we've constructed from the `document` DOM element. Because this is a common task, the `$()` function provides a shortcut for us. When called with no arguments, the function behaves as though `document` were passed in. This means that instead of:

```
$(document).ready(function() {
  // Our code here...
});
```

we can write:

```
$().ready(function() {
  // Our code here...
});
```

In addition, the factory function can take another function as an argument. When we do this, jQuery performs an implicit call to `.ready()`, so for the same result we can write:

```
$(function() {
  // Our code here...
});
```

While these other syntaxes are shorter, the authors prefer the longer version to make it clearer what the code is doing.

Simple Events

There are many other times apart from the loading of the page at which we might want to perform a task. Just as JavaScript allows us to intercept the page load event with `<body onload="">` or `window.onload`, it provides similar hooks for user-initiated events such as mouse clicks (`onclick`), form fields being modified (`onchange`), and windows changing size (`onresize`). When assigned directly to elements in the DOM, these hooks have similar drawbacks to the ones we outlined for `onload`. Therefore, jQuery offers an improved way of handling these events as well.

A Simple Style Switcher

To illustrate some event handling techniques, suppose we wish to have a single page rendered in several different styles based on user input. We will allow the user to click buttons to toggle between a normal view, a view in which the text is constrained to a narrow column, and a view with large print for the content area.

In a real-world example, a good web citizen will employ the principle of progressive enhancement here. The style switcher should either be hidden when JavaScript is unavailable or, better yet, should still function through links to alternative versions of the page. For the purposes of this tutorial, we'll assume that all users have JavaScript turned on.

The HTML markup for the style switcher is as follows:

```
<div id="switcher">
  <h3>Style Switcher</h3>
  <div class="button selected" id="switcher-normal">Normal</div>
  <div class="button" id="switcher-narrow">Narrow Column</div>
  <div class="button" id="switcher-large">Large Print</div>
</div>
```

Combined with the rest of the page's HTML markup and some basic CSS, we get a page that looks like the following figure:

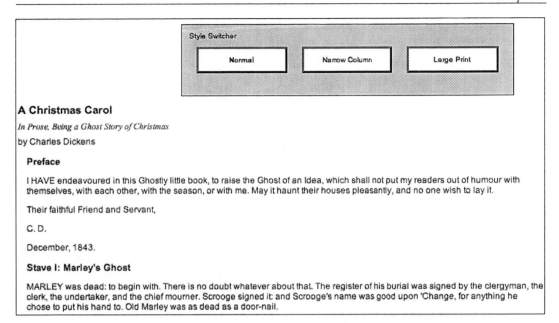

To begin, we'll make the **Large Print** button function. We need a bit of CSS to implement our alternative view of the page:

```
body.large .chapter {
    font-size: 1.5em;
}
```

Our goal, then, is to apply the large class to the body tag. This will allow the stylesheet to reformat the page appropriately. We already know the statement needed to accomplish this:

```
$('body').addClass('large');
```

However, we want this to occur when the button is clicked. To do this, we'll introduce the .bind() method. This method allows us to specify any JavaScript event, and to attach a behavior to it. In this case, the event is called **click**, and the behavior is a function consisting of our one-liner above:

```
$(document).ready(function() {
  $('#switcher-large').bind('click', function() {
    $('body').addClass('large');
  });
});
```

Now when the button gets clicked, our code runs and we see the resulting screen as shown in the following figure:

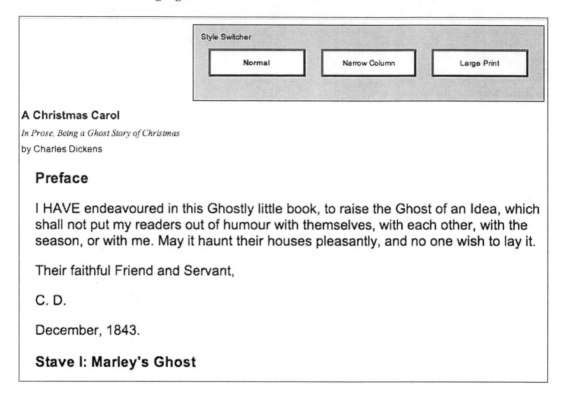

That's all there is to binding an event. The advantages we discussed with the `.ready()` method apply here, as well. Multiple calls to `.bind()` coexist nicely, appending additional behaviors to the same event as necessary.

This is not necessarily the most elegant or efficient way to accomplish this task. As we proceed through this chapter, we will extend and refine this code into something we can be proud of.

Enabling the Other Buttons

We now have a **Large Print** button that works as advertised, but we need to apply similar handling to the other two buttons to make them perform their tasks. This is straightforward; we use `.bind()` to add a click handler to each of them, removing and adding classes as necessary. The new code reads as follows:

```
$(document).ready(function() {
  $('#switcher-normal').bind('click', function() {
    $('body').removeClass('narrow');
```

```
      $('body').removeClass('large');
    });
    $('#switcher-narrow').bind('click', function() {
      $('body').addClass('narrow');
      $('body').removeClass('large');
    });
    $('#switcher-large').bind('click', function() {
      $('body').removeClass('narrow');
      $('body').addClass('large');
    });
  });
```

This is combined with a CSS rule for the `narrow` class:

```
body.narrow .chapter {
  width: 400px;
}
```

Now, after clicking the **Narrow Column** button, its corresponding CSS is applied and the page looks like the following figure:

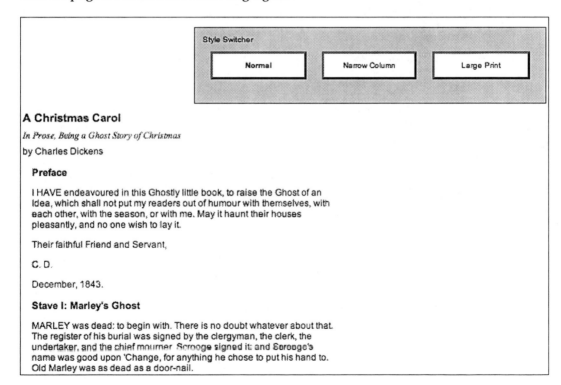

Event Handler Context

Our switcher is functioning correctly, but we are not giving the user any feedback about which button is currently active. Our approach for handling this will be to apply the `selected` class to the button when it is clicked, and remove this class from the other buttons. The `selected` class simply makes the button's text bold:

```
.selected {
  font-weight: bold;
}
```

We could accomplish this class modification as we do above, by referring to each button by ID and applying or removing classes as necessary; but instead we'll explore a more elegant and scalable solution that exploits the context in which event handlers run.

When any event handler is triggered, the keyword `this` refers to the DOM element to which the behavior was attached. Earlier we noted that the `$()` function could take a DOM element as its argument; this is one of the key reasons that facility is available. By writing `$(this)` within the event handler, we create a jQuery object corresponding to the element, and can act on it just as if we had located it with a CSS selector.

With this in mind, we can write:

```
$(this).addClass('selected');
```

Placing this line in each of the three handlers will add the class when a button is clicked. To remove the class from the other buttons, we can take advantage of jQuery's implicit iteration feature, and write:

```
$('#switcher .button').removeClass('selected');
```

This line removes the class from every button inside the style switcher. So, placing these in the correct order, we have the code as:

```
$(document).ready(function() {
  $('#switcher-normal').bind('click', function() {
    $('body').removeClass('narrow');
    $('body').removeClass('large');
    $('#switcher .button').removeClass('selected');
    $(this).addClass('selected');
  });
  $('#switcher-narrow').bind('click', function() {
    $('body').addClass('narrow');
    $('body').removeClass('large');
    $('#switcher .button').removeClass('selected');
```

```
      $(this).addClass('selected');
    });
    $('#switcher-large').bind('click', function() {
      $('body').removeClass('narrow');
      $('body').addClass('large');
      $('#switcher .button').removeClass('selected');
      $(this).addClass('selected');
    });
  });
```

Now the style switcher gives appropriate feedback as shown in the following figure:

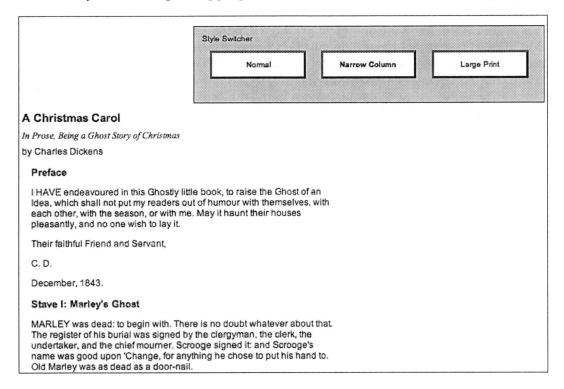

Generalizing the statements by using the handler context allows us to be yet more efficient. Because the button highlighting code is the same for all three buttons, we can factor it out into a separate handler as the following code:

```
  $(document).ready(function() {
    $('#switcher-normal').bind('click', function() {
      $('body').removeClass('narrow').removeClass('large');
    });
    $('#switcher-narrow').bind('click', function() {
```

```
      $('body').addClass('narrow').removeClass('large');
    });
    $('#switcher-large').bind('click', function() {
      $('body').removeClass('narrow').addClass('large');
    });

    $('#switcher .button').bind('click', function() {
      $('#switcher .button').removeClass('selected');
      $(this).addClass('selected');
    });
  });
```

This optimization takes advantage of the three jQuery features we have discussed. First, implicit iteration is once again useful where we bind the same click handler to each button with a single call to `.bind()`. Second, behavior queueing allows us to bind two functions to the same click event, without the second overwriting the first. Lastly, we're using jQuery's chaining capabilities to collapse the adding and removing of classes into a single line of code each time.

Further Consolidation

Now let's look at the behaviors we have bound to each button once again. The `.removeClass()` method's parameter is optional; when omitted, it removes *all* classes from the element. We can streamline our code a bit by exploiting this as follows:

```
$(document).ready(function() {
  $('#switcher-normal').bind('click', function() {
    $('body').removeClass();
  });
  $('#switcher-narrow').bind('click', function() {
    $('body').removeClass().addClass('narrow');
  });
  $('#switcher-large').bind('click', function() {
    $('body').removeClass().addClass('large');
  });

  $('#switcher .button').bind('click', function() {
    $('#switcher .button').removeClass('selected');
    $(this).addClass('selected');
  });
});
```

Now we are executing some of the same code in each of the button handlers. This can be easily factored out into our general button click handler:

```
$(document).ready(function() {
  $('#switcher .button').bind('click', function() {
    $('body').removeClass();
    $('#switcher .button').removeClass('selected');
    $(this).addClass('selected');
  });

  $('#switcher-narrow').bind('click', function() {
    $('body').addClass('narrow');
  });
  $('#switcher-large').bind('click', function() {
    $('body').addClass('large');
  });
});
```

Note that we need to move the general handler above the specific ones now. The `.removeClass()` needs to happen before the `.addClass()`, and we can count on this because jQuery always triggers event handlers in the order in which they were registered.

 We can only safely remove all classes because we are in charge of the HTML in this case. When we are writing code for reuse (such as for a plug-in), we need to respect any classes that might be present and leave them intact.

Finally, we can get rid of the specific handlers entirely by once again exploiting event context. Since the context keyword `this` gives us a DOM element rather than a jQuery object, we can use native DOM properties to determine the ID of the element that was clicked. We can thus bind the same handler to all the buttons, and within the handler perform different actions for each button:

```
$(document).ready(function() {
  $('#switcher .button').bind('click', function() {
    $('body').removeClass();
    if (this.id == 'switcher-narrow') {
      $('body').addClass('narrow');
    }
    else if (this.id == 'switcher-large') {
      $('body').addClass('large');
    }
```

```
      $('#switcher .button').removeClass('selected');
      $(this).addClass('selected');
    });
  });
```

Shorthand Events

Binding a handler for an event (like a simple click event) is such a common task that jQuery provides an even terser way to accomplish it; **shorthand event methods** work in the same way as their `.bind()` counterparts with a couple fewer keystrokes.

For example, our style switcher could be written using `.click()` instead of `.bind()` as follows:

```
$(document).ready(function() {
  $('#switcher .button').click(function() {
    $('body').removeClass();
    if (this.id == 'switcher-narrow') {
      $('body').addClass('narrow');
    }
    else if (this.id == 'switcher-large') {
      $('body').addClass('large');
    }
    $('#switcher .button').removeClass('selected');
    $(this).addClass('selected');
  });
});
```

Compound Events

Most of jQuery's event-handling methods directly respond to native JavaScript events. A handful, however, are custom handlers added for convenience and cross-browser optimization. One of these, the `.ready()` method, we have discussed in detail already. The `.toggle()` and `.hover()` methods are two more custom event handlers; they are both referred to as **compound event handlers** because they intercept combinations of user actions, and respond to them using more than one function.

Showing and Hiding Advanced Features

Suppose that we wanted to be able to hide our style switcher when it is not needed. One convenient way to hide advanced features is to make them collapsible. We will allow one click on the label to hide the buttons, leaving the label alone. Another click on the label will restore the buttons. We need another class to handle the hidden buttons:

```
.hidden {
  display: none;
}
```

We could implement this feature by storing the current state of the buttons in a variable, and checking its value each time the label is clicked to know whether to add or remove the `hidden` class on the buttons. We could also directly check for the presence of the class on a button, and use this information to decide what to do. Instead, jQuery provides the `.toggle()` method, which performs this housekeeping task for us. There are in fact two `.toggle()` methods defined by jQuery. For information on the effect method of this name, see:

```
http://docs.jquery.com/Effects#toggle.28.29
```

The `.toggle()` method takes two arguments, both of which are functions. The first click on the element causes the first function to execute; the second click triggers the second function. The two functions continue to alternate every other click thereafter. With `.toggle()`, we can implement our collapsible style switcher quite easily:

```
$(document).ready(function() {
  $('#switcher h3').toggle(function() {
    $('#switcher .button').addClass('hidden');
  }, function() {
    $('#switcher .button').removeClass('hidden');
  });
});
```

After the first click, the buttons are all hidden as shown in the following screenshot:

And a second click returns them to visibility as shown in the following screenshot:

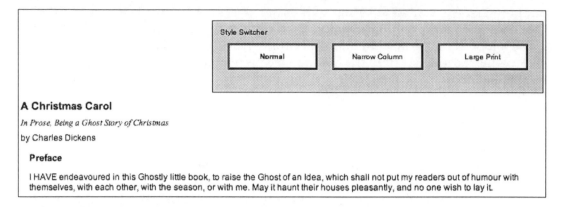

Once again we rely on implicit iteration; this time to hide all the buttons in one fell swoop without requiring an enclosing element.

For this specific case, jQuery provides another mechanism for the collapsing we are performing. We can use the `.toggleClass()` method to automatically check for the presence of the class before applying or removing it:

```
$(document).ready(function() {
  $('#switcher h3').click(function() {
    $('#switcher .button').toggleClass('hidden');
  });
});
```

In this case, `.toggleClass()` is probably the more elegant solution, but `.toggle()` is a more versatile way to perform two different actions in alternation.

Highlighting Clickable Items

In illustrating the ability of the click event to operate on normally non-clickable page elements, we have crafted an interface that gives few hints that the buttons are actually *live*. To remedy this, we can give the buttons a rollover state, making it clear that they interact in some way with the mouse:

```
#switcher .hover {
  cursor: pointer;
  background-color: #afa;
}
```

The CSS specification incorporates a pseudo-class called :hover, which allows a stylesheet to affect an element's appearance when the user's mouse cursor is inside it. In Internet Explorer 6, this capability is restricted to link elements, so we can't use it for other items in cross-browser code. Instead, jQuery allows us to perform arbitrary actions both when the mouse cursor enters an element and when it leaves the element.

The .hover() method takes two function arguments, just as .toggle() does. In this case, the first function will be executed when the mouse cursor enters the selected element, and the second is fired when the cursor leaves. We can modify the classes applied to the buttons at these times to achieve a rollover effect:

```
$(document).ready(function() {
  $('#switcher .button').hover(function() {
    $(this).addClass('hover');
  }, function() {
    $(this).removeClass('hover');
  });
});
```

We once again use implicit iteration and event context for short, simple code. Now when hovering over any button, we see our class applied as shown in the following screenshot:

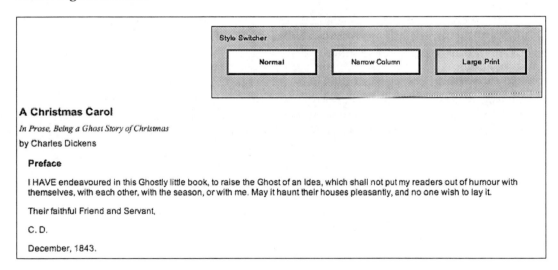

The use of .hover() also means we avoid headaches caused by **event propagation** in JavaScript. To understand this, we need to take a look at how JavaScript decides which element gets to handle a given event.

The Journey of an Event

When an event occurs on a page, an entire hierarchy of DOM elements gets a chance to handle the event. Consider a page model like this:

```
<div class="foo">
  <span class="bar"><a href="http://www.example.com/">The quick brown
                        fox jumps over the lazy dog.</a></span>
  <p>How razorback-jumping frogs can level six piqued gymnasts!</p>
</div>
```

We then visualize the code as a set of nested elements as shown in the following figure:

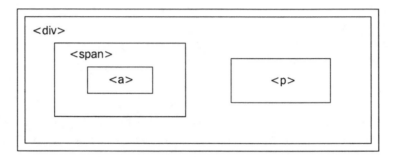

When the anchor on this page is clicked, for example, the `<div>`, `<span>`, and `<a>` all should get the opportunity to respond to the click. After all, the three are all under the user's mouse cursor at the time.

One strategy for allowing multiple elements to respond to a click is called **event capturing**. With event capturing, the event is first given to the most all-encompassing element, and then to successively more specific ones. In our example, this means that first the `<div>` gets passed the event, then the `<span>`, and finally the `<a>`.

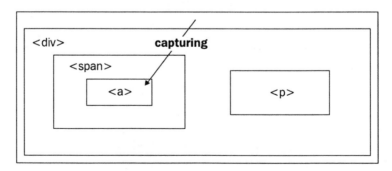

Technically, in browser implementations of event capturing, specific elements register to listen for events that occur among their descendants. The approximation provided here is close enough for our needs.

The opposite strategy is called **event bubbling**. The event gets sent to the most specific element, and after this element has an opportunity to react, the event bubbles up to more general elements. In our example, the <a> would be handed the event first, and then the <span> and <div> in that order.

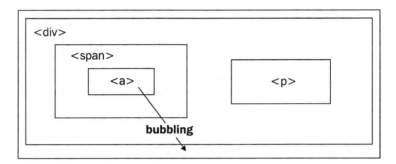

Unsurprisingly, different browser developers originally decided on different models for event propagation. The DOM standard that eventually developed thus specified that both strategies should be used; first the event is captured from general to specific, and then the event bubbles back up to the top of the DOM tree. Event handlers can be registered for either part of the process.

Not all browsers have been updated to match this new standard, and in those that support capturing it typically must be specifically enabled. To provide cross-browser consistency, therefore, jQuery always registers event handlers for the bubbling phase of the model. We can always assume that the most specific element will get the first opportunity to respond to any event.

Side Effects of Event Bubbling

Event bubbling can cause unexpected behavior, especially when the wrong element responds to a mouseover or mouseout. Consider a mouseout event handler attached to the <div> in our example. When the user's mouse cursor exits the <div>, the mouseout handler is run as anticipated. Since this is at the top of the hierarchy, no other elements get the event. On the other hand, when the cursor exits the <a> element, a mouseout event is sent to that. This event will then bubble up to the

`<span>` and then to the `<div>`, firing the same event handler. This bubbling sequence is likely not desired; for the buttons in our style switcher example, it could mean the highlight was turned off prematurely.

The `.hover()` method is aware of these bubbling issues, and when we use that method to attach events, we can ignore the problems caused by the wrong element getting a `mouseover` or `mouseout` event. This makes `.hover()` a very attractive alternative to binding the individual mouse events.

Limiting and Ending Events

The `mouseout` scenario just described illustrates the need to constrain the scope of an event. While `.hover()` handles this specific case, we will encounter other situations in which we need to limit an event spatially (preventing the event from being sent to certain elements) or temporally (preventing the event from being sent at certain times).

Preventing Event Bubbling

We have already seen one situation in which event bubbling can cause problems. To show a case in which `.hover()` does not help our cause, we'll alter the collapsing behavior we implemented earlier.

Suppose we wish to expand the clickable area that triggers the collapsing or expanding of the style switcher. One way to do this is to move the event handler from the label to the containing `<div>` element:

```
$(document).ready(function() {
  $('#switcher').click(function() {
    $('#switcher .button').toggleClass('hidden');
  });
});
```

This alteration makes the entire area of the style switcher clickable to toggle its visibility. The downside is that clicking on the buttons collapses the style switcher after the style on the content has been altered. This is due to event bubbling; the event is first handled by the buttons, then passed up to the DOM tree until it reaches the `<div id="switcher">`, which hides the buttons.

To solve this problem, we need access to the **event object**. This is a JavaScript construct that is passed to each event handler as elements get an opportunity to handle the event. It provides information about the event, such as where the mouse cursor was at the time. It also provides some methods that can be used to affect the progress of the event through the DOM.

To use the event object in our handlers, we only need to add a parameter to the function:

```
$(document).ready(function() {
  $('#switcher').click(function(event) {
    $('#switcher .button').toggleClass('hidden');
  });
});
```

Event Targets

Now we have the event object available in the variable `event` within our handler. The property `event.target` can be helpful in controlling where an event takes effect. This property is a part of the DOM API, but is not implemented in all browsers; jQuery extends the event object as necessary to provide the property in every browser. With `.target`, we can determine which element in the DOM was the first to receive the event (the actual item clicked on). Remembering that `this` gives us the DOM element handling the event, we can write the following code:

```
$(document).ready(function() {
  $('#switcher').click(function(event) {
    if (event.target == this) {
      $('#switcher .button').toggleClass('hidden');
    }
  });
});
```

This code ensures that the item clicked on was `<div id="switcher">`, not one of its sub-elements. Now clicking on buttons will not collapse the style switcher, and clicking on the border will. However, clicking on the label now does nothing, because it too is a sub-element. Instead of placing this check here, then, we can modify the behavior of the buttons to achieve our goals.

Stopping Event Propagation

The event object provides the `.stopPropagation()` method, which can eliminate bubbling completely for the event. Like `.target`, this method is a plain JavaScript feature, but cannot be safely used across all browsers. As long as we register all of our event handlers using jQuery, though, we can use it with impunity.

We'll remove the `e.target == this` check we just added, and instead add some code in our buttons' click handlers:

```
$(document).ready(function() {
  $('#switcher .button').click(function(event) {
```

```
    $('body').removeClass();
    if (this.id == 'switcher-narrow') {
      $('body').addClass('narrow');
    }
    else if (this.id == 'switcher-large') {
      $('body').addClass('large');
    }
    $('#switcher .button').removeClass('selected');
    $(this).addClass('selected');
    event.stopPropagation();
  });
});
```

As before, we need to add a parameter to the function we're using as the click handler, so we have access to the event object. Then we simply call `event.stopPropagation()` to prevent any other DOM element from responding to the event. Now our click is handled by the buttons, and only the buttons; clicks anywhere else on the style switcher will collapse or expand it.

Default Actions

Were our click event handler registered on an anchor element rather than a generic `<div>`, we would face another problem. When a user clicks on a link, the browser loads a new page. This behavior is not an event handler in the same sense as the ones we have been discussing; instead, this is the **default action** for a click on an anchor element. Similarly, when the *Enter* key is pressed while the user is editing a form, the `submit` event is triggered on the form, but then the form submission actually occurs after this.

If these default actions are undesired, calling `.stopPropagation()` on the event will not help. These actions occur nowhere in the normal flow of event propagation. Instead, the `.preventDefault()` method will serve to stop the event in its tracks before the default action is triggered.

Calling `.preventDefault()` is often useful after we have done some tests on the environment of the event. For example, during a form submission we might wish to check that required fields are filled in, and prevent the default action only if they are not. We'll see this in action in Chapter 8.

Event propagation and default actions are independent mechanisms; either can be stopped while the other still occurs. If we wish to halt both, we can return `false` from our event handler, which is a shortcut for calling both `.stopPropagation()` and `.preventDefault()` on the event.

Removing an Event Handler

There are times when we will be done with an event handler we previously registered. Perhaps the state of the page has changed such that the action no longer makes sense. It is typically possible to handle this situation with conditional statements inside our event handlers, but it may be more elegant to remove the handler entirely.

Suppose that we want our collapsible style switcher to remain expanded whenever the page is not using the normal style. We can accomplish this by calling the .unbind() method to remove the handler when one of the style switcher buttons is clicked. First, we should give our handler function a name so that we can use it more than once without repeating ourselves:

```
$(document).ready(function() {
  var toggleStyleSwitcher = function() {
    $('#switcher .button').toggleClass('hidden');
  };

  $('#switcher').click(toggleStyleSwitcher);
});
```

Note that we are using yet another syntax for defining a function. Rather than defining the function by leading with the function keyword, we assign an anonymously-created function to a local variable. This is a stylistic choice to make our event handlers and other function definitions resemble each other more closely; the two syntaxes are functionally equivalent.

Now that the function has a name, we can remove it as a handler when necessary:

```
$(document).ready(function() {
  var toggleStyleSwitcher = function() {
    $('#switcher .button').toggleClass('hidden');
  };

  $('#switcher').click(toggleStyleSwitcher);

  $('#switcher-narrow, #switcher-large').click(function() {
    $('#switcher').unbind('click', toggleStyleSwitcher);
  });
});
```

The .unbind() method here takes an event type as its first argument, and the function to remove as the second argument. We could have omitted the function with the same result here, as the default behavior of .unbind() is to remove all handlers that have been registered for the event. However, being more specific is safer, because we need not fear interference with other code that may wish to bind behaviors to the element.

The code now prevents the collapse functionality after either of the buttons is clicked. However, we have no code in place to restore the behavior when the style is turned back to normal. To do this we add another behavior to the **Normal** button:

```
$(document).ready(function() {
  var toggleStyleSwitcher = function() {
    $('#switcher .button').toggleClass('hidden');
  };

  $('#switcher').click(toggleStyleSwitcher);

  $('#switcher-normal').click(function() {
    $('#switcher').click(toggleStyleSwitcher);
  });
  $('#switcher-narrow, #switcher-large').click(function() {
    $('#switcher').unbind('click', toggleStyleSwitcher);
  });
});
```

Now the toggle behavior is bound when the document is loaded, unbound when **Narrow Column** or **Large Print** is clicked, and rebound when **Normal** is clicked after that.

We have sidestepped a potential pitfall here. Remember that when a handler is bound to an event in jQuery, previous handlers remain in effect. This could mean that if **Normal** was clicked twice in a row, the toggling behavior could be triggered twice. Indeed, if we had used anonymous functions throughout our example, this would be the case. But since we gave the function a name and used the same function throughout the code, the behavior is only bound once. The .bind() function will not attach an event handler to an element if it has already been attached.

In jQuery 1.0, unbinding event handlers was possible by using shorthand event methods, just like their binding counterparts. For example, .unclick() was a synonym for .unbind('click'). This facility was rarely used, so to prevent unnecessary library size and API complexity, the 1.1 release removed these shorthand event methods.

Reintroducing a removed shorthand event method is straightforward. We will discuss how to achieve this in Chapter 10, as an example of how to extend jQuery's functionality.

A shortcut is also available for the situation in which we want to unbind an event handler immediately after the first time it is triggered. This shortcut, called `.one()`, is used like this:

```
$(document).ready(function() {
  $('#switcher').one('click', toggleStyleSwitcher);
});
```

This would cause the toggle action to occur once, and not again.

Simulating User Interaction

At times it is convenient to execute code that we have bound to an event, even if the normal circumstances of the event are not occurring. For example, suppose we wanted our style switcher to begin in its collapsed state. We could accomplish this by hiding buttons from within the stylesheet, or by calling the `.hide()` method from a `$(document).ready()` handler. Another way, though, is to simulate a click on the style switcher so that the toggling mechanism we've already established is triggered.

The `.trigger()` method allows us to do just this:

```
$(document).ready(function() {
  $('#switcher').trigger('click');
});
```

Now right when the page loads, the switcher is collapsed, just as if it had been clicked as shown in the following screenshot:

Style Switcher

A Christmas Carol

In Prose, Being a Ghost Story of Christmas

by Charles Dickens

Preface

I HAVE endeavoured in this Ghostly little book, to raise the Ghost of an Idea, which shall not put my readers out of humour with themselves, with each other, with the season, or with me. May it haunt their houses pleasantly, and no one wish to lay it.

Note that event propagation does not occur when an event is triggered by jQuery in this way; only the handlers attached directly to the element are executed. We must perform our trigger on `$('#switcher')`, not `$('#switcher h3')`, if we want it to operate correctly, because that is where the behaviors have been attached.

The `.trigger()` method provides the same set of shortcuts that `.bind()` does. When these shortcuts are used with no arguments, the behavior is to trigger the action rather than bind it:

```
$(document).ready(function() {
  $('#switcher').click();
});
```

Summary

The abilities we've discussed in this chapter allow us to:

- React to a user's click on a page element with `.bind()` or `.click()` and change the styles used on the page

- Use event context to perform different actions depending on the page element clicked, even when the handler is bound to several elements

- Alternately expand and collapse a page element by using `.toggle()`

- Highlight page elements under the mouse cursor by using `.hover()`

- Influence which elements get to respond to an event with `.stopPropagation()` and `.preventDefault()`

- Call `.unbind()` to remove an event handler we're done with

- Cause bound event handlers to execute with `.trigger()`.

Taken together, we can use these capabilities to build quite interactive pages. In the next chapter, we'll learn how to provide visual feedback to the user during these interactions.

4
Effects—How to Add Flair to Your Actions

Move it up and down now
Move it all around now
— Devo,
"Gut Feeling"

If actions speak louder than words, then in the JavaScript world, effects make actions speak louder still. With jQuery, we can easily add impact to our actions through a set of simple visual effects, and even craft our own, more sophisticated animations.

jQuery effects certainly add flair, as is evident when we see an element gradually slide into view instead of appearing all at once. However, they can also provide important usability enhancements that help orient the user when there is some change on a page (especially common in AJAX applications). In this chapter, we will explore a number of these effects and combine them in interesting ways.

Inline CSS Modification

Before we jump into the nifty jQuery effects, a quick look at CSS is in order. In previous chapters we have been modifying a document's appearance by defining styles for classes in a separate stylesheet and then adding or removing those classes with jQuery. Typically, this is the preferred process for injecting CSS into HTML because it respects the stylesheet's role in dealing with the presentation of a page. However, there may be times when we need to apply styles that haven't been, or can't easily be, defined in a stylesheet. Fortunately, jQuery has a `.css()` method for such occasions.

This method acts as both a **getter** and a **setter**. To get the value of a style property, we simply pass the name of the property as a string, like `.css('backgroundColor')`.

Multi-word properties can be interpreted by jQuery when hyphenated, as they are in CSS notation (`background-color`), or camel-cased, as they are in DOM notation (`backgroundColor`). For setting style properties, the `.css()` method comes in two flavors—one that takes a single style property and its value and one that takes a **map** of property-value pairs:

- `.css('property','value')`
- `.css({property1: 'value1', 'property-2': 'value2'})`

Experienced JavaScript developers will recognize these jQuery maps as JavaScript object literals.

 Numeric values do not take quotation marks while string values do. But, when using the map notation, quotation marks are not required for property names if they are written in camel-cased DOM notation.

We use the `.css()` method the same way we've been using `.addClass()`—by chaining it to a selector and binding it to an event. To demonstrate this, we'll return to the style switcher example, using slightly different HTML this time:

```
<div id="switcher">
  <div class="label">Style Switcher</div>
  <div class="button" id="switcher-large">Increase Text Size</div>
  <div class="button" id="switcher-small">Decrease Text size</div>
</div>
<div class="speech">
  <p>Fourscore and seven years ago our fathers brought forth on
     this continent a new nation, conceived in liberty, and dedicated
     to the proposition that all men are created equal.</p>
</div>
```

By linking to a stylesheet with a few basic style rules, the page can initially look like the following screenshot:

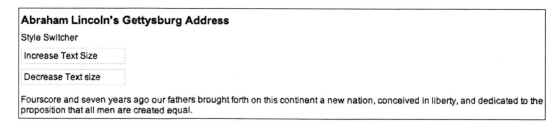

In this version of the style switcher, we have two buttons in `div` elements. Clicking on the `switcher-large` div will increase the text size of the `speech` div, and clicking on the `switcher-small` div will decrease it.

If all we wanted were to increase and decrease the size a single time to a predetermined value, we could still use the .addClass() method. But let's suppose that now we want the text to continue increasing or decreasing incrementally each time the respective button is clicked. Although it might be possible to define a separate class for each click and iterate through them, a more straightforward approach would be to compute the new text size each time by getting the current size and multiplying it by a set number.

Our code will start with the $(document).ready() and $('#switcher-large').click() event handlers:

```
$(document).ready(function() {
  $('#switcher-large').click(function() {
  });
});
```

Next, the font size can be easily discovered: $('div.speech').css('fontSize'). However, because the returned value will include both the number and the unit of measurement, we'll need to store each part in its own variable, after which we can multiply the number and reattach the unit. Also, when we plan to use a jQuery object more than once, it's generally a good idea to store that in a variable as well.

```
$(document).ready(function() {
  $('#switcher-large').click(function() {
    var $speech = $('div.speech');
    var currentSize = $speech.css('fontSize');
    var num = parseFloat(currentSize, 10);
    var unit = currentSize.slice(-2);
  });
});
```

The first line inside .click() stores a variable for the speech div itself.

Notice the use of a $ in the variable name, $speech. Since $ is a legal character in JavaScript variables, we can use it as a reminder that the variable is storing a jQuery object. The next line stores the font size of the speech div—for example, 12px.

After that, we use parseFloat() and .slice(). The parseFloat() function looks at a string from left to right until it encounters a non-numeric character. The string of digits is converted into a floating-point (decimal) number. For example, it would convert the string 12 to the number 12. In addition, it strips non-numeric trailing characters from the string, so 12px becomes 12 as well. If the string begins with a non-numeric character, parseFloat() returns NaN, which stands for *Not a Number*. The second argument for parseFloat() allows us to ensure that the number is interpreted as base-10 instead of octal or some other representation.

The `.slice()` method returns a substring beginning at the specified character in the string. Because the unit of measurement that we are using (px) is two characters long, we indicate that the substring should begin two characters before the end.

All that's left is to multiply `num` by 1.4 and then set the font size by concatenating the two parsed variables, `num` and `unit`:

```
$(document).ready(function() {
  $('#switcher-large').click(function() {
    var $speech = $('div.speech');
    var currentSize = $speech.css('fontSize');
    var num = parseFloat(currentSize, 10);
    var unit = currentSize.slice(-2);
    num *= 1.4;
    $speech.css('fontSize', num + unit);
  });
});
```

The equation num *= 1.4 is shorthand for num = num * 1.4. We can use the same type of shorthand for the other basic mathematical operations, as well: addition, num += 1.4; subtraction, num -= 1.4; division, num /= 1.4; and modulus (division remainder), num %= 1.4.

Now when a user clicks on the `switcher-large` div, the text becomes larger as shown in the following screenshot:

Abraham Lincoln's Gettysburg Address

Style Switcher

Increase Text Size

Decrease Text size

Fourscore and seven years ago our fathers brought forth on this continent a new nation, conceived in liberty, and dedicated to the proposition that all men are created equal.

Another click, and the text becomes larger still.

To get the `switcher-small` div to decrease the font size, we will divide rather than multiply—`num /= 1.4`. Better still, we can combine the two into a single `.click()` handler on the `button` class. Then, after setting the variables, we can either multiply or divide depending on the ID of the div that was clicked. Here is what that code would look like:

```
$(document).ready(function() {
  $('div.button').click(function() {
    var $speech = $('div.speech');
    var currentSize = $speech.css('fontSize');
    var num = parseFloat(currentSize, 10);
    var unit = currentSize.slice(-2);
    if (this.id == 'switcher-large') {
      num *= 1.4;
    } else if (this.id == 'switcher-small') {
      num /= 1.4;
    }
    $speech.css('fontSize', num + unit);
  });
});
```

Recall from Chapter 3 that we can access the id property of the DOM element referred to by this, which appears here inside the if and else if statements. Here, it is more efficient to use this than to create a jQuery object just to test the value of a property.

Basic Hide and Show

Basic .hide() and .show(), without any parameters, can be thought of as smart shorthand methods for .css('display', 'string'), where string is the appropriate display value. The effect, as might be expected, is that the matched set of elements will be immediately hidden or shown, with no animation.

The .hide() method sets the inline style attribute of the matched set of elements to display:none. The smart part here is that it remembers the value of the display property—typically block or inline—before it was changed to none. Conversely, the .show() method restores the matched set of elements to whatever visible display property they had before display:none was applied.

This feature of .show() and .hide() is especially helpful when hiding elements whose default display property is overridden in a stylesheet. For example, the <li> element has the property display:block by default, but we might want to change it to display:inline for a horizontal menu. Fortunately, using the .show() method on a hidden element such as one of these <li> tags would not merely reset it to its default display:block, because that would put the <li> on its own line. Instead, the element is restored to its previous display:inline state, thus preserving the horizontal design.

A quick demonstration of these two methods can be set up by adding an ellipsis at the end of the paragraph, followed by another paragraph, to our example HTML:

```
<div id="switcher">
  <div class="label">Style Switcher</div>
  <div class="button" id="switcher-large">
                                    Increase Text Size</div>
  <div class="button" id="switcher-small">
                            Decrease Text size</div>         </div>
<div class="speech">
  <p>Fourscore and seven years ago our fathers brought forth on
      this continent a new nation, conceived in liberty, and dedicated
      to the proposition that all men are created equal.
  <span class="more">. . .</span></p>
  <p>Now we are engaged in a great civil war, testing whether that
  nation, or any nation so conceived and so dedicated, can long
  endure. We are met on a great battlefield of that war. We have come
  to dedicate a portion of that field as a final resting-place for
  those who here gave their lives that the nation might live. It is
  altogether fitting and proper that we should do this. But, in a
  larger sense, we cannot dedicate, we cannot consecrate, we cannot
  hallow, this ground.</p>
</div>
```

When the DOM is ready, the second paragraph will be hidden:

```
$(document).ready(function() {
  $('p:eq(1)').hide();
});
```

And the speech will look like the following screenshot:

Fourscore and seven years ago our fathers brought forth on this continent a new nation, conceived in liberty, and dedicated to the proposition that all men are created equal....

Then, when the user clicks on the ellipsis (. . .) at the end of the first paragraph, the ellipsis will be hidden and the second paragraph will be shown:

```
$(document).ready(function() {
  $('p:eq(1)').hide();
  $('span.more').click(function() {
    $('p:eq(1)').show();
    $(this).hide();
  });
});
```

Now the speech will look like this:

> Fourscore and seven years ago our fathers brought forth on this continent a new nation, conceived in liberty, and dedicated to the proposition that all men are created equal.
>
> Now we are engaged in a great civil war, testing whether that nation, or any nation so conceived and so dedicated, can long endure. We are met on a great battlefield of that war. We have come to dedicate a portion of that field as a final resting-place for those who here gave their lives that the nation might live. It is altogether fitting and proper that we should do this. But, in a larger sense, we cannot dedicate, we cannot consecrate, we cannot hallow, this ground.

The .hide() and .show() methods are quick and useful, but they aren't very flashy. To add some flair, we can give them a speed.

Effects and Speed

When we include a speed with .show() or .hide(), it becomes animated—occurring over a specified period of time. The .hide('speed') method, for example, will decrease an element's height, width, and opacity simultaneously until all three reach zero, at which point the CSS rule display:none is applied. The .show('speed') method will increase the element's height from top to bottom, width from left to right, and opacity from 0 to 1 until its contents are completely visible.

Speeding In

With any jQuery effect, we can use one of three speeds: slow, normal, and fast. Using .show('slow') would make the show effect complete in .6 seconds, .show('normal') in .4 seconds, and .show('fast') in .2 seconds. For even greater precision we can specify a number of milliseconds, for example .show(850). Unlike the speed names, the numbers are not wrapped in quotation marks.

Let's include a speed in our example when showing the second paragraph of Lincoln's Gettysburg Address:

```
$(document).ready(function() {
  $('p:eq(1)').hide();
  $('span.more').click(function() {
    $('p:eq(1)').show('slow');
    $(this).hide();
  });
});
```

If we were able to capture the paragraph's appearance at roughly halfway through the effect, we would see something like the following:

> Fourscore and seven years ago our fathers brought forth on this continent a new nation, conceived in liberty, and dedicated to the proposition that all men are created equal.
>
> Now we are engaged in a great civil war, testing whether that nation, or any nation so conceived and so dedicated, can long endure. We are met on a great battlefield

Fading In and Fading Out

If we wanted the whole paragraph to appear just by gradually increasing the opacity, we could use `.fadeIn('slow')` instead:

```
$(document).ready(function() {
  $('p:eq(1)').hide();
  $('span.more').click(function() {
    $('p:eq(1)').fadeIn('slow');
    $(this).hide();
  });
});
```

This time if we captured the paragraph's appearance halfway, it would now be seen as:

> Fourscore and seven years ago our fathers brought forth on this continent a new nation, conceived in liberty, and dedicated to the proposition that all men are created equal.
>
> Now we are engaged in a great civil war, testing whether that nation, or any nation so conceived and so dedicated, can long endure. We are met on a great battlefield of that war. We have come to dedicate a portion of that field as a final resting-place for those who here gave their lives that the nation might live. It is altogether fitting and proper that we should do this. But, in a larger sense, we cannot dedicate, we cannot consecrate, we cannot hallow, this ground.

The difference here is that the `.fadeIn()` effect starts by setting the dimensions of the paragraph so that the contents can simply fade into it. Similarly, to gradually decrease the opacity we could use `.fadeOut()`.

Multiple Effects

Of the simple effects bundled in the jQuery core, only `show()` and `hide()` modify more than one style property at a time—height, width, and opacity. The others change a single property:

- `fadeIn()` and `fadeOut()`: opacity
- `fadeTo()`: opacity
- `slideDown()` and `slideUp()`: height

However, jQuery also provides a powerful `animate()` method that allows us to create our own custom animations with multiple effects. The `animate` method takes four arguments:

1. A **map** of style properties and values—similar to the `.css()` map discussed earlier in this chapter

2. An optional **speed**—which can be one of the preset strings or a number of milliseconds

3. An optional **easing type**—an advanced option discussed in Chapter 10

4. An optional **callback function**—which will be discussed later in this chapter

All together, the three arguments would look like this:

```
.animate({param1: 'value1', param2: 'value2'}, speed, function() {
  alert('The animation is finished.');
});
```

Building an Animated show()

Let's take another look at our code that makes the second **Gettysburg Address** paragraph gradually appear:

```
$(document).ready(function() {
  $('p:eq(1)').hide();
  $('span.more').click(function() {
    $('p:eq(1)').show('slow');
    $(this).hide();
  });
});
```

Remember that `.show('slow')` simultaneously modifies the width, height, and opacity. In fact, this method is really just a shortcut for the `.animate()` method, with a specific set of built-in style properties. If we wanted to build it on our own with `.animate()`, the code would look like this:

```
$(document).ready(function() {
  $('p:eq(1)').hide();
  $('span.more').click(function() {
    $('p:eq(1)'). animate({height: 'show', width: 'show',
                                     opacity: 'show'}, 'slow');
    $(this).hide();
  });
});
```

Apparently, `.animate()` has a few shortcuts of its own! We just used the `show` shortcut to restore width and height to their values before they were hidden. We can also use `hide`, `toggle` or any appropriate numeric value.

Creating a Custom Animation

With the `.animate()` method, we have at our disposal not only the style properties used for the other effect methods, but also other properties such as `left` and `top`. The extra properties allow us to create much more sophisticated effects. We could, for example, move an item from the left side of the page to the right while increasing its height to 50 pixels.

So, let's do that with our style switcher buttons. Here is how they look before we animate them:

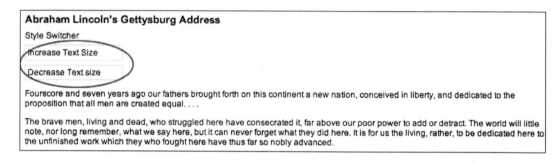

We'll make the buttons move to the right and increase their height. Let's trigger this animation by clicking on the **Style Switcher** text just above the links. Here is what the code should look like:

```
$(document).ready(function() {
  $('div.label').click(function() {
    $('div.button').animate({left: 650, height: 38}, 'slow');
  });
});
```

This code will increase the heights of the buttons, but at the moment their position cannot be changed. We still need to enable changing their position in the CSS.

Positioning with CSS

When working with `.animate()`, it's important to keep in mind the limitations that CSS imposes on the elements that we wish to change. For example, adjusting the `left` property will have no effect on the matching elements unless those elements have their CSS position set to `relative` or `absolute`. The default CSS position for all block-level elements is `static`, which accurately describes how those elements will remain if we try to move them without first changing their position value.

 For more information on absolute and relative positioning, see Joe Gillespie's article, *Absolutely Relative* at: `http://www.wpdfd.com/editorial/wpd0904news.htm#feature`

A peek at our stylesheet shows that we have set both the `<div id="switcher">` container and the individual buttons to be relatively positioned:

```
#switcher {
  position: relative;
}
.button {
  position: relative;
  width: 140px;
  padding: 5px;
  border: 1px solid #e3e3e3;
  margin: .5em 0;
}
```

With the CSS taken into account, the result of clicking on the **Style Switcher**, when the animation has completed, will look like this:

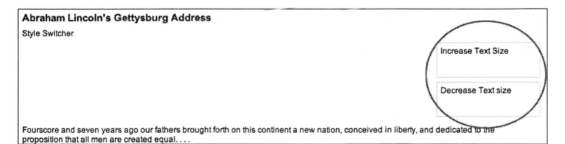

Making Sense of the Numbers

As we examine the code more closely, note the two values — 650 for `left` and 38 for `height`:

```
$('div.button').animate({left: 650, height: 38}, 'slow');
```

Why these two numbers? Why not 750 or 800 for the left position? And more important, why not 50 for the height?

As far as the left position is concerned, well, let's just admit it: We're cheating! We're only guessing how wide the page is. For all we know, somebody could be looking at our page with a super-widescreen, high-resolution monitor, which might leave our buttons sitting somewhere near the middle of the page.

The 38-pixel height, on the other hand, is intentional. The buttons, in addition to being set as `position: relative`, have `padding: 5px` and `border: 1px solid #e3e3e3` applied to them. The height property, however, does not take the padding or the borders into account. So, in order to arrive at 50 pixels, we need to subtract the height of the top padding and the bottom padding and the width of the top and bottom border from it. We're using the shorthand `padding` and `border` properties; but they amount to the same as if we set each side's padding to 5 pixels and each side's border-width to 1 pixel, like:

```css
.button {
  position: relative;
  width: 140px;
 /* each side's padding . . . */
  padding-top: 5px;
  padding-right: 5px;
  padding-bottom: 5px;
  padding-left: 5px;

 /* each side's border-width . . . */
  border-top-width: 1px;
  border-right-width: 1px;
  border-bottom-width: 1px;
  border-left-width: 1px;
  border-style: solid;
  border-color: #e3e3e3;
  margin: .5em 0;
}
```

So, we need to calculate the following:

```
height - (padding-top + padding-bottom) - (border-top-width
                                        + border-bottom-width)
```

Substituting our values, we get this:

```
50 - (5 + 5) - (1 + 1)
```

And the result, of course, is 38!

These calculations are based on the *W3C's box model* for CSS. The full specification for this model can be found at `http://www.w3.org/TR/REC-CSS2/box.html`.

Improving the Custom Animation

Now let's return to the problem we encountered with our custom animation's resulting left position. It certainly would be nice to be able to move those buttons so that their right sides line up with the right sides of the paragraphs below (approximately, because the paragraphs aren't right-justified). Here's how we can do it:

1. Get the width of the paragraphs.
2. Get the width of the buttons, including their left and right padding and borders.
3. Subtract the width of the buttons from the width of the paragraphs.
4. Use the result of our calculation, in the form of a variable, as our .animate method's left value.

In order to calculate the buttons' total width and to keep our code somewhat readable, we need to set a lot of variables. Here is what the new and improved code looks like:

```
$(document).ready(function() {
  $('div.label').click(function() {
    //get all of the widths...
    var paraWidth = $('div.speech p').width();
    var $button = $('div.button');
    var buttonWidth = $button.width();
    var paddingRight = $button.css('paddingRight');
    var paddingLeft = $button.css('paddingLeft');
    var borderRightWidth = $button.css('borderRightWidth');
    var borderLeftWidth = $button.css('borderLeftWidth');

    // calculate the total width...
    var totalButtonWidth = parseInt(
            buttonWidth, 10) + parseInt(paddingRight, 10) + parseInt(
            paddingLeft, 10) + parseInt(borderRightWidth, 10) +
            parseInt(borderLeftWidth, 10);
    var rightSide = paraWidth - totalButtonWidth;
    $button.animate({left: rightSide, height: 38}, 'slow');
  });
});
```

Now we can see the buttons lining up nicely with the right side of the paragraphs:

Abraham Lincoln's Gettysburg Address

Style Switcher

Increase Text Size

Decrease Text size

Fourscore and seven years ago our fathers brought forth on this continent a new nation, conceived in liberty, and dedicated to the proposition that all men are created equal. . . .

The brave men, living and dead, who struggled here have consecrated it, far above our poor power to add or detract. The world will little note, nor long remember, what we say here, but it can never forget what they did here. It is for us the living, rather, to be dedicated here to the unfinished work which they who fought here have thus far so nobly advanced.

In addition to adding a number of variables, the preceding code makes heavy use of the JavaScript `parseInt()` function, which is similar to `parseFloat()`, except that it returns an integer rather than a floating-point number. Each value returned by our instances of `.css()` has px appended to the number. For example, the value of `paddingRight` is 5px. If we want to do any adding and subtracting (and we do), we need to remove px from those variables, so we're left with actual numbers. Note that only pixel values are safe to use in these calculations, because Internet Explorer may misinterpret values expressed in other units.

jQuery does, however, give us the `width()` shorthand method, which returns the same number as `.css('width')`, but without the unit of measurement.

Simultaneous versus Queued Effects

The `.animate` method, as we've just discovered, is very useful for creating **simultaneous** effects in a particular set of elements. There may be times, however, when we want to **queue** our effects, having them occur one after the other.

Working with a Single Set of Elements

When applying multiple effects to the same set of elements, queuing is easily achieved by chaining those effects. To demonstrate this queuing, let's take another look at our simpler example of moving the switcher buttons to the right and enlarging them:

```
$(document).ready(function() {
  $('div.label').click(function() {
    $('div.button').animate({left: 650, height: 38}, 'slow');
  });
});
```

As we've already noted, the two animations — left:650 and height:38 — occur virtually simultaneously. To queue these effects, we simply chain them instead:

```
$(document).ready(function() {
  $('div.label').click(function() {
    $('div.button')
      .animate({left: 650}, 'slow')
      .animate({height: 38}, 'slow');
  });
});
```

Now, our buttons first move 650 pixels to the right, and then they grow to a height of 50 pixels (38 + top and bottom padding and borders). If we wanted to increase the height first, all we'd need to do is reverse the order of the two animations in our code.

Recall that chaining permits us to keep the two .animate() methods on the same line, but here we have indented them and put each on its own line for greater readability.

We can queue any of the jQuery effects, not just .animate(), by chaining them. We can, for example, queue effects on the buttons in the following order:

1. Fade their opacity to .5, making them semi-transparent.

2. Move them 650 pixels to the right.

3. Fade them back in to full opacity.

4. Hide them by sliding them up.

All we need to do is chain the effects in the same order in our code:

```
$(document).ready(function() {
  $('div.label').click(function() {
    $('div.button')
      .fadeTo('slow',0.5)
      .animate({left: 650}, 'slow')
      .fadeTo('slow',1.0)
      .slideUp('slow');
  });
});
```

One final observation about queuing effects on a single set of elements is that queuing does not apply to other, non-effect methods such as .css(). So let's suppose we wanted to change the buttons' background color to red at the end of our animation instead of sliding them up and out of sight. We could try doing it like this:

```
$(document).ready(function() {
  $('div.label').click(function() {
    $('div.button')
      .fadeTo('slow',0.5)
      .animate({left: 650}, 'slow')
      .fadeTo('slow',1.0)
      .css('backgroundColor','#f00');
  });
});
```

However, even though the background-changing code is placed at the end of the chain, it occurs immediately upon the click. What if we take `.css()` out of the chain and repeat the selector expression instead?

```
$(document).ready(function() {
  $('div.label').click(function() {
    $('div.button')
    .fadeTo('slow',0.5)
    .animate({left: 650}, 'slow')
    .fadeTo('slow',1.0);
    $('div.button').css('backgroundColor','#f00');
  });
});
```

We get the same result—the buttons' background color changes immediately when the switcher label is clicked.

So, how then can we queue these non-effect methods? We'll discover the answer as we examine effects with multiple sets of elements.

Working with Multiple Sets of Elements

Unlike with a single set of elements, when we apply effects to different sets, they occur at virtually the same time. To see these simultaneous effects in action, we'll slide one paragraph down while sliding another paragraph up. First, we'll add the remaining portion of the **Gettysburg Address** to the HTML, dividing it into two separate paragraphs:

```
<div id="switcher">
  <div class="label">Style Switcher</div>
  <div class="button" id="switcher-large">Increase Text Size</div>
  <div class="button" id="switcher-small">Decrease Text size</div>
</div>
<div class="speech">
```

```
<p>Fourscore and seven years ago our fathers brought forth on this
continent a new nation, conceived in liberty, and dedicated to the
proposition that all men are created equal.<span class="more">. .
.</span></p>
<p>Now we are engaged in a great civil war, testing whether that
nation, or any nation so conceived and so dedicated, can long
endure. We are met on a great battlefield of that war. We have come
to dedicate a portion of that field as a final resting-place for
those who here gave their lives that the nation might live. It is
altogether fitting and proper that we should do this. But, in a
larger sense, we cannot dedicate, we cannot consecrate, we cannot
hallow, this ground.</p>
<p>The brave men, living and dead, who struggled here have
consecrated it, far above our poor power to add or detract. The
world will little note, nor long remember, what we say here, but it
can never forget what they did here. It is for us the living,
rather, to be dedicated here to the unfinished work which they who
fought here have thus far so nobly advanced.</p>
<p>It is rather for us to be here dedicated to the great task
remaining before us&mdash;that from these honored dead we take
increased devotion to that cause for which they gave the last full
measure of devotion&mdash;that we here highly resolve that these
dead shall not have died in vain&mdash;that this nation, under God,
shall have a new birth of freedom and that government of the
people, by the people, for the people, shall not perish from the
earth.</p>
</div>
```

Next, to help us see what's happening during the effect, we'll give the third paragraph a light-blue background and the fourth paragraph a lavender background. We'll also hide the fourth paragraph when the DOM is ready:

```
$(document).ready(function() {
  $('p:eq(3)').css('backgroundColor', '#fcf').hide();
  $('p:eq(2)').css('backgroundColor', '#cff');
});
```

Finally, we'll add the `.click()` method to the third paragraph, so that when it is clicked the third paragraph will slide up (and out of view) while the fourth paragraph slides down (and into view):

```
$(document).ready(function() {
  $('p:eq(3)').css('backgroundColor', '#fcf').hide();
  $('p:eq(2)').css('backgroundColor', '#cff').click(function() {
    $(this).slideUp('slow').next().slideDown('slow');
  });
});
```

A screenshot of these two effects in *mid-slide* confirms that they do, indeed, occur virtually simultaneously:

Abraham Lincoln's Gettysburg Address

Style Switcher

Increase Text Size

Decrease Text size

Fourscore and seven years ago our fathers brought forth on this continent a new nation, conceived in liberty, and dedicated to the proposition that all men are created equal. . . .

The brave men, living and dead, who struggled here have consecrated it, far above our poor power to add or detract. The world will little note, nor long remember, what we say here, but it can never forget what they did here. It is for us the living, rather, to be dedicated here to

It is rather for us to be here dedicated to the great task remaining before us—that from these honored dead we take increased devotion to that cause for which they gave the last full measure of devotion—that we here highly resolve that these dead shall not have died in

The light-blue paragraph, which started visible, is halfway through sliding up at the same time as the lavender paragraph, which started hidden, is halfway through sliding down.

Callbacks

In order to allow queuing effects on different elements, jQuery provides **callback** functions. As we have seen with event handlers, callbacks are simply functions passed as method arguments. In the case of effects, they appear as the last argument of the method.

If we use a callback to queue the two slide effects, we can have the fourth paragraph slide down before the third paragraph slides up. Let's first look at how to set up the `.slideDown()` method with the callback:

```
$(document).ready(function() {
  $('p:eq(3)')
    .css('backgroundColor', '#fcf')
    .hide();
  $('p:eq(2)')
    .css('backgroundColor', '#cff')
    .click(function() {
      $(this).next().slideDown('slow',function() {
      // slideUp() here will start after the slideDown has ended
      });
    });
});
```

We do need to be careful here, however, about what is actually going to slide up. Because the callback is inside the `.slideDown()` method, the context has changed for `$(this)`. Now, `$(this)` is no longer the third paragraph, as it was at the point of the `.click()` method; rather, since the `.slideDown()` method is attached to `$(this).next()`, everything within that method now sees `$(this)` as the next sibling, or the fourth paragraph. Therefore, if we put `$(this).slideUp('slow')` inside the callback, we would end up hiding the same paragraph that we had just made visible.

A simple way to keep the reference of `$(this)` stable is to store it in a variable right away within the `.click()` method, like `var $thisPara = $(this)`.

Now `$thisPara` will refer to the third paragraph, both outside and inside the callback. Here is what the code looks like using our new variable:

```
$(document).ready(function() {
  $('p:eq(3)')
    .css('backgroundColor', '#fcf')
    .hide();
  $('p:eq(2)')
    .css('backgroundColor', '#cff')
    .click(function() {
      var $thisPara = $(this);
      $thisPara.next().slideDown('slow',function() {
        $thisPara.slideUp('slow');
      });
    });
});
```

Using `$thisPara` inside the `.slideDown()` callback creates a closure. We'll be discussing this topic in Appendix C.

This time a snapshot halfway through the effects will reveal that both the third and the fourth paragraphs are visible; the fourth has finished sliding down and the third is about to begin sliding up:

Abraham Lincoln's Gettysburg Address

Style Switcher

Increase Text Size

Decrease Text size

Fourscore and seven years ago our fathers brought forth on this continent a new nation, conceived in liberty, and dedicated to the proposition that all men are created equal. . . .

The brave men, living and dead, who struggled here have consecrated it, far above our poor power to add or detract. The world will little note, nor long remember, what we say here, but it can never forget what they did here. It is for us the living, rather, to be dedicated here to the unfinished work which they who fought here have thus far so nobly advanced.

It is rather for us to be here dedicated to the great task remaining before us—that from these honored dead we take increased devotion to that cause for which they gave the last full measure of devotion—that we here highly resolve that these dead shall not have died in vain—that this nation, under God, shall have a new birth of freedom and that government of the people, by the people, for the people, shall not perish from the earth.

Now that we've discussed callbacks, we can return to the code from earlier in this chapter in which we wanted to queue a background-color change at the end of a series of effects. Rather than chaining the .css() method, as we previously attempted unsuccessfully, we can put it inside the last effect's callback:

```
$(document).ready(function() {
  $('div.label').click(function() {
    $('div.button')
      .fadeTo('slow',0.5)
      .animate({left: 650}, 'slow')
      .fadeTo('slow',1.0, function() {
        $(this).css('backgroundColor','#f00');
      });
  });
});
```

Now we've managed to get the buttons to turn red after they have faded out to 50 percent opacity, moved slowly to the right 650 pixels and faded back in to 100 percent opacity.

In a Nutshell

With all the variations to consider when applying effects, it can become difficult to remember whether the effects will occur simultaneously or sequentially. A brief outline might help:

1. Effects on a single set of elements are:
   ° simultaneous when applied as multiple properties in a single .animate() method
   ° queued when applied in a chain of methods

2. Effects on multiple sets of elements are:
   ° simultaneous by default
   ° queued when applied within the callback of an event handler

Summary

By using effect methods that we have explored in this chapter, we should now be able to incrementally increase and decrease text size by using the .css() method. We should also be able to apply various effects to gradually hide and show page elements in different ways and also to animate elements, simultaneously or sequentially, in a number of ways.

In the first four chapters of the book, all of our examples have involved manipulating elements that have been *hard-coded* into the page's HTML. In Chapter 5 we will explore ways in which we can use jQuery to create new elements and insert them into the DOM wherever we choose.

5
DOM Manipulation— How to Change Your Page on Command

Something's changed
Everything's rearranged
— Devo,
"Let's Talk"

Like a magician who appears to produce a bouquet of flowers out of thin air, jQuery can create elements, attributes, and text in a web page—as if by magic. But wait, there's more! With jQuery, we can also make any of these things vanish. And, we can take that bouquet of flowers and transform it into a `<div class="magic" id="flowers-to-dove">dove</div>`.

Manipulating Attributes

Throughout the first four chapters of this book, we have been using the `.addClass()` and `.removeClass()` methods to demonstrate how we can change the appearance of elements on a page. Effectively, what these two methods are doing is manipulating the `class` attribute (or, in DOM scripting parlance, the `className` property). The `.addClass()` method creates or adds to the attribute, while `.removeClass()` deletes or shortens it. Add to these the `.toggleClass()` method, which alternates between adding and removing a class, and we have an efficient and robust way of handling classes.

Nevertheless, the `class` attribute is only one of several attributes that we may need to access or change: for example, `id` and `rel` and `href`. For these attributes, jQuery has the `.attr()` and `.removeAttr()` methods. We could even use `.attr()` and `.removeAttr()` instead of their respective `.class()` methods, if we wanted to do it the hard way (but we don't).

Non-class Attributes

Some attributes are not so easily manipulated without the help of jQuery; jQuery lets us modify more than one attribute at a time, similar to the way we worked with multiple CSS properties using the `.css()` method in Chapter 4.

For example, we can easily set the `id`, `rel`, and `title` attributes for links, all at once. Let's start with some sample HTML:

```
<h1 id="f-title">Flatland: A Romance of Many Dimensions</h1>
<div id="f-author">by Edwin A. Abbott</div>
<h2>Part 1, Section 3</h2>
<h3 id="f-subtitle">Concerning the Inhabitants of Flatland</h3>
<div id="excerpt">an excerpt</div>

<div class="chapter">
  <p class="square">Our Professional Men and Gentlemen are Squares
    (to which class I myself belong) and Five-Sided Figures or <a
    href="http://en.wikipedia.org/wiki/Pentagon">Pentagons</a>.
  </p>

  <p class="nobility hexagon">Next above these come the Nobility, of
    whom there are several degrees, beginning at Six-Sided Figures,
    or <a href="http://en.wikipedia.org/wiki/Hexagon">Hexagons</a>,
    and from thence rising in the number of their sides till they
    receive the honourable title of <a href="http://en.wikipedia.org/
    wiki/Polygon">Polygonal</a>, or many-Sided. Finally when the
    number of the sides becomes so numerous, and the sides themselves
    so small, that the figure cannot be distinguished from a <a
    href="http://en.wikipedia.org/wiki/Circle">circle</a>, he is
    included in the Circular or Priestly order; and this is the
    highest class of all.
  </p>

  <p><span class="pull-quote">It is a <span class="drop">Law of
    Nature</span> with us that a male child shall have <strong>one
    more side</strong> than his father</span>, so that each
    generation shall rise (as a rule) one step in the scale of
    development and nobility. Thus the son of a Square is a Pentagon;
    the son of a Pentagon, a Hexagon; and so on.
  </p>
  <!-- . . . code continues . . . -->

</div>
```

Now we can iterate through each of the links inside `<div class="chapter">` and apply attributes to them one by one. If we only needed to set a common attribute value for all of the links, we could do so with a single line of code within our `$(document).ready` handler:

```
$(document).ready(function() {
  $('div.chapter a').attr({'rel': 'external'});
});
```

However, for any given document, each `id` must be unique if we want our JavaScript code to behave predictably. To set a unique `id` for each link, we abandon the single-line solution in favor of jQuery's `.each()` method.

```
$(document).ready(function() {
  $(' div.chapter a').each(function(index) {
    $(this).attr({
      'rel': 'external',
      'id': 'wikilink-' + index
    });
  });
});
```

The `.each()` method, which acts as an iterator, is actually a more convenient form of the `for` loop. It can be employed when the code we want to use on each item in the selector's set of matched elements is too complex for the implicit iteration syntax. In our situation, the `.each()` method's anonymous function is passed an `index` that we can append to each `id`. This `index` argument acts as a counter, starting at 0 for the first link and incrementing by 1 with each successive link. Thus, setting the `id` to `'wikilink-' + index` gives the first link an `id` of `wikilink-0`, the second an `id` of `wikilink-1`, and so on.

We'll use the `title` attribute to invite people to learn more about the linked term at **Wikipedia**. In our example HTML, all of the links point to Wikipedia, but it's probably a good idea to make the selector expression a little more specific, selecting only links that contain `wikipedia` in the `href`, just in case we decide to add a non-Wikipedia link to the HTML at a later time:

```
$(document).ready(function() {
  $('div.chapter a[@href*=wikipedia]').each(function(index) {
    var $thisLink = $(this);
    $thisLink.attr({
      'rel': 'external',
      'id': 'wikilink-' + index,
      'title': 'learn more about ' + $thisLink.text() + ' at Wikipedia'
    });
  });
});
```

One thing worth noting here is that we're now storing $(this) in a variable called $thisLink, simply because we end up using it more than once.

With all three attributes set, the first link, for example, now looks like this:

```
<a href="http://en.wikipedia.org/wiki/Pentagon" rel="external"
   id="wikilink-0" title="learn more about Pentagons at Wikipedia">
   Pentagons
</a>
```

The $() Factory Function Revisited

From the start of this book, we've been using the $() function to access elements in a document. In a sense, this function lies at the very heart of the jQuery library, as it is used every time we attach an effect, event, or property to a matched set of elements.

What's more, the $() function has yet another trick within its parentheses — a feature so powerful that it can change not only the visual appearance but also the actual contents of a page. Simply by inserting a set of HTML elements inside the parentheses, we can change the whole structure of the DOM.

We should keep in mind, once again, the inherent danger in making certain functionality, visual appeal, or textual information available only to those with web browsers capable of (and enabled for) using JavaScript. Important information should be accessible to all, not just people who happen to be using the right software.

A feature commonly seen on FAQ pages is the **Back to top** link that appears after each question-and-answer pair. It could be argued that these links serve no semantic purpose and therefore can be included via JavaScript legitimately as an enhancement for a subset of the visitors to a page. For our example, we'll add a **Back to top** link after each paragraph, as well as the anchor to which the **Back to top** links will take us. To begin, we simply create the new elements:

```
$(document).ready(function() {
  $('<a href="#top">back to top</a>');
  $('<a id="top"></a>');
});
```

Here is what the page looks like at this point:

Flatland: A Romance of Many Dimensions
by Edwin A. Abbott

Part 1, Section 3

Concerning the Inhabitants of Flatland
an excerpt

Our Professional Men and Gentlemen are Squares (to which class I myself belong) and Five-Sided Figures or Pentagons.

Next above these come the Nobility, of whom there are several degrees, beginning at Six-Sided Figures, or Hexagons, and from thence rising in the number of their sides till they receive the honourable title of Polygonal, or many-Sided. Finally when the number of the sides becomes so numerous, and the sides themselves so small, that the figure cannot be distinguished from a circle, he is included in the Circular or Priestly order; and this is the highest class of all.

It is a Law of Nature with us that a male child shall have **one more side** than his father, so that each generation shall rise (as a rule) one step in the scale of development and nobility. Thus the son of a Square is a Pentagon; the son of a Pentagon, a Hexagon; and so on.

But where are the **Back to top** links and the anchor? Shouldn't they appear on the page? In short, **no**. While the two lines do create the elements, they don't yet add the elements to the page. To do that, we can use one of the many jQuery insertion methods.

Inserting New Elements

jQuery has two methods for inserting elements before other elements: `.insertBefore()` and `.before()`. These two methods have the same function; their difference lies only in how they are chained to other methods. Another two methods, `.insertAfter()` and `.after()`, bear the same relationship with each other, but as their names suggest, they insert elements after other elements. For the **Back to top** links we'll use the `.insertAfter()` method:

```
$(document).ready(function() {
  $('<a href="#top">back to top</a>').insertAfter('div.chapter p');
  $('<a id="top"></a>');
});
```

The `.after()` method would accomplish the same thing as `.insertAfter()`, but with the selector expression preceding the method rather than following it. Using `.after()`, the first line inside `$(document).ready()` would look like this:

```
$('div.chapter p').after('<a href="#top">back to top</a>');
```

With `.insertAfter()`, we can continue acting on the created `<a>` element by chaining additional methods. With `.after()`, additional methods would act on the elements matched by the `$('div.chapter p')` selector instead.

So, now that we've actually inserted the links into the page (and into the DOM) after each paragraph that appears within `<div class="chapter">`, the **Back to top** links will appear:

Flatland: A Romance of Many Dimensions
by Edwin A. Abbott

Part 1, Section 3

Concerning the Inhabitants of Flatland
an excerpt

Our Professional Men and Gentlemen are Squares (to which class I myself belong) and Five-Sided Figures or Pentagons.

back to top

Next above these come the Nobility, of whom there are several degrees, beginning at Six-Sided Figures, or Hexagons, and from thence rising in the number of their sides till they receive the honourable title of Polygonal, or many-Sided. Finally when the number of the sides becomes so numerous, and the sides themselves so small, that the figure cannot be distinguished from a circle, he is included in the Circular or Priestly order; and this is the highest class of all.

back to top

It is a Law of Nature with us that a male child shall have **one more side** than his father, so that each generation shall rise (as a rule) one step in the scale of development and nobility. Thus the son of a Square is a Pentagon; the son of a Pentagon, a Hexagon; and so on.

back to top

Unfortunately, the links won't work yet. We still need to insert the anchor with `id="top"`. For this, we can use one of the methods that insert elements inside of other elements.

```
$(document).ready(function() {
  $('<a href="#top">back to top</a>').insertAfter('div.chapter p');
  $('<a id="top" name="top"></a>').prependTo('body');
});
```

This additional code inserts the anchor right at the beginning of the `<body>`; in other words, at the top of the page. Now, with the `.insertAfter` method for the links and the `.prependTo()` method for the anchor, we have a fully functioning set of **Back to top** links for the page.

With **Back to top** links, it doesn't make much sense to have them appear when the top of the page is still visible. A quick improvement to the script would start the links only after, say, the fourth paragraph, which is easy to accomplish with a little change to the selector expression: `.insertAfter('div.chapter p:gt(2)')`. Why the 2 here? Remember that JavaScript indexing starts at `0`; therefore, the first paragraph is indexed at `0`, the second is `1`, the third is `2`, and the fourth paragraph is `3`. Our selector expression begins inserting the links after each paragraph when the index reaches `3`, because that is the first one greater than `2`.

The effect of this selector-expression change is evident with the addition of a few more paragraphs to the HTML:

Concerning the Inhabitants of Flatland
an excerpt

Our Professional Men and Gentlemen are Squares (to which class I myself belong) and Five-Sided Figures or Pentagons.

Next above these come the Nobility, of whom there are several degrees, beginning at Six-Sided Figures, or Hexagons, and from thence rising in the number of their sides till they receive the honourable title of Polygonal, or many-Sided. Finally when the number of the sides becomes so numerous, and the sides themselves so small, that the figure cannot be distinguished from a circle, he is included in the Circular or Priestly order; and this is the highest class of all.

It is a Law of Nature with us that a male child shall have **one more side** than his father, so that each generation shall rise (as a rule) one step in the scale of development and nobility. Thus the son of a Square is a Pentagon; the son of a Pentagon, a Hexagon; and so on.

But this rule applies not always to the Tradesman, and still less often to the Soldiers, and to the Workmen; who indeed can hardly be said to deserve the name of human Figures, since they have not all their sides equal. With them therefore the Law of Nature does not hold; and the son of an Isosceles (i.e. a Triangle with two sides equal) remains Isosceles still. Nevertheless, all hope is not such out, even from the Isosceles, that his posterity may ultimately rise above his degraded condition....

back to top

Rarely—in proportion to the vast numbers of Isosceles births—is a genuine and certifiable Equal-Sided Triangle produced from Isosceles parents. [1] Such a birth requires, as its antecedents, not only a series of carefully arranged intermarriages, but also a long-continued exercise of frugality and self-control on the part of the would-be ancestors of the coming Equilateral, and a patient, systematic, and continuous development of the Isosceles intellect through many generations.

back to top

Moving Elements

With the **Back to top** links, we created new elements and inserted them on the page. It's also possible to take elements from one place on the page and insert them into another place. A practical application of this type of insertion is the dynamic placement and formatting of footnotes. One footnote already appears in the original **Flatland** text that we are using for this example, but we'll designate a couple of other portions of the text as footnotes, too, for the purpose of this demonstration:

```
<p>Rarely&mdash;in proportion to the vast numbers of Isosceles
   births&mdash;is a genuine and certifiable Equal-Sided Triangle
   produced from Isosceles parents. <span class="footnote">"What need
   of a certificate?" a Spaceland critic may ask: "Is not the
   procreation of a Square Son a certificate from Nature herself,
   proving the Equal-sidedness of the Father?" I reply that no Lady
   of any position will marry an uncertified Triangle. Square
   offspring has sometimes resulted from a slightly Irregular
   Triangle; but in almost every such case the Irregularity of the
   first generation is visited on the third; which either fails to
   attain the Pentagonal rank, or relapses to the Triangular.</span>
   Such a birth requires, as its antecedents, not only a series of
   carefully arranged intermarriages, but also a long-continued
   exercise of frugality and self-control on the part of the would-be
   ancestors of the coming Equilateral, and a patient, systematic,
   and continuous development of the Isosceles intellect through many
   generations.
</p>
<p>The birth of a True Equilateral Triangle from Isosceles parents
   is the subject of rejoicing in our country for many furlongs
   round. After a strict examination conducted by the Sanitary and
   Social Board, the infant, if certified as Regular, is with solemn
   ceremonial admitted into the class of Equilaterals. He is then
   immediately taken from his proud yet sorrowing parents and adopted
   by some childless Equilateral. <span class="footnote">The
   Equilateral is bound by oath never to permit the child henceforth
   to enter his former home or so much as to look upon his relations
   again, for fear lest the freshly developed organism may, by force
   of unconscious imitation, fall back again into his hereditary
   level.</span>
</p>
<p>How admirable is the Law of Compensation! <span class="footnote">
   And how perfect a proof of the natural fitness and, I may almost
   say, the divine origin of the aristocratic constitution of the
   States of Flatland!</span> By a judicious use of this Law of
   Nature, the Polygons and Circles are almost always able to stifle
   sedition in its very cradle, taking advantage of the irrepressible
   and boundless hopefulness of the human mind.&hellip;</p>
```

Each of these three paragraphs has a single footnote wrapped inside
`<span class="footnote"></span>`. By marking up the HTML in this way, we can
preserve the context of the footnote. With a CSS rule applied in the stylesheet, the
three paragraphs look like this:

Rarely—in proportion to the vast numbers of Isosceles births—is a genuine and certifiable Equal-Sided Triangle produced from Isosceles parents. *"What need of a certificate?"* a Spaceland critic may ask: *"Is not the procreation of a Square Son a certificate from Nature herself, proving the Equal-sidedness of the Father?"* I reply that no Lady of any position will marry an uncertified Triangle. *Square offspring has sometimes resulted from a slightly Irregular Triangle; but in almost every such case the Irregularity of the first generation is visited on the third; which either fails to attain the Pentagonal rank, or relapses to the Triangular.* Such a birth requires, as its antecedents, not only a series of carefully arranged intermarriages, but also a long-continued exercise of frugality and self-control on the part of the would-be ancestors of the coming Equilateral, and a patient, systematic, and continuous development of the Isosceles intellect through many generations.

back to top

The birth of a True Equilateral Triangle from Isosceles parents is the subject of rejoicing in our country for many furlongs round. After a strict examination conducted by the Sanitary and Social Board, the infant, if certified as Regular, is with solemn ceremonial admitted into the class of Equilaterals. He is then immediately taken from his proud yet sorrowing parents and adopted by some childless Equilateral. *The Equilateral is bound by oath never to permit the child henceforth to enter his former home or so much as to look upon his relations again, for fear lest the freshly developed organism may, by force of unconscious imitation, fall back again into his hereditary level.*

back to top

How admirable is the Law of Compensation! *And how perfect a proof of the natural fitness and, I may almost say, the divine origin of the aristocratic constitution of the States of Flatland!* By a judicious use of this Law of Nature, the Polygons and Circles are almost always able to stifle sedition in its very cradle, taking advantage of the irrepressible and boundless hopefulness of the human mind....

Now we can grab the footnotes and insert them in between `<div class="chapter">` and `<div id="footer">`. Here we need to keep in mind that even in cases of implicit iteration the order of insertion is predefined, starting at the top of the DOM tree and working its way down. Since it's important to maintain the correct order of the footnotes in their new place on the page, we should use `.insertBefore('#footer')`. This will place each footnote directly before the `<div id="footer">`, so that *footnote 1* is placed between `<div class="chapter">` and `<div id="footer">`, *footnote 2* is placed between *footnote 1* and `<div id="footer">`, and so on. Using `.insertAfter('div.chapter')`, on the other hand, would have the footnotes appear in reverse order. So far, our code looks like this:

```
$(document).ready(function() {
  $('span.footnote').insertBefore('#footer');
});
```

Unfortunately, though, we've run into a big problem. The **footnotes** are in `<span>` tags, which means they display inline by default, one right after the other with no separation:

> *"What need of a certificate?" a Spaceland critic may ask: "Is not the procreation of a Square Son a certificate from Nature herself, proving the Equal-sidedness of the Father?" I reply that no Lady of any position will marry an uncertified Triangle. Square offspring has sometimes resulted from a slightly Irregular Triangle; but in almost every such case the Irregularity of the first generation is visited on the third; which either fails to attain the Pentagonal rank, or relapses to the Triangular. The Equilateral is bound by oath never to permit the child henceforth to enter his former home or so much as to look upon his relations again, for fear lest the freshly developed organism may, by force of unconscious imitation, fall back again into his hereditary level. And how perfect a proof of the natural fitness and, I may almost say, the divine origin of the aristocratic constitution of the States of Flatland!*

One solution to this problem is to modify the CSS, making the `<span>` elements display as blocks, but only if they are not inside `<div class="chapter">`:

```
span.footnote {
   font-style: italic;
   font-family: "Times New Roman", Times, serif;
   display: block;
}
.chapter span.footnote {
   display: inline;
}
```

The footnotes are now beginning to take shape:

> *"What need of a certificate?" a Spaceland critic may ask: "Is not the procreation of a Square Son a certificate from Nature herself, proving the Equal-sidedness of the Father?" I reply that no Lady of any position will marry an uncertified Triangle. Square offspring has sometimes resulted from a slightly Irregular Triangle; but in almost every such case the Irregularity of the first generation is visited on the third; which either fails to attain the Pentagonal rank, or relapses to the Triangular.*
>
> *The Equilateral is bound by oath never to permit the child henceforth to enter his former home or so much as to look upon his relations again, for fear lest the freshly developed organism may, by force of unconscious imitation, fall back again into his hereditary level.*
>
> *And how perfect a proof of the natural fitness and, I may almost say, the divine origin of the aristocratic constitution of the States of Flatland!*

At least they are distinct footnotes now; yet there is still a lot of work that can be done to them. A more robust footnote solution should:

1. Mark the location in the text from which each footnote is pulled.

2. Number each location, and provide a matching number for the footnote itself.

3. Create a link from the text location to its matching footnote, and from the footnote back to the text location.

These steps can be accomplished from within an `.each()` method; but first we'll set up a container element for the notes at the bottom of the page:

```
$(document).ready(function() {
  $('<ol id="notes"></ol>').insertAfter('div.chapter');
});
```

It seems reasonable enough to use an ordered list `<ol id="notes"></ol>` for the footnotes; after all, we want them to be numbered. Why not use an element that numbers them for us automatically? We've given the list an ID of `notes` and have inserted it after `<div class="chapter">`.

Marking, Numbering, and Linking the Context

Now we're ready to mark and number the place from which we're pulling the footnote:

```
$(document).ready(function() {
  $('<ol id="notes"></ol>').insertAfter('div.chapter');
  $('span.footnote').each(function(index) {
    $(this)
      .before('<a href="#foot-note-' + (index+1) +
              '"id="context-' + (index+1) + '" class="context"><sup>'
                                + (index+1) + '</sup></a>');
  });
});
```

Here we start with the same selector as we used with the simpler footnote example, but we chain the `.each()` method to it.

Inside the `.each()` we begin with `$(this)`, which represents each footnote in succession, and we chain the `.before()` method to it.

Everything that appears inside the `.before()` method's parentheses will be inserted before the footnote `<span>`. It's a pretty long concatenated string, but all it really does is build a superscripted link. Perhaps a closer look is in order.

The first two parts form the beginning of the opening `a` tag, along with an `href` attribute. The `href` is particularly important because it must exactly match the footnote's `id` attribute (not including the # of course):

```
.before('<a href="#foot-note-' + (index+1) + '" id="context-' +
    (index+1) + '" class="context"><sup>' + (index+1) + '</sup></a>');
```

Because counting begins at 0, we need to add 1 to index to start the hrefs at #foot-note-1. Next come the id and class attributes:

```
.before('<a href="#foot-note-' + (index+1) + '" id="context-' +
                    (index+1) + '" class="context"><sup>'
                        + (index+1) + '</sup></a>');
```

This part starts by closing the href with a quotation mark. The id comes next, with index + 1 added to context- so that the numbering matches that of the href. We give it a class of context in case we'd like to style it later.

Finally, we insert the link text—which, again, is a number starting at 1—inside a <sup> element and close the link:

```
.before('<a href="#foot-note-' + (index+1) + '" id="context-' +
                    (index+1) + '" class="context"><sup>'
                        + (index+1) + '</sup></a>');
```

Our three linked footnote markers now look like this:

> Rarely—in proportion to the vast numbers of Isosceles births—is a genuine and certifiable Equal-Sided Triangle produced from Isosceles parents. [1] Such a birth requires, as its antecedents, not only a series of carefully arranged intermarriages, but also a long-continued exercise of frugality and self-control on the part of the would-be ancestors of the coming Equilateral, and a patient, systematic, and continuous development of the Isosceles intellect through many generations.
>
> back to top
>
> The birth of a True Equilateral Triangle from Isosceles parents is the subject of rejoicing in our country for many furlongs round. After a strict examination conducted by the Sanitary and Social Board, the infant, if certified as Regular, is with solemn ceremonial admitted into the class of Equilaterals. He is then immediately taken from his proud yet sorrowing parents and adopted by some childless Equilateral. [2]
>
> back to top
>
> How admirable is the Law of Compensation! [3] By a judicious use of this Law of Nature, the Polygons and Circles are almost always able to stifle sedition in its very cradle, taking advantage of the irrepressible and boundless hopefulness of the human mind....

Appending Footnotes

The next step is to move the <span class="footnote"> elements, as we did with the simpler example. This time, however, we drop them into the newly created <ol id="notes">. We'll use .appendTo() here, again to maintain proper ordering, as each successive footnote will be inserted at the end of the element:

```
$(document).ready(function() {
  $('<ol id="notes"></ol>').insertAfter('div.chapter');
  $('span.footnote').each(function(index) {
    $(this)
      .before('<a href="#foot-note-' + (index+1) +
        '" id="context-' + (index+1) + '" class="context"><sup>'
                                     + (index+1) + '</sup></a>')
      .appendTo('#notes')
  });
});
```

It's important to remember that `.appendTo()` is still being chained to `$(this)`, so that jQuery is saying, *Append the* `footnote` *span to the element with an ID of* `notes`.

To each of the footnotes we just moved, we'll append another link—this one back to the number in the text:

```
$(document).ready(function() {
  $('<ol id="notes"></ol>').insertAfter('div.chapter');
  $('span.footnote').each(function(index) {
    $(this)
      .before('<a href="#foot-note-' + (index+1) + '"
              id="context-' + (index+1) + '" class="context"><sup>' +
                                  (index+1) + '</sup></a>')
      .appendTo('#notes')
      .append( ' (<a href="#context-' + (index+1) +
                                    '">context </a>)' )
  });
});
```

Notice that the `href` points back to the `id` of the corresponding marker. Here you can see the footnotes again with a link appended to each:

> *"What need of a certificate?" a Spaceland critic may ask: "Is not the procreation of a Square Son a certificate from Nature herself, proving the Equal-sidedness of the Father?" I reply that no Lady of any position will marry an uncertified Triangle. Square offspring has sometimes resulted from a slightly Irregular Triangle; but in almost every such case the Irregularity of the first generation is visited on the third; which either fails to attain the Pentagonal rank, or relapses to the Triangular. (context)*
>
> *The Equilateral is bound by oath never to permit the child henceforth to enter his former home or so much as to look upon his relations again, for fear lest the freshly developed organism may, by force of unconscious imitation, fall back again into his hereditary level. (context)*
>
> *And how perfect a proof of the natural fitness and, I may almost say, the divine origin of the aristocratic constitution of the States of Flatland! (context)*

The footnotes still lack their numbers, however. Even though they have been placed within an `<ol>`, each one must also be individually wrapped in an `<li>`.

Wrapping Elements

jQuery's method for wrapping elements around other elements is the appropriately named `.wrap()`. Because we want each `$(this)` to be wrapped in `<li></li>`, we can complete our footnote code like so:

```
$(document).ready(function() {
  $('<ol id="notes"></ol>').insertAfter('div.chapter');
  $('span.footnote').each(function(index) {
    $(this)
      .before('<a href="#foot-note-' + (index+1) +
          '"id="context-' + (index+1) + '" class="context"><sup>' +
                                      (index+1) + '</sup></a>')
      .appendTo('#notes')
      .append( ' (<a href="#context-' + (index+1) + '">
                                      context </a>)' )
      .wrap('<li id="foot-note-' + (index+1) + '"></li>');
  });
});
```

Now each of the `<li>` elements comes complete with an `id` that matches the marker's `href`. At last, we have a set of numbered, linked footnotes:

---

1. *"What need of a certificate?" a Spaceland critic may ask: "Is not the procreation of a Square Son a certificate from Nature herself, proving the Equal-sidedness of the Father?" I reply that no Lady of any position will marry an uncertified Triangle. Square offspring has sometimes resulted from a slightly Irregular Triangle; but in almost every such case the Irregularity of the first generation is visited on the third; which either fails to attain the Pentagonal rank, or relapses to the Triangular. (context)*

2. *The Equilateral is bound by oath never to permit the child henceforth to enter his former home or so much as to look upon his relations again, for fear lest the freshly developed organism may, by force of unconscious imitation, fall back again into his hereditary level. (context)*

3. *And how perfect a proof of the natural fitness and, I may almost say, the divine origin of the aristocratic constitution of the States of Flatland! (context)*

Of course, the numbers could have been inserted before each footnote the same way they were in the paragraphs, but there is something deeply satisfying about having semantic markup dynamically generated by JavaScript.

Copying Elements

So far in this chapter we have inserted newly created elements, moved elements from one location in the document to another, and wrapped new elements around existing ones. Sometimes, though, we may want to copy elements. For example, a navigation menu that appears in the page's header could be copied and placed in the footer as well. In fact, whenever elements can be copied to enhance a page visually, it's a good opportunity to do it with code. After all, why write something twice and double our chance of error when we can write it once and let jQuery do the heavy lifting?

For copying elements, jQuery's `.clone()` method is just what we need; it takes any set of matched elements and creates a copy of them for later use. As with the element-creation process we explored earlier in this chapter, the copied elements will not appear in the document until we apply one of the insertion methods. For example, the following line creates a copy of the first paragraph inside `<div class="chapter">`:

```
$('div.chapter p:eq(0)').clone();
```

So far, the content on the page hasn't changed:

Concerning the Inhabitants of Flatland
an excerpt

Our Professional Men and Gentlemen are Squares (to which class I myself belong) and Five-Sided Figures or Pentagons.

Next above these come the Nobility, of whom there are several degrees, beginning at Six-Sided Figures, or Hexagons, and from thence rising in the number of their sides till they receive the honourable title of Polygonal, or many-Sided. Finally when the number of the sides becomes so numerous, and the sides themselves so small, that the figure cannot be distinguished from a circle, he is included in the Circular or Priestly order; and this is the highest class of all.

It is a Law of Nature with us that a male child shall have **one more side** than his father, so that each generation shall rise (as a rule) one step in the scale of development and nobility. Thus the son of a Square is a Pentagon; the son of a Pentagon, a Hexagon; and so on.

To continue the example, we can make the cloned paragraph appear before `<div class="chapter">`:

```
$('div.chapter p:eq(0)').clone().insertBefore('div.chapter');
```

Now the first paragraph appears twice, and because the first instance of it is no longer inside `<div class="chapter">`, it does not retain the styles associated with the div (most noticeably, the width):

Concerning the Inhabitants of Flatland
an excerpt

Our Professional Men and Gentlemen are Squares (to which class I myself belong) and Five-Sided Figures or Pentagons.

Our Professional Men and Gentlemen are Squares (to which class I myself belong) and Five-Sided Figures or Pentagons.

Next above these come the Nobility, of whom there are several degrees, beginning at Six-Sided Figures, or Hexagons, and from thence rising in the number of their sides till they receive the honourable title of Polygonal, or many-Sided. Finally when the number of the sides becomes so numerous, and the sides themselves so small, that the figure cannot be distinguished from a circle, he is included in the Circular or Priestly order; and this is the highest class of all.

It is a Law of Nature with us that a male child shall have **one more side** than his father, so

---

So, using an analogy that most people should be familiar with, `.clone()` is to the insertion methods as copy is to paste.

Clone Depth

The `.clone` method by default copies not only the matched element, but also all of its descendant elements. However, it has a parameter that, when set to `false`, clones only the matched element itself. As we have already seen, `$('div.chapter p:eq(0)').clone()` copies the following HTML:

```
<p class="square">Our Professional Men and Gentlemen are Squares (to
    which class I myself belong) and Five-Sided Figures or Pentagons.
</p>
```

Let's place `false` inside the parentheses, like so:

```
$('div.chapter p:eq(0)').clone(false);
```

This time we've copied only the paragraph element:

```
<p class="square"></p>
```

The text inside is not copied along with the element because text is itself a DOM node.

 The `.clone()` method does not clone events along with the elements. We should remember to reapply the handlers by calling the function that attached them in the first place. An alternative is to clone events directly using Brandon Aaron's plug-in method, `.cloneWithEvents()`. More information on plug-ins can be found in Chapter 10.

Cloning for Pull Quotes

Many websites, like their print counterparts, use **pull quotes** to emphasize small portions of text and attract the reader's eye. We can easily accomplish this embellishment with the `.clone()` method. First, let's take another look at the third paragraph of our example text:

```
<p>
  <span class="pull-quote">It is a Law of Nature <span class="drop">
  with us</span> that a male child shall have <strong>one more side
  </strong> than his father</span>, so that each generation shall
  rise (as a rule) one step in the scale of development and nobility.
  Thus the son of a Square is a Pentagon; the son of a Pentagon, a
  Hexagon; and so on.
</p>
```

Notice that the paragraph begins with `<span class="pull-quote">`. This is the class we will be targeting for cloning. Once the copied text inside that `<span>` is pasted into another place, we need to modify its style properties to set it apart from the rest of the text.

A CSS Diversion

To accomplish this styling, we'll add a `pulled` class to the copied `<span>` and give the class the following style rule in the stylesheet:

```
.pulled {
  background: #e5e5e5;
  position: absolute;
  width: 145px;
  top: -20px;
  right: -180px;
  padding: 12px 5px 12px 10px;
  font: italic 1.4em "Times New Roman", Times, serif;
}
```

The `pull-quote` now gets a light-gray background, some padding, and a different font. Most important, it's absolutely positioned, 20 pixels above and 20 pixels to the right of the nearest (absolute or relative) positioned ancestor in the DOM. If no ancestor has positioning applied (other than `static`), the pull quote will be positioned relative to the document `<body>`. Because of this, we'll need to make sure in the jQuery code that the cloned `pull-quote`'s parent element has `position:relative`.

While the top positioning is fairly intuitive, it may not be clear at first how the `pull-quote` box will be located 20 pixels to the left of its positioned parent. We derive the number first from the total width of the `pull-quote` box, which is the value of the `width` property plus the left and right padding, or 145px + 5px + 10px, or 160px. We then set the `right` property of the `pull-quote`. A value of 0 would align the `pull-quote`'s right side with that of its parent. Therefore, to make its left side 20px to the right of the parent, we need to move it in a negative direction 20 pixels more than its total width, or -180px.

Back to the Code

Now we can get into the jQuery. Let's start with a selector expression for all of the `<span class="pull-quote">` elements, and attach an `.each()` method so that we can perform multiple actions as we iterate through them:

```
$(document).ready(function() {
  $('span.pull-quote').each(function(index) {
```

```
  . . .
  });
});
```

Next, we find the parent paragraph of each `pull-quote` and apply the CSS `position` property:

```
$(document).ready(function() {
  $('span.pull-quote').each(function(index) {
    var $parentParagraph = $(this).parent('p');
    $parentParagraph.css('position', 'relative');
  });
});
```

Notice here that we stored the parent paragraph in a variable. That's because we'll be using it a little later as well. It's always a good idea to use variables for jQuery objects when we need to refer to them more than once. This improves performance by traversing the DOM with jQuery's `$()` factory function only once, rather than each time the object is needed.

We can be sure now that the CSS is all set and ready for the `pull-quote`. At this point we can clone each `<span>`, add the `pulled` class to the copy, and insert it into the beginning of the paragraph:

```
$(document).ready(function() {
  $('span.pull-quote').each(function(index) {
    var $parentParagraph = $(this).parent('p');
    $parentParagraph.css('position', 'relative');
    $(this).clone()
      .addClass('pulled')
      .prependTo($parentParagraph);
  });
});
```

Because we're using `absolute` positioning for the `pull-quote`, the placement of it within the paragraph is irrelevant. As long as it remains inside the paragraph, it will be positioned in relation to the top and right of the paragraph, based on our CSS rules. If, however, we wanted to apply a `float` to the pull quote instead, its placement within the paragraph would affect its vertical position.

The paragraph, together with its `pull-quote`, now looks like this:

> highest class of all.
>
> It is a Law of Nature with us that a male child shall have **one more side** than his father, so that each generation shall rise (as a rule) one step in the scale of development and nobility. Thus the son of a Square is a Pentagon; the son of a Pentagon, a Hexagon; and so on.
>
> But this rule applies not always to the Tradesman, and still less often to the Soldiers, and to the Workmen; who indeed can hardly be said to deserve the name of human Figures, since they have not all their sides equal. With them therefore the Law of Nature does not hold; and the son of an Isosceles (i.e. a Triangle with two sides equal) remains Isosceles still.
>
> *It is a Law of Nature with us that a male child shall have **one more side** than his father*

This is a good start, but pull quotes typically do not retain font formatting as this one does with bold **one more side**. What we want is the text of `<span class="pull-quote">`, stripped of any `<strong>`, `<em>`, `<a href>` or other inline tags. Additionally it would be nice to be able to modify the `pull-quote` a bit, dropping some words and replacing them with ellipses. For this, we have wrapped `<span class="drop">` around some text in our example:

```
<p>
  <span class="pull-quote">It is a Law of Nature <span class="drop">
  with us</span> that a male child shall have <strong>one more side
  </strong> than his father</span>, so that each generation shall
  rise (as a rule) one step in the scale of development and nobility.
  Thus the son of a Square is a Pentagon; the son of a Pentagon, a
  Hexagon; and so on.
</p>
```

We'll apply the ellipsis first, and then replace all of the `pull-quote` HTML with a stripped, text-only version:

```
$(document).ready(function() {
  $('span.pull-quote').each(function(index) {
    var $parentParagraph = $(this).parent('p');
    $parentParagraph.css('position', 'relative');
    var $clonedCopy = $(this).clone();
    $clonedCopy
      .addClass('pulled')
      .find('span.drop')
        .html('&hellip;')
      .end()
      .prependTo($parentParagraph);
    var clonedText = $clonedCopy.text();
    $clonedCopy.html(clonedText);
  });
});
```

So, we start the cloning process this time by storing the clone in a variable. The variable is necessary this time because we can't work on it completely within the same chain. Notice, too, that after we find `<span class="drop">` and replace its HTML with an ellipsis (`&hellip;`), we use `.end()` to back out of the last query, `.find('span.drop')`. This way, we're inserting the whole copy, not just the ellipsis, at the beginning of the paragraph.

At the end, we set one more variable, `clonedText`, to the text-only contents of the copy; then we use these text-only contents as a replacement for the HTML of the copy. Now, the `pull-quote` looks like this:

It is a Law of Nature with us that a male child shall have **one more side** than his father, so that each generation shall rise (as a rule) one step in the scale of development and nobility. Thus the son of a Square is a Pentagon; the son of a Pentagon, a Hexagon; and so on.

It is a Law of Nature ... that a male child shall have one more side than his father

But this rule applies not always to the Tradesman, and still less often to the Soldiers, and to the Workmen; who indeed can hardly be said to deserve the name of human Figures, since they have not all their sides equal. With them therefore the Law of Nature does not hold; and the son of an Isosceles (i.e. a Triangle with two sides equal) remains Isosceles still. Nevertheless, all hope is not such out, even from the Isosceles, that his posterity may ultimately rise above his degraded condition....

back to top

Rarely—in proportion to the vast numbers of Isosceles births—is a genuine and certifiable Equal-Sided Triangle produced from Isosceles parents. [1] Such a birth requires, as its antecedents, not only a series of carefully arranged intermarriages, but also a long-continued exercise of frugality and self-control on the part of the would-be ancestors of the coming Equilateral, and a patient, systematic, and continuous development of the Isosceles intellect through many generations.

back to top

The birth of a True Equilateral Triangle from Isosceles parents is the subject of rejoicing in our country for many furlongs round. After a strict examination conducted by the Sanitary and Social Board, the infant, if certified as Regular, is with solemn ceremonial admitted into the class of Equilaterals. He is then immediately taken from his proud yet sorrowing parents and adopted by some childless Equilateral. [2]

back to top

The birth of a True Equilateral Triangle from Isosceles parents is the subject of rejoicing in our country ....

Evidently, another `<span class="pull-quote">` has been added to a later paragraph to ensure that the code works for multiple elements.

Prettifying the Pull Quotes

The `pull-quotes` are now working as expected, with child elements stripped and ellipses added where text should be dropped.

Since one of the goals is to add visual appeal, though, we would do well to give the `pull-quotes` rounded corners with drop shadows. However, variable height of the `pull-quote` boxes is problematic because we'll need to apply two background images to a single element, an impossibility for every browser at the moment except the most recent builds of Safari.

To overcome this limitation, we can wrap another **wrapper** `<div>` around the
`pull-quotes`:

```
$(document).ready(function() {
  $('span.pull-quote').each(function(index) {
    var $parentParagraph = $(this).parent('p');
    $parentParagraph.css('position', 'relative');
    var $clonedCopy = $(this).clone();
    $clonedCopy
      .addClass('pulled')
      .find('span.drop')
        .html('&hellip;')
      .end()
      .prependTo($parentParagraph)
      .wrap('<div class="pulled-wrapper"></div>');
    var clonedText = $clonedCopy.text();
    $clonedCopy.html(clonedText);
  });
});
```

We also need to modify the CSS, of course, to account for the new `<div>` and the two
background images:

```
.pulled-wrapper {
  background: url(pq-top.jpg) no-repeat left top;
  position: absolute;
  width: 160px;
  right: -180px;
  padding-top: 18px;
}
.pulled {
  background: url(pq-bottom.jpg) no-repeat left bottom;
  position: relative;
  display: block;
  width: 140px;
  padding: 0 10px 24px 10px;
  font: italic 1.4em "Times New Roman", Times, serif;
}
```

Here, some of the rules formerly applied to `.pulled` are applied to `.pulled-wrapper`
instead. A couple of `width` and `padding` adjustments take into account the design
of the background images' borders, and `.pulled` has its `position` and `display`
properties modified in order to appear correctly for all browsers.

Here is one final look at the newly primped `pull-quotes` in their native habitat:

highest class of all.

It is a Law of Nature with us that a male child shall have **one more side** than his father, so that each generation shall rise (as a rule) one step in the scale of development and nobility. Thus the son of a Square is a Pentagon; the son of a Pentagon, a Hexagon; and so on.

But this rule applies not always to the Tradesman, and still less often to the Soldiers, and to the Workmen; who indeed can hardly be said to deserve the name of human Figures, since they have not all their sides equal. With them therefore the Law of Nature does not hold; and the son of an Isosceles (i.e. a Triangle with two sides equal) remains Isosceles still. Nevertheless, all hope is not such out, even from the Isosceles, that his posterity may ultimately rise above his degraded condition....

back to top

Rarely—in proportion to the vast numbers of Isosceles births—is a genuine and certifiable Equal-Sided Triangle produced from Isosceles parents. [1] Such a birth requires, as its antecedents, not only a series of carefully arranged intermarriages, but also a long-continued exercise of frugality and self-control on the part of the would-be ancestors of the coming Equilateral, and a patient, systematic, and continuous development of the Isosceles intellect through many generations.

back to top

The birth of a True Equilateral Triangle from Isosceles parents is the subject of rejoicing in our country for many furlongs round. After a strict examination conducted by the Sanitary and Social Board, the infant, if certified as Regular, is with solemn ceremonial admitted into the class of Equilaterals. He is then immediately taken from his proud yet sorrowing parents and adopted by some childless Equilateral. [2]

back to top

How admirable is the Law of Compensation! [3] By a judicious use of this Law of Nature, the Polygons and Circles are almost always able to stifle sedition in its very cradle, taking advantage of the irrepressible and boundless hopefulness of the human mind....

It is a Law of Nature ... that a male child shall have one more side than his father

The birth of a True Equilateral Triangle from Isosceles parents is the subject of rejoicing in our country ....

DOM Manipulation Methods in a Nutshell

The extensive DOM manipulation methods that jQuery provides vary according to their task and their location. The following outline can serve as a reminder of which methods we can use to accomplish any of these tasks, just about anywhere.

1. To **insert** new element(s) **inside** every matched element, use:
   - `.append()`
   - `.appendTo()`
   - `.prepend()`
   - `.prependTo()`

2. To **insert** new element(s) **adjacent to** every matched element, use:
   - `.after()`
   - `.insertAfter()`
   - `.before()`
   - `.insertBefore()`

3. To **insert** new element(s) **around** every matched element, use:

    - `.wrap()`

4. To **replace** every matched element with new element(s) or text, use:

    - `.html()`

    - `.text()`

5. To **remove** element(s) **inside** every matched element, use:

    - `.empty()`

6. To **remove** every matched element and descendants from the document without actually deleting them, use:

    - `.remove()`

Summary

In this chapter we have created, copied, reassembled, and embellished content using jQuery's DOM modification methods. We've applied these methods to a single web page, transforming a handful of generic paragraphs to a footnoted, pull-quoted, linked, and stylized literary excerpt.

The tutorial section of the book is nearly over, but before we move on to examine more complex, expanded examples, let's take a round-trip journey to the server via jQuery's AJAX methods.

6
AJAX—How to Make Your Site Buzzword-Compliant

Life's a bee without a buzz
It's going great till you get stung
— Devo,
"That's Good"

AJAX was the name of a great Greek warrior (actually, two Greek warriors) whose adventures were chronicled in Homer's epic, *The Iliad*. The term was later re-coined as the name of a household cleanser. It was then re-re-coined as a label for a group of web technologies.

In this last, most modern sense, AJAX is an acronym standing for **Asynchronous JavaScript and XML**. The technologies involved in an AJAX solution include:

- JavaScript, to capture interactions with the user or other browser-related events
- The XMLHttpRequest object, which allows requests to be made to the server without interrupting other browser tasks
- XML files on the server, or possibly other similar data formats
- More JavaScript, to interpret the data from the server and present it on the page

AJAX technology has been hailed as the savior of the web landscape, transforming static web pages into interactive web applications. Because of the inconsistencies in the browsers' implementations of the XMLHttpRequest object, many frameworks have sprung up to assist developers in taming it, and jQuery is no exception.

Can AJAX truly help us perform miracles?

Loading Data on Demand

Underneath all the hype and trappings, AJAX is just a means of loading data from the server to the web browser without a visible page refresh. This data can take many forms, and we have many options for what to do with it when it arrives. We'll see this by performing the same basic task in many ways.

Suppose we have a page that displays entries from a dictionary. The HTML inside the body of the page looks like this:

```
<div id="dictionary">
</div>
```

Yes, really! Our page will have no content to begin with. We are going to use jQuery's various AJAX methods to populate this <div> with dictionary entries.

We're going to need a way to trigger the loading process, so we'll add some buttons for our event handlers to latch onto:

```
<div class="letters">
  <div class="letter" id="letter-a">
    <h3>A</h3>
    <div class="button">Load</div>
  </div>
  <div class="letter" id="letter-b">
    <h3>B</h3>
    <div class="button">Load</div>
  </div>
  <div class="letter" id="letter-c">
    <h3>C</h3>
    <div class="button">Load</div>
  </div>
  <div class="letter" id="letter-d">
    <h3>D</h3>
    <div class="button">Load</div>
  </div>
</div>
```

Adding a few CSS rules, we get a page that looks like this:

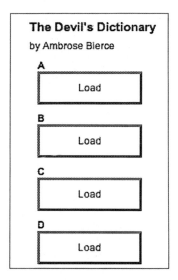

Now we can focus on getting content onto the page.

Appending HTML

AJAX applications are often no more than a request for a chunk of HTML. This technique, sometimes referred to as AHAH (Asynchronous HTTP and HTML), is almost trivial to implement with jQuery. First we need some HTML to insert, which we'll place in a file called a.html alongside our main document. This secondary HTML file begins:

```
<div class="entry">
  <h3 class="term">ABDICATION</h3>
  <div class="part">n.</div>
  <div class="definition">
    An act whereby a sovereign attests his sense of the high
    temperature of the throne.
    <div class="quote">
      <div class="quote-line">Poor Isabella's Dead, whose
                                             abdication</div>
      <div class="quote-line">Set all tongues wagging in the Spanish
                                             nation,</div>
      <div class="quote-line">For that performance 'twere unfair to
                                             scold her:</div>
      <div class="quote-line">She wisely left a throne too hot to
                                             hold her.</div>
```

```
            <div class="quote-line">To History she'll be no royal riddle
                                                    &mdash;</div>
            <div class="quote-line">Merely a plain parched pea that jumped
                                                    the griddle.</div>
            <div class="quote-author">G.J.</div>
        </div>
      </div>
    </div>

    <div class="entry">
      <h3 class="term">ABSOLUTE</h3>
      <div class="part">adj.</div>
      <div class="definition">
        Independent, irresponsible.  An absolute monarchy is one in which
        the sovereign does as he pleases so long as he pleases the
        assassins.  Not many absolute monarchies are left, most of them
        having been replaced by limited monarchies, where the sovereign's
        power for evil (and for good) is greatly curtailed, and by
        republics, which are governed by chance.
      </div>
    </div>
```

Rendered on its own, this file is quite plain:

ABDICATION

n.
An act whereby a sovereign attests his sense of the high temperature of the throne.
Poor Isabella's Dead, whose abdication
Set all tongues wagging in the Spanish nation.
For that performance 'twere unfair to scold her.
She wisely left a throne too hot to hold her.
To History she'll be no royal riddle —
Merely a plain parched pea that jumped the griddle.
G.J.

ABSOLUTE

adj.
Independent, irresponsible. An absolute monarchy is one in which the sovereign does as he pleases so long as he pleases the assassins. Not many absolute monarchies are left, most of them having been replaced by limited monarchies, where the sovereign's power for evil (and for good) is greatly curtailed, and by republics, which are governed by chance.

ACKNOWLEDGE

v.t.
To confess. Acknowledgement of one another's faults is the highest duty imposed by our love of truth.

AFFIANCED

pp.
Fitted with an ankle-ring for the ball-and-chain.

Note that a.html is not a true HTML document; it contains no <html>, <head>, or <body>, all of which are normally required. The file's only purpose is to be inserted into another HTML document, which we'll accomplish now:

```
$(document).ready(function() {
  $('#letter-a .button').click(function() {
    $('#dictionary').load('a.html');
  });
});
```

The .load() method does all our heavy lifting for us! We specify the target location for the HTML snippet by using a normal jQuery selector, and then pass the URL of the file to be loaded as a parameter to the method. Now, when the first button is clicked, the file is loaded and placed inside <div id="dictionary">. The browser will render the new HTML as soon as it is inserted:

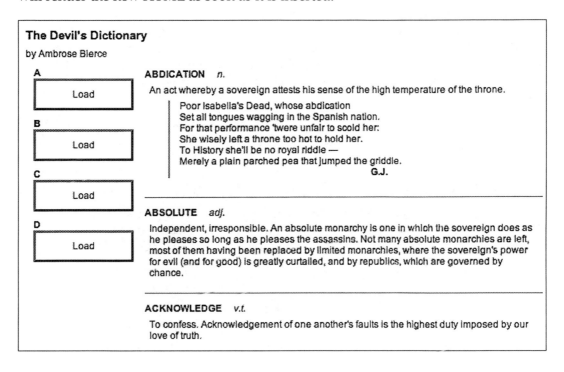

Note that the HTML is now styled, whereas before it was plain. This is due to the CSS rules in the main document; as soon as the new HTML snippet is inserted, the rules apply to its tags as well.

In this example, the dictionary definitions will probably appear instantaneously when the button is clicked. This is a hazard of working on our applications locally; it is hard to account for delays in transferring documents across the network. Suppose we added an alert box to display after the definitions are loaded:

```
$(document).ready(function() {
  $('#letter-a .button').click(function() {
    $('#dictionary').load('a.html');
    alert('Loaded!');
  });
});
```

We might assume from the structure of this code that the alert can only be displayed after the load has been performed. However, the alert will quite possibly have come and gone before the load has completed, due to network lag. All AJAX calls are by default **asynchronous**. Otherwise, we'd have to call it **SJAX**, which hardly has the same ring to it! Asynchronous loading means that the HTTP request to retrieve the HTML snippet is issued, and script execution immediately resumes without waiting. At some later time, the browser receives the response from the server and handles it. This is generally desired behavior; it is unfriendly to lock up the whole web browser while waiting for data to be retrieved.

If actions must be delayed until the load has been completed, jQuery provides a **callback** for this. An example will be provided below.

Working with JavaScript Objects

Pulling in fully-formed HTML on demand is very convenient, but there are times when we want our script to be able to do some processing of the data before it is displayed. In this case, we need to retrieve the data in a structure that we can traverse with JavaScript.

Retrieving a JavaScript Object

With jQuery's selectors, we could traverse the HTML we get back and manipulate it, but it must first be inserted into the document. A more native JavaScript data format can mean even less code.

As we have often seen, JavaScript objects are just sets of key-value pairs, and can be defined succinctly using curly braces ({ }). JavaScript arrays, on the other hand, are defined on the fly with square brackets ([ ]). Combining these two syntaxes, we can easily express some very complex and rich data structures.

The term **JavaScript Object Notation (JSON)** was coined by Douglas Crockford to capitalize on this simple syntax. This notation can offer a concise alternative to the sometimes-bulky XML format:

```
{
  "key": "value",
  "key 2": [
    "array",
    "of",
    "items"
  ]
}
```

For information on some of the potential advantages of JSON, as well as implementations in many programming languages, visit http://json.org/.

We can encode our definitions in this format in many ways. We'll place some dictionary entries in a JSON file we'll call b.json:

```
[
  {
    "term": "BACCHUS",
    "part": "n.",
    "definition": "A convenient deity invented by the ancients as an
                                        excuse for getting drunk.",
    "quote": [
      "Is public worship, then, a sin,",
      "That for devotions paid to Bacchus",
      "The lictors dare to run us in,",
      "And resolutely thump and whack us?"
    ],
    "author": "Jorace"
  },
  {
    "term": "BACKBITE",
    "part": "v.t.",
    "definition": "To speak of a man as you find him when he can't
                                        find you."
  },
  {
    "term": "BEARD",
    "part": "n.",
    "definition": "The hair that is commonly cut off by those who
      justly execrate the absurd Chinese custom of shaving the head."
  },
```

To retrieve this data, we'll use the `$.getJSON()` method, which fetches the file and processes it, providing the code with the resulting JavaScript object.

Global jQuery Functions

To this point, all jQuery methods that we've used have been attached to a jQuery object that we've built with the `$()` factory function. The selectors have allowed us to specify a set of DOM nodes to work with, and the methods have operated on them in some way. This `$.getJSON()` function, however, is different. There is no logical DOM element to which it could apply; the resulting object has to be provided to the script, not injected into the page. For this reason, `getJSON()` is defined as a method of the global jQuery object, rather than of an individual jQuery object instance.

If JavaScript had classes like other object-oriented languages, we'd call `$.getJSON()` a **class method**. For our purposes, we'll refer to this type of method as a **global function**; in effect, they are functions that use the jQuery namespace so as not to conflict with other function names.

To use this function, we pass it the file name as before:

```
$(document).ready(function() {
  $('#letter-b .button').click(function() {
    $.getJSON('b.json');
  });
});
```

This code has no apparent effect when we click the button. The function call loads the file, but we have not told JavaScript what to do with the resulting data. For this, we need to use a callback.

The `$.getJSON()` function takes a second argument, which is a function to be called when the load is complete. As mentioned before, AJAX calls are asynchronous, and the callback provides a way to wait for the data to be transmitted rather than executing code right away. The callback function also takes an argument, which is filled with the resulting data. So, we write:

```
$(document).ready(function() {
  $('#letter-b .button').click(function() {
    $.getJSON('b.json', function(data) {
    });
  });
});
```

Inside this function, we can use the `data` variable to traverse the data structure as necessary. We'll need to iterate over the top-level array, building the HTML for each item. We could do this with a standard `for` loop, but instead we'll introduce another of jQuery's useful global functions, `$.each()`. We saw its counterpart, the `.each()` method, in Chapter 5. Instead of operating on a jQuery object, this function takes an array or map as its first parameter and a callback function as its second. The current iteration index and the current item in the array or map each time through the loop are passed as two parameters to the callback function:

```
$(document).ready(function() {
  $('#letter-b .button').click(function() {
    $.getJSON('b.json', function(data) {
      $('#dictionary').empty();
      $.each(data, function(entryIndex, entry) {
        var html = '<div class="entry">';
        html += '<h3 class="term">' + entry['term'] + '</h3>';
        html += '<div class="part">' + entry['part'] + '</div>';
        html += '<div class="definition">';
        html += entry['definition'];
        html += '</div>';
        html += '</div>';
        $('#dictionary').append(html);
      });
    });
  });
});
```

Before the loop, we empty out `<div id="dictionary">` so that we can fill it with our newly-constructed HTML. Then we use `$.each()` to examine each item in turn, building an HTML structure using the contents of the `entry` map. Finally, we turn this HTML into a DOM tree by append it to the `<div>`.

 This approach presumes that the data is safe for HTML consumption; it should not contain any stray < characters, for example.

All that's left is to handle the entries with quotations, which takes another `$.each()` loop:

```
$(document).ready(function() {
  $('#letter-b .button').click(function() {
    $.getJSON('b.json', function(data) {
      $('#dictionary').empty();
      $.each(data, function(entryIndex, entry) {
```

```
var html = '<div class="entry">';
html += '<h3 class="term">' + entry['term'] + '</h3>';
html += '<div class="part">' + entry['part'] + '</div>';
html += '<div class="definition">';
html += entry['definition'];
if (entry['quote']) {
  html += '<div class="quote">';
  $.each(entry['quote'], function(lineIndex, line) {
    html += '<div class="quote-line">' + line + '</div>';
  });
  if (entry['author']) {
    html += '<div class="quote-author">' + entry['author'] +
                                              '</div>';
  }
  html += '</div>';
}
html += '</div>';
html += '</div>';
$('#dictionary').append($(html));
      });
    });
  });
});
```

With this code in place, we can click the next button and confirm our results:

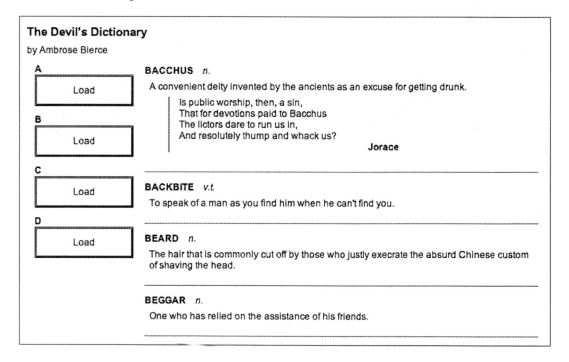

The JSON format is concise, but not forgiving. Every bracket, brace, quote and comma must be present and accounted for, or the file will not load. In most browsers, we won't even get an error message; the script will just silently fail.

Executing a Script

Occasionally we don't want to retrieve all the JavaScript we will need when the page is first loaded. We might not know what scripts will be necessary until some user interaction occurs. We could introduce `<script>` tags on the fly when they are needed, but a more elegant way to inject additional code is to have jQuery load the `.js` file directly.

Pulling in a script is about as simple as loading an HTML fragment. In this case, we use the global function `$.getScript()`, which, like its siblings, accepts a URL locating the script file:

```
$(document).ready(function() {
  $('#letter-c .button').click(function() {
    $.getScript('c.js');
  });
});
```

In our last example, we then needed to process the result data so that we could do something useful with the loaded file. With a script file, though, the processing is automatic; the script is simply run.

Scripts fetched in this way are run in the global context of the current page. This means they have access to all globally-defined functions and variables, notably including jQuery itself. We can therefore mimic the JSON example to prepare and insert HTML on the page when the script is executed, and place this code in `c.js`:

```
var entries = [
  {
    "term": "CALAMITY",
    "part": "n.",
    "definition": "A more than commonly plain and unmistakable
                   reminder that the affairs of this life are not of
                   our own ordering.  Calamities are of two kinds:
                   misfortune to ourselves, and good fortune to
                   others."
  },
  {
    "term": "CANNIBAL",
    "part": "n.",
```

```
            "definition": "A gastronome of the old school who preserves the
                          simple tastes and adheres to the natural diet of
                          the pre-pork period."
        },
        {
          "term": "CHILDHOOD",
          "part": "n.",
          "definition": "The period of human life intermediate between the
                        idiocy of infancy and the folly of youth &mdash;
                        two removes from the sin of manhood and three from
                        the remorse of age."
        }
    ];

    var html = '';

    $.each(entries, function() {
      html += '<div class="entry">';
      html += '<h3 class="term">' + this['term'] + '</h3>';
      html += '<div class="part">' + this['part'] + '</div>';
      html += '<div class="definition">' + this['definition'] + '</div>';
      html += '</div>';
    });

    $('#dictionary').html(html);
```

Now clicking on the third button has the expected result:

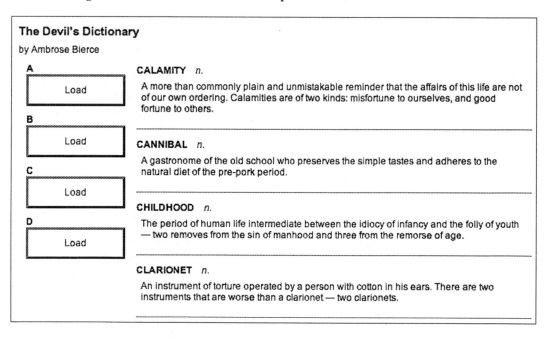

Loading an XML Document

XML is part of the acronym AJAX, but we haven't actually loaded any XML yet. Doing so is straightforward, and mirrors the JSON technique fairly closely. First we'll need an XML file `d.xml` containing some data we wish to display:

```
<?xml version="1.0" encoding="UTF-8"?>
<entries>
  <entry term="DANCE" part="v.i.">
    <definition>
      To leap about to the sound of tittering music, preferably with
      arms about your neighbor's wife or daughter.  There are many
      kinds of dances, but all those requiring the participation of
      the two sexes have two characteristics in common:  they are
      conspicuously innocent, and warmly loved by the vicious.
    </definition>
  </entry>
  <entry term="DAY" part="n.">
    <definition>
      A period of twenty-four hours, mostly misspent.  This period is
      divided into two parts, the day proper and the night, or day
      improper <![CDATA[&mdash;]]> the former devoted to sins of
      business, the latter consecrated to the other sort.  These two
      kinds of social activity overlap.
    </definition>
  </entry>
  <entry term="DEBT" part="n.">
    <definition>
      An ingenious substitute for the chain and whip of the
      slave-driver.
    </definition>
    <quote author="Barlow S. Vode">
      <line>As, pent in an aquarium, the troutlet</line>
      <line>Swims round and round his tank to find an outlet,</line>
      <line>Pressing his nose against the glass that holds him,</line>
      <line>Nor ever sees the prison that enfolds him;</line>
      <line>So the poor debtor, seeing naught around him,</line>
      <line>Yet feels the narrow limits that impound him,</line>
      <line>Grieves at his debt and studies to evade it,</line>
      <line>And finds at last he might as well have paid it.</line>
    </quote>
  </entry>
  <entry term="DEFAME" part="v.t.">
    <definition>
      To lie about another.  To tell the truth about another.
    </definition>
  </entry>
</entries>
```

This data could be expressed in many ways, of course, and some would more closely mimic the structure we established for the HTML or JSON used earlier. Here, though, we're illustrating some of the features of XML designed to make it more readable to humans, such as the use of attributes for `term` and `part` rather than tags.

We'll start off our function in a familiar manner:

```
$(document).ready(function() {
  $('#letter-d .button').click(function() {
    $.get('d.xml', function(data) {
    });
  });
});
```

This time it's the `$.get()` function that does our work. In general, this function simply fetches the file at the supplied URL and provides the plain text to the callback. However, if the response is known to be XML because of its server-supplied MIME type, the callback will be handed the XML DOM tree.

Fortunately, we have already seen jQuery's substantial DOM-traversing capabilities. We can use the normal `.find()`, `.filter()` and other traversal methods on the XML document just as we would on HTML:

```
$(document).ready(function() {
  $('#letter-d .button').click(function() {
    $.get('d.xml', function(data) {
      $('#dictionary').empty();
      $(data).find('entry').each(function() {
        var $entry = $(this);
        var html = '<div class="entry">';
        html += '<h3 class="term">' + $entry.attr('term') + '</h3>';
        html += '<div class="part">' + $entry.attr('part') + '</div>';
        html += '<div class="definition">'
        html += $entry.find('definition').text();
        var $quote = $entry.find('quote');
        if ($quote.length) {
          html += '<div class="quote">';
          $quote.find('line').each(function() {
            html += '<div class="quote-line">' + $(this).text() +
                                                 '</ div>';
          });
          if ($quote.attr('author')) {
            html += '<div class="quote-author">' +
                                $quote.attr('author') + '</div>';
          }
          html += '</div>';
```

```
      }
      html += '</div>';
      html += '</div>';
      $('#dictionary').append($(html));
    });
  });
  });
});
```

This has the expected effect when the fourth button is pressed:

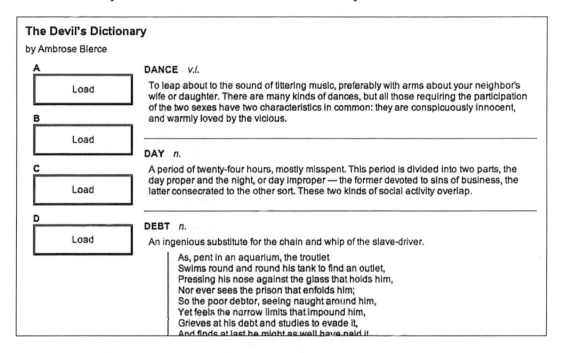

This is a new use for the DOM traversal methods we already know, shedding some light on the utility of jQuery's **XPath support**. While the CSS syntax of selectors is typically the natural one for dealing with HTML pages, XPath was built for XML. This means that while there are ways to locate desired DOM elements using either syntax, we can sometimes reuse existing XPath expressions from other systems that use the same XML files.

XML's usage of arbitrary tags and attributes, rather than relying on classes for identification, makes XPath especially convenient for traversing it. For example, suppose we wanted to limit the displayed entries to those that have quotes that in turn have attributed authors. We can limit the entries to those with nested quote elements by changing entry to entry[quote]. Then we can further restrict the entries to those with `author` attributes on the quote elements by writing `entry[quote[@author]]`. The line with the initial selector now reads:

```
$(data).find('entry[quote[@author]]').each(function() {
```

This new selector expression restricts the returned entries correspondingly:

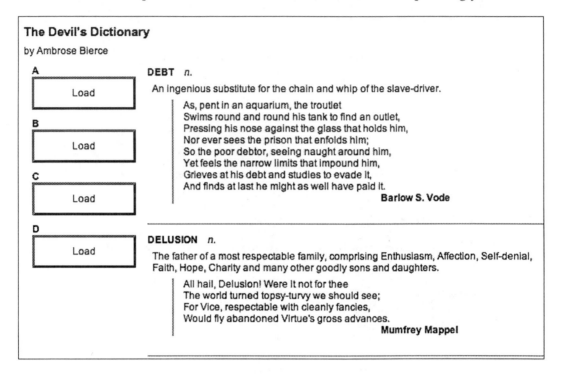

Choosing a Data Format

We have looked at four formats for our external data, each of which is handled natively by jQuery's AJAX functions. We have also verified that all four can handle the task at hand, loading information onto an existing page when the user requests it and not before. How, then, do we decide which one to use in our applications?

HTML snippets require very little work to implement. The external data can be loaded and inserted into the page with one simple method, which does not even require a callback function. No traversal of the data is necessary for the straightforward task of adding the new HTML into the existing page. On the other hand, the data is not necessarily structured in a way that makes it reusable for other applications. The external file is tightly coupled with its intended container.

JSON files are structured for simple reuse. They are compact, and easy to read. The data structure must be traversed to pull out the information and present it on the page, but this can be done with standard JavaScript techniques. Since the files can be parsed with a single call to JavaScript's `eval()`, reading in a JSON file is extremely fast. Any use of `eval()` does carry inherent risks, however. Errors in the JSON file can cause silent failure or even side effects on the page, so the data must be crafted carefully by a trusted party.

JavaScript files offer the ultimate in flexibility, but are not really a data storage mechanism. Because the files are language-specific, they cannot be used to provide the same information to disparate systems. Instead, the ability to load a JavaScript file means that behaviors that are rarely needed can be factored out into external files, reducing code size unless and until it is needed.

XML documents are the kings of portability. Because XML has become the *lingua franca* of the web service world, providing data in this format makes it very likely the data can be reused elsewhere. For example, Flickr (`http://flickr.com/`), del.icio.us (`http://del.icio.us/`) and Upcoming (`http://upcoming.org/`) all export XML representations of their data, which has allowed many interesting mashups of their data to arise. The XML format is somewhat bulky, though, and can be a bit slower to parse and manipulate than other options.

With these characteristics in mind, it is typically easiest to provide external data as HTML snippets, as long as the data is not needed in other applications as well. In cases where the data will be reused but the other applications can also be influenced, JSON is often a good choice due to its performance and size. When the remote application is not known, XML provides the greatest assurance that interoperability will be possible.

More than any other consideration, we should determine if the data is already available. If it is, chances are it's in one of these formats to begin with, so our decision may be made for us.

Passing Data to the Server

Our examples to this point have focused on the task of retrieving static data files from the web server. However, the AJAX technique really comes into its own only when the server can dynamically shape the data based on input from the browser. We're helped along by jQuery in this task as well; all of the methods we've covered so far can be modified so that data transfer becomes a two-way street.

Since demonstrating these techniques requires interaction with the web server, we'll need to use server-side code for the first time here. The examples given will use the PHP scripting language, which is very widely used as well as freely available. We will not cover how to set up a web server with PHP here; help on this can be found on the websites of Apache (http://apache.org/) or PHP (http://php.net/), or from your site's hosting company.

Performing a GET Request

To illustrate this communication between client and server, we'll write a script that only sends one dictionary entry to the browser on each request. The entry chosen will depend on a parameter sent from the browser. Our script will pull its data from an internal data structure like this:

```php
<?php
$entries = array(
  'EAVESDROP' => array(
    'part' => 'v.i.',
    'definition' => 'Secretly to overhear a catalogue of the crimes
                                and vices of another or yourself.',
    'quote' => array(
      'A lady with one of her ears applied',
      'To an open keyhole heard, inside,',
      'Two female gossips in converse free &mdash;',
      'The subject engaging them was she.',
      '"I think," said one, "and my husband thinks',
      'That she\'s a prying, inquisitive minx!"',
      'As soon as no more of it she could hear',
      'The lady, indignant, removed her ear.',
      '"I will not stay," she said, with a pout,',
      '"To hear my character lied about!"',
    ),
    'author' => 'Gopete Sherany',
  ),
  'EDIBLE' => array(
    'part' => 'adj.',
    'definition' => 'Good to eat, and wholesome to digest, as a worm
                    to a toad, a toad to a snake, a snake to a pig,
                    a pig to a man, and a man to a worm.',
  ),
  'EDUCATION' => array(
    'part' => 'n.',
```

```php
        'definition' => 'That which discloses to the wise and disguises
                         from the foolish their lack of understanding.',
    ),
);
?>
```

In a production version of this example, the data would probably be stored in a database and loaded on demand. Since the data is a part of the script here, the code to retrieve it is quite straightforward. We examine the data that has been posted and craft the HTML snippet to display:

```php
<?php
if (isset($entries[strtoupper($_REQUEST['term'])])) {
  $entry = $entries[strtoupper($_REQUEST['term'])];

  $html = '<div class="entry">';
  $html .= '<h3 class="term">';
  $html .= strtoupper($_REQUEST['term']);
  $html .= '</h3>';
  $html .= '<div class="part">';
  $html .= $entry['part'];
  $html .= '</div>';
  $html .= '<div class="definition">';
  $html .= $entry['definition'];
  if (isset($entry['quote'])) {
    $html .= '<div class="quote">';
    foreach ($entry['quote'] as $line) {
      $html .= '<div class="quote-line">'. $line .'</div>';
    }
    if (isset($entry['author'])) {
      $html .= '<div class="quote-author">'. $entry['author'] .
                                                    '</div>';
    }
    $html .= '</div>';
  }
  $html .= '</div>';

  $html .= '</div>';

  print($html);
}
?>
```

Now requests to this script, which we'll call `e.php`, will return the HTML snippet corresponding to the term that was sent in the GET parameters. For example, when accessing the script with `e.php?term=eavesdrop`, we get back:

EAVESDROP

v.i.
Secretly to overhear a catalogue of the crimes and vices of another or yourself.
A lady with one of her ears applied
To an open keyhole heard, inside,
Two female gossips in converse free —
The subject engaging them was she.
"I think," said one, "and my husband thinks
That she's a prying, inquisitive minx!"
As soon as no more of it she could hear
The lady, indignant, removed her ear.
"I will not stay," she said, with a pout,
"To hear my character lied about!"
Gopete Sherany

Once again we note the lack of formatting we saw with earlier HTML snippets, because CSS rules have not been applied.

Since we're showing how data is passed to the server, we will use a different method to request entries than the solitary buttons we've been relying on so far. Instead, we'll present a list of links for each term, and cause a click on any of them to load the corresponding definition. The HTML we'll add for this looks like:

```
<div class="letter" id="letter-e">
  <h3>E</h3>
  <ul>
    <li><a href="e.php?term=Eavesdrop">Eavesdrop</a></li>
    <li><a href="e.php?term=Edible">Edible</a></li>
    <li><a href="e.php?term=Education">Education</a></li>
    <li><a href="e.php?term=Eloquence">Eloquence</a></li>
    <li><a href="e.php?term=Elysium">Elysium</a></li>
    <li><a href="e.php?term=Emancipation">Emancipation</a></li>
    <li><a href="e.php?term=Emotion">Emotion</a></li>
    <li><a href="e.php?term=Envelope">Envelope</a></li>
    <li><a href="e.php?term=Envy">Envy</a></li>
    <li><a href="e.php?term=Epitaph">Epitaph</a></li>
    <li><a href="e.php?term=Evangelist">Evangelist</a></li>
  </ul>
</div>
```

Now we need to get our JavaScript code to call the PHP script with the right parameters. We could do this with the normal `.load()` mechanism, appending the query string right to the URL and fetching data with addresses like `e.php?term=eavesdrop` directly. Instead, though, we can have jQuery construct the query string based on a map we provide to the `$.get()` function:

```
$(document).ready(function() {
  $('#letter-e a').click(function() {
    $.get('e.php', {'term': $(this).text()}, function(data) {
      $('#dictionary').html(data);
    });
    return false;
  });
});
```

Now that we have seen other AJAX interfaces that jQuery provides, the operation of this function seems familiar. The only difference is the second parameter, which allows us to supply a map of keys and values that become part of the query string. In this case, the key is always `term` but the value is taken from the text of each link. Now, clicking on the first link in the list causes its definition to appear:

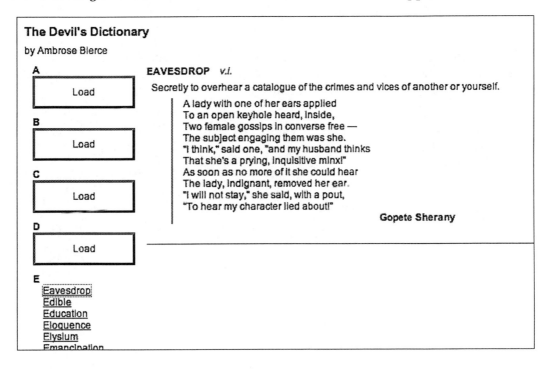

All the links here have addresses given, even though we are not using them in the code. This provides an alternative method of navigating the information for users who have JavaScript turned off or unavailable. To prevent the links from being followed normally when clicked, the event handler has to return `false`.

Performing a POST Request

HTTP requests using the POST method are almost identical to those using GET. One of the most visible differences is that GET places its arguments in the query string portion of the URL, whereas POST requests do not. However, in AJAX calls, even this distinction is invisible to the average user. Generally, the only reason to choose one method over the other is to conform to the norms of the server-side code, or to provide for large amounts of transmitted data; GET has a more stringent limit. We have coded our PHP example to cope equally well with either method, so we can change from GET to POST simply by changing the jQuery function we call:

```
$(document).ready(function() {
  $('#letter-e a').click(function() {
    $.post('e.php', {'term': $(this).text()}, function(data) {
      $('#dictionary').html(data);
    });
    return false;
  });
});
```

The arguments are the same, and the request will now be made via POST. We can further simplify the code by using the .load() method, which uses POST by default when it is supplied with a map of arguments:

```
$(document).ready(function() {
  $('#letter-e a').click(function() {
    $('#dictionary').load('e.php', {'term': $(this).text()});
    return false;
  });
});
```

This cut-down version functions the same way when a link is clicked:

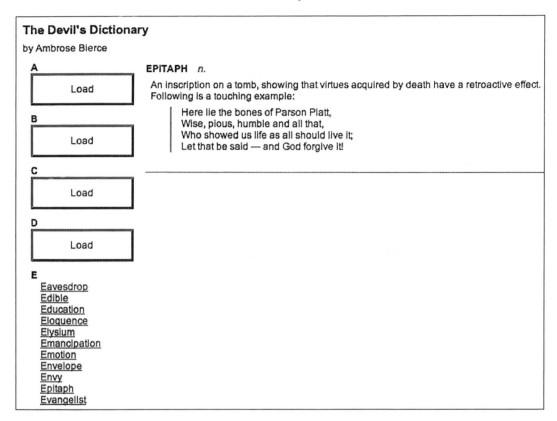

Serializing a Form

Sending data to the server often involves the user filling out forms. Rather than relying on the normal form submission mechanism, which will load the response in the entire browser window, we can use jQuery's AJAX toolkit to submit the form asynchronously and place the response inside the current page.

To try this out, we'll need to construct a simple form:

```
<div class="letter" id="letter-f">F
  <form>
    <input type="text" name="term" value="" id="term">
    <input type="submit" name="search" value="search" id="search">
  </form>
</div>
```

This time we'll return a set of entries from the PHP script by searching for the supplied search term as a substring of a dictionary term. The data structure will be of the same format as before, but the logic will be a bit different:

```php
foreach ($entries as $term => $entry) {
  if (strpos($term, strtoupper($_REQUEST['term'])) !== FALSE) {
    $html = '<div class="entry">';
    $html .= '<h3 class="term">';
    $html .= $term;
    $html .= '</h3>';
    $html .= '<div class="part">';
    $html .= $entry['part'];
    $html .= '</div>';
    $html .= '<div class="definition">';
    $html .= $entry['definition'];
    if (isset($entry['quote'])) {
      foreach ($entry['quote'] as $line) {
        $html .= '<div class="quote-line">'. $line .'</div>';
      }
      if (isset($entry['author'])) {
        $html .= '<div class="quote-author">'. $entry['author']
                                              .'</div>';
      }
    }
    $html .= '</div>';
    $html .= '</div>';
    print($html);
  }
}
```

The call to `strpos()` scans the word for the supplied search string. Now we can react to a form submission and craft the proper query parameters by traversing the DOM tree:

```javascript
$(document).ready(function() {
  $('#letter-f form').submit(function() {
    $('#dictionary').load('f.php', {'term': $('input[@name="term"]').
val()});
    return false;
  });
});
```

This code has the intended effect, but searching for input fields by name and appending them to a map one by one is cumbersome. The approach particularly does not scale well as the form becomes more complex. Fortunately, jQuery offers a shortcut for this often-used idiom. The `.serialize()` method acts on a jQuery object and translates the matched DOM elements into a query string that can be passed along with an AJAX request. We can generalize our submission handler as follows:

```
$(document).ready(function() {
  $('#letter-f form').submit(function() {
    $.get('f.php', $(this).find('input').serialize(), function(data)
    {
      $('#dictionary').html(data);
    });
    return false;
  });
});
```

Now the same script will work to submit the form, even as the number of fields increases. When we perform a search, the matched entries are displayed:

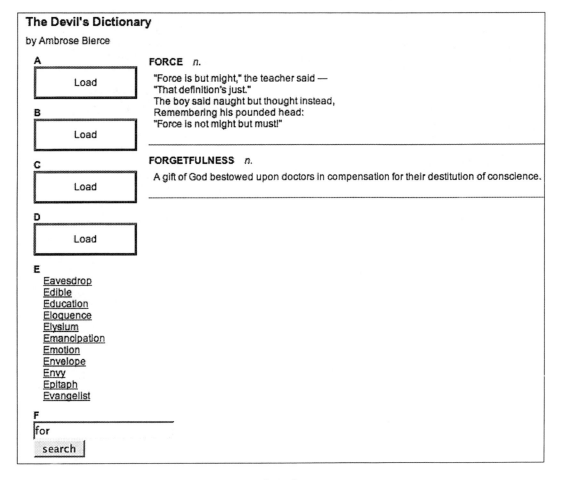

While the `.serialize()` method is convenient, it does not perfectly mimic the submit action of a browser. In particular, multiple-select fields will be reduced to a single selection when serialized. Use this method with caution. For an exact imitation of a browser's normal form submission behavior, we can instead turn to the `form.js` jQuery plug-in. More information on this tool can be found in Chapter 10.

Keeping an Eye on the Request

So far, it has been sufficient for us to make a call to an AJAX method and patiently await the response. At times, though, it is handy to know a bit more about the HTTP request as it progresses. If such a need arises, jQuery offers a suite of functions that can be used to register callbacks when various AJAX-related events occur.

The `.ajaxStart()` and `.ajaxStop()` methods are two examples of these *observer* functions, and are attached to any jQuery object. When an AJAX call begins with no other transfer in progress, the `.ajaxStart()` callback is fired. Conversely, when the last active request ends, the callback attached with `.ajaxStop()` will be executed. All of the observers are **global**, in that they are called when any AJAX communication occurs, regardless of what code initiates it.

We can use these methods to provide some feedback to the user in case of a slow network connection. The HTML for the page can have a suitable loading message appended:

```
<div id="loading">
  Loading...
</div>
```

This could also include an animated GIF image to provide a **throbber**. We add styles to the CSS file, so that on initial load the page looks like:

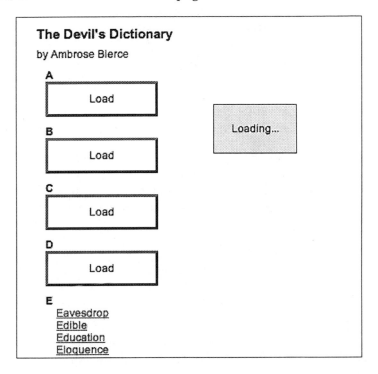

Now we add a `display: none;` style rule so that the message is initially hidden. To display it at the right time, we just register it as an observer with `.ajaxStart()`:

```
$(document).ready(function() {
  $('#loading').ajaxStart(function() {
    $(this).show();
  });
});
```

We can chain the hiding behavior right onto this:

```
$(document).ready(function() {
  $('#loading').ajaxStart(function() {
    $(this).show();
  }).ajaxStop(function() {
    $(this).hide();
  });
});
```

Voilà! We have our loading feedback.

Once again, note that these methods have no association with the particular ways in which the AJAX communications begin. The .load() on the first button and the .getJSON() on the second both cause these actions to occur. In this case, the global behavior is desirable. If we need to get more specific, we have a few options at our disposal. Some of the observer methods, like .ajaxError(), send their callback a reference to the XMLHttpRequest object. This can be used to differentiate one request from another and provide different behaviors. Other more specific handling can be achieved by using the low-level $.ajax() function. All of the AJAX functions we've discussed call $.ajax() internally. This function provides a wide array of options, several of which are handlers for specific events relating to the AJAX request.

The most common way of interacting with the request, though, which we have already covered, is the success callback. We have used this in several of our examples to interpret the data coming back from the server and to populate the page with the results. It can be used for other feedback too, of course. Consider once again our .load() example:

```
$(document).ready(function() {
  $('#letter-a .button').click(function() {
    $('#dictionary').load('a.html');
  });
});
```

We can create a small enhancement here by making the loaded content fade into view rather than appearing suddenly. The .load() can take a callback to be fired on completion:

```
$(document).ready(function() {
  $('#letter-a .button').click(function() {
    $('#dictionary').hide().load('a.html', function() {
      $(this).fadeIn();
    });
  });
});
```

First we hide the target element, and then initiate the load. When the load is complete, we use the callback to show the newly-populated element by fading it in.

AJAX and Events

Suppose we wanted to highlight all the <h3> elements on the page when they are clicked. By now the code to perform such a task is almost second-nature:

```
$(document).ready(function() {
  $('h3').click(function() {
```

```
         $(this).toggleClass('highlighted');
      });
   });
```

All is well, in that clicking on the letters on the left side of the page highlights them. But the dictionary terms are also <h3> elements, and they do not get the highlight. Why?

The dictionary terms are not yet part of the DOM when the page is loaded, so the event handlers are never bound. This is an example of a general issue with event handlers and AJAX calls: loaded elements must have their event handlers bound at the appropriate time.

A first pass at solving this problem is to factor the binding out into a function, and call that function both at the time when the document is ready and after the AJAX call:

```
$(document).ready(function() {
   var bindBehaviors = function() {
      $('h3').click(function() {
         $(this).toggleClass('highlighted');
      });
   };

   bindBehaviors();

   $('#letter-a .button').click(function() {
      $('#dictionary').hide().load('a.html', function() {
         bindBehaviors();
         $(this).fadeIn();
      });
   });
});
```

Now we can put all our event handlers in the bindBehaviors() function, and call that whenever the DOM changes. Clicking on a dictionary term now highlights it, as we intended. Unfortunately, we've also managed to cause very strange behavior when the letters are clicked. At first they highlight correctly, but after the button is clicked (loading the dictionary entries), they no longer highlight on subsequent clicks.

Closer inspection reveals that, after the AJAX call, the highlighting breaks because the click handler is fired twice. A doubled .toggleClass() is the same as none at all, so the click seems not to work. The culprit here is bindBehaviors(), which binds the click event to all <h3> elements each time. After a button click, there are actually two event handlers for clicks on an <h3>, which happen to do the exact same thing.

Scoping an Event-Binding Function

A nice way around this double-firing is to pass some context into `bindBehaviors()` each time we call it. The `$()` function can take a second argument, a DOM node to which the search is restricted. By using this feature in `bindBehaviors()`, we can avoid multiple event bindings:

```
$(document).ready(function() {
  var bindBehaviors = function(scope) {
    $('h3', scope).click(function() {
      $(this).toggleClass('highlighted');
    });
  };

  bindBehaviors(this);

  $('#letter-a .button').click(function() {
    $('#dictionary').hide().load('a.html', function() {
      bindBehaviors(this);
      $(this).fadeIn();
    });
  });
});
```

The first time `bindBehaviors()` is called, the scope is `document`, so all `<h3>` elements in the document are matched and have the click event bound. After an AJAX load, the scope is instead the `<div id="dictionary">` element, so the letters are not matched and are left alone.

Using Event Bubbling

Adding scope to a behavior-binding function is often a very elegant solution to the problem of binding event handlers after an AJAX load. We can often avoid the issue entirely, however, by exploiting event bubbling. We can bind the handler not to the elements that are loaded, but to a common ancestor element:

```
$(document).ready(function() {
  $('body').click(function(event) {
    if ($(event.target).is('h3')) {
      $(event.target).toggleClass('highlighted');
    }
  });
});
```

Here we bind the click event handler to the `<body>` element. Because this is not in the portion of the document that is changed when the AJAX call is made, the event handler never has to be re-bound. However, the event context is now wrong, so we compensate for this by checking what the event's `target` attribute is. If the target is of the right type, we perform our normal action; otherwise, we do nothing.

Security Limitations

For all its utility in crafting dynamic web applications, `XMLHttpRequest` (the underlying browser technology behind jQuery's AJAX implementation) is subject to strict boundaries. To prevent various cross-site scripting attacks, it is not generally possible to request a document from a server other than the one that hosts the original page.

This is generally a positive situation. For example, some cite the implementation of JSON parsing by using `eval()` as insecure. If malicious code is present in the data file, it could be run by the `eval()` call. However, since the data file must reside on the same server as the web page itself, the ability to inject code in the data file is largely equivalent to the ability to inject code in the page directly. This means that, for the case of loading trusted JSON files, `eval()` is not a significant security concern.

There are many cases, though, in which it would be beneficial to load data from a third-party source. There are several ways to work around the security limitations and allow this to happen.

One method is to rely on the server to load the remote data, and then provide it when requested by the client. This is a very powerful approach, as the server can perform pre-processing on the data as needed. For example, we could load XML files containing RSS news feeds from several sources, aggregate them into a single feed on the server, and publish this new file for the client when it is requested.

To load data from a remote location without server involvement, we have to get sneakier. A popular approach for the case of loading foreign JavaScript files is injecting `<script>` tags on demand. Since jQuery can help us insert new DOM elements, it is simple to do this:

```
$(document.createElement('script'))
    .attr('src', 'http://example.com/example.js').appendTo('head');
```

The browser will execute the loaded script, but there is no mechanism to retrieve results from the script. For this reason, the technique requires cooperation from the remote host. The loaded script must take some action, such as setting a global variable that has an effect on the local environment. Services that publish scripts that are executable in this way will also provide an API with which to interact with the remote script.

Another option is to use the `<iframe>` HTML tag to load remote data. This element allows any URL to be used as the source for its data fetching, even if it does not match the host page's server. The data can be loaded and easily displayed on the current page. Manipulating the data, however, typically requires the same cooperation needed for the `<script>` tag approach; scripts inside the `<iframe>` need to explicitly provide the data to objects in the parent document.

Summary

We have learned that AJAX methods provided by jQuery can help us to load data in several different formats from the server without a page refresh. We can execute scripts from the server on demand, and send data back to the server.

We've also learned how to deal with common challenges of asynchronous loading techniques, such as keeping handlers bound after a load has occurred and loading data from a third-party server.

This concludes the tutorial portion of the book. We are armed with the main tools offered by jQuery: selectors, events, effects, DOM manipulation, and asynchronous server requests. The reference section will step through each method available to us in these categories. But first, we'll examine a few combinations of these techniques that enhance our web pages in new and interesting ways.

7
Table Manipulation

Let 'em wear gaudy colors
Or avoid display
> *— Devo,*
> *"Wiggly World"*

In the first six chapters, we explored the jQuery library in a series of tutorials that focused on each jQuery component and used examples as a way to see those components in action. In Chapters 7 through 9 we invert the process; we'll begin with the examples and see how we can use jQuery methods to achieve them.

Here we will use an online bookstore as our model website, but the techniques we cook up can be applied to a wide variety of other sites as well, from weblogs to portfolios, from market-facing business sites to corporate intranets. Chapters 7 and 8 focus on two common elements of most sites—tables and forms—while Chapter 9 examines a couple of ways to visually enhance sets of information using animated shufflers and rotators.

In this chapter, we will use jQuery to apply techniques for increasing the readability, usability, and visual appeal of tables, though we are not dealing with tables used for layout and design. In fact, as the web standards movement has become more pervasive in the last few years, table-based layout has increasingly been abandoned in favor of CSS-based designs. Although tables were often employed as a somewhat necessary stopgap measure in the 1990s to create multi-column and other complex layouts, they were never intended to be used in that way, whereas CSS is a technology expressly created for presentation.

But this is not the place for an extended discussion on the proper role of tables. Suffice it to say that in this chapter we will explore ways to display and interact with tables used as semantically marked up containers of tabular data. For a closer look at applying semantic, accessible HTML to tables, a good place to start is Roger Johansson's blog entry, *Bring on the Tables* at `http://www.456bereastreet.com/archive/200410/bring_on_the_tables/`.

Some of the techniques we apply to tables in this chapter can be found in plug-ins such as Christian Bach's *Table Sorter*. For more information, visit the *jQuery Plug-in Repository* at http://jquery.com/Plugins.

Sorting

One of the most common tasks performed with tabular data is **sorting**. In a large table, being able to rearrange the information that we're looking for is invaluable. Unfortunately, this helpful operation is one of the trickiest to put into action. We can achieve the goal of sorting in two ways, namely Server-Side Sorting and JavaScript Sorting.

Server-Side Sorting

A common solution for data sorting is to perform it on the server side. Data in tables often comes from a database, which means that the code that pulls it out of the database can request it in a given sort order (using, for example, the SQL language's ORDER BY clause). If we have server-side code at our disposal, it is straightforward to begin with a reasonable default sort order.

Sorting is most useful when the user can determine the sort order. A common idiom is to make the headers of sortable columns into links. These links can go to the current page, but with a query string appended indicating the column to sort by:

```
<table id="my-data">
  <tr>
    <th class="name"><a href="index.php?sort=name">Name</a></th>
    <th class="date"><a href="index.php?sort=date">Date</a></th>
  </tr>
  ...
</table>
```

The server can react to the query string parameter by returning the database contents in a different order.

Preventing Page Refreshes

This setup is simple, but requires a page refresh for each sort operation. As we have seen, jQuery allows us to eliminate such page refreshes by using AJAX methods. If we have the column headers set up as links as before, we can add jQuery code to change those links into AJAX requests:

```
$(document).ready(function() {
  $('#my-data .name a').click(function() {
```

```
    $('#my-data').load('index.php?sort=name&type=ajax');
    return false;
  });
  $('#my-data .date a').click(function() {
    $('#my-data').load('index.php?sort=date&type=ajax');
    return false;
  });
});
```

Now when the anchors are clicked, jQuery sends an AJAX request to the server for the same page. We add an additional parameter to the query string so that the server can determine that an AJAX request is being made. The server code can be written to send back only the table itself, and not the surrounding page, when this parameter is present. This way we can take the response and insert it in place of the table.

This is an example of **progressive enhancement**. The page works perfectly well without any JavaScript at all, as the links for server-side sorting are still present. When JavaScript is present, however, the AJAX hijacks the page request and allows the sort to occur without a full page load.

JavaScript Sorting

There are times, though, when we either don't want to wait for server responses when sorting, or don't have a server-side scripting language available to us. A viable alternative in this case is to perform the sorting entirely on the browser using JavaScript client-side scripting.

For example, suppose we have a table listing books, along with their authors, release dates, and prices:

```
<table class="sortable">
  <thead>
    <tr>
      <th></th>
      <th>Title</th>
      <th>Author(s)</th>
      <th>Publish Date</th>
      <th>Price</th>
    </tr>
  </thead>
  <tbody>
    <tr>
      <td>
        <img src="../covers/small/1847192386.png" width="49"
             height="61" alt="Building Websites with
```

```
                                                      Joomla! 1.5 Beta 1" />
        </td>
        <td>Building Websites with Joomla! 1.5 Beta 1</td>
        <td>Hagen Graf</td>
        <td>Feb 2007</td>
        <td>$40.49</td>
      </tr>
      <tr>
        <td><img src="../covers/small/1904811620.png" width="49"
                height="61" alt="Learning Mambo: A Step-by-Step
                Tutorial to Building Your Website" /></td>
        <td>Learning Mambo: A Step-by-Step Tutorial to Building Your
            Website</td>
        <td>Douglas Paterson</td>
        <td>Dec 2006</td>
        <td>$40.49</td>
      </tr>
      ...
    </tbody>
</table>
```

We'd like to turn the table headers into buttons that sort by their respective columns. Let us look into ways of doing this.

Row Grouping Tags

Note our use of the `<thead>` and `<tbody>` tags to segment the data into row groupings. Many HTML authors omit these implied tags, but they can prove useful in supplying us with more convenient CSS selectors to use. For example, suppose we wish to apply typical even/odd row striping to this table, but only to the body of the table:

```
$(document).ready(function() {
  $('table.sortable tbody tr:odd').addClass('odd');
  $('table.sortable tbody tr:even').addClass('even');
});
```

This will add alternating colors to the table, but leave the header untouched:

	Title	Author(s)	Publish Date	Price
	Building Websites with Joomla! 1.5 Beta 1	Hagen Graf	Feb 2007	$40.49
	Learning Mambo: A Step-by-Step Tutorial to Building Your Website	Douglas Paterson	Dec 2006	$40.49
	Moodle E-Learning Course Development	William Rice	May 2006	$35.99
	AJAX and PHP: Building Responsive Web Applications	Cristian Darie, Mihai Bucica, Filip Cherecheş-Toşa, Bogdan Brinzarea	Mar 2006	$31.49

Basic Alphabetical Sorting

Now let's perform a sort on the **Title** column of the table. We'll need a class on the table header cell so that we can select it properly:

```
<thead>
  <tr>
    <th></th>
    <th class="sort-alpha">Title</th>
    <th>Author(s)</th>
    <th>Publish Date</th>
    <th>Price</th>
  </tr>
</thead>
```

To perform the actual sort, we can use JavaScript's built in .sort() method. It does an in-place sort on an array, and can take a function as an argument. This function compares two items in the array and should return a positive or negative number depending on the result. Our initial sort routine looks like this:

```
$(document).ready(function() {
  $('table.sortable').each(function() {
    var $table = $(this);
    $('th', $table).each(function(column) {
      if ($(this).is('.sort-alpha')) {
```

```
            $(this).addClass('clickable').hover(function() {
              $(this).addClass('hover');
            }, function() {
              $(this).removeClass('hover');
            }).click(function() {
              var rows = $table.find('tbody > tr').get();
              rows.sort(function(a, b) {
                var keyA = $(a).children('td').eq(column).text()
                                                   .toUpperCase();
                var keyB = $(b).children('td').eq(column).text()
                                                   .toUpperCase();
                if (keyA < keyB) return -1;
                if (keyA > keyB) return 1;
                return 0;
              });
              $.each(rows, function(index, row) {
                $table.children('tbody').append(row);
              });
            });
        }
      });
    });
  });
```

The first thing to note is our use of the `.each()` method to make iteration explicit. Even though we could bind a click handler to all headers with the `sort-alpha` class just by calling `$('table.sortable th.sort-alpha').click()`, this wouldn't allow us to easily capture a crucial bit of information—the column index of the clicked header. Because `.each()` passes the iteration index into its callback function, we can use it to find the relevant cell in each row of the data later.

Once we have found the header cell, we retrieve an array of all of the data rows. This is a great example of how `.get()` is useful in transforming a jQuery object into an array of DOM nodes; even though jQuery objects act like arrays in many respects, they don't have any of the native array methods available, such as `.sort()`.

With `.sort()` at our disposal, the rest is fairly straightforward. The rows are sorted by comparing the textual contexts of the relevant table cell. We know which cell to look at because we captured the column index in the enclosing `.each()` call. We convert the text to uppercase because string comparisons in JavaScript are case-sensitive and we wish our sort to be case-insensitive. Finally, with the array sorted, we loop through the rows and reinsert them into the table. Since `.append()` does not clone nodes, this moves them rather than copying them. Our table is now sorted.

This is an example of progressive enhancement's counterpart, **graceful degradation**. Unlike with the AJAX solution discussed earlier, we cannot make the sort work without JavaScript, as we are assuming the server has no scripting language available to it in this case. The JavaScript is required for the sort to work, so by adding the "clickable" class only through code, we make sure not to indicate with the interface that sorting is even possible unless the script can run. The page *degrades* into one that is still functional, albeit without sorting available.

We have moved the actual rows around, hence our alternating row colors are now out of whack:

	Title	Author(s)	Publish Date	Price
	Advanced Microsoft Content Management Server Development	Angus Logan, Stefan Goßner, Lim Mei Ying, Andrew Connell	Nov 2005	$53.99
	AJAX and PHP: Building Responsive Web Applications	Cristian Darie, Mihai Bucica, Filip Chereches-Toşa, Bogdan Brinzarea	Mar 2006	$31.49
	Alfresco Enterprise Content Management Implementation	Munwar Shariff	Jan 2007	$53.99
	BPEL Cookbook: Best Practices for SOA-based integration and composite applications development	Jerry Thomas, Doug Todd, Harish Gaur, Lawrence Pravin, Arun Poduval, The Hoa Nguyen, Yves Coene, Jeremy Bolie, Stany Blanvalet, Markus Zim, Matjaz Juric, Sean Carey, Michael Cardella, Kevin Geminiuc, Praveen Ramachandran	Jul 2006	$40.49

We need to reapply the row colors after the sort is performed. We can do this by pulling the coloring code out into a function that we call when needed:

```
$(document).ready(function() {
  var alternateRowColors = function($table) {
    $('tbody tr:odd', $table).removeClass('even').addClass('odd');
    $('tbody tr:even', $table).removeClass('odd').addClass('even');
  };

  $('table.sortable').each(function() {
    var $table = $(this);
    alternateRowColors($table);
    $('th', $table).each(function(column) {
      if ($(this).is('.sort-alpha')) {
        $(this).addClass('clickable').hover(function() {
          $(this).addClass('hover');
        }, function() {
```

```
                $(this).removeClass('hover');
        }).click(function() {
            var rows = $table.find('tbody > tr').get();
            rows.sort(function(a, b) {
                var keyA = $(a).children('td').eq(column).text()
                                                    .toUpperCase();
                var keyB = $(b).children('td').eq(column).text()
                                                    .toUpperCase();
                if (keyA < keyB) return -1;
                if (keyA > keyB) return 1;
                return 0;
            });
            $.each(rows, function(index, row) {
                $table.children('tbody').append(row);
            });
            alternateRowColors($table);
        });
    }
    });
  });
});
```

This corrects the row coloring after the fact, fixing our issue:

	Title	Author(s)	Publish Date	Price
	Advanced Microsoft Content Management Server Development	Angus Logan, Stefan Goßner, Lim Mei Ying, Andrew Connell	Nov 2005	$53.99
	AJAX and PHP: Building Responsive Web Applications	Cristian Darie, Mihai Bucica, Filip Chereches-Toşa, Bogdan Brinzarea	Mar 2006	$31.49
	Alfresco Enterprise Content Management Implementation	Munwar Shariff	Jan 2007	$53.99
	BPEL Cookbook: Best Practices for SOA-based integration and composite applications development	Jerry Thomas, Doug Todd, Harish Gaur, Lawrence Pravin, Arun Poduval, The Hoa Nguyen, Yves Coene, Jeremy Bolie, Stany Blanvalet, Markus Zirn, Matjaz Juric, Sean Carey, Michael Cardella, Kevin Geminiuc, Praveen Ramachandran	Jul 2006	$40.49

The Power of Plug-ins

The `alternateRowColors()` function that we wrote is a perfect candidate to become a jQuery plug-in. In fact, any operation that we wish to apply to a set of DOM elements can easily be expressed as a plug-in. In this case, we only need to modify our existing function a little bit:

```
jQuery.fn.alternateRowColors = function() {
  $('tbody tr:odd', this).removeClass('even').addClass('odd');
  $('tbody tr:even', this).removeClass('odd').addClass('even');
  return this;
};
```

We have made three important changes to the function.

- It is defined as a new property of `jQuery.fn` rather than as a standalone function. This registers the function as a plug-in method.

- We use the keyword `this` as a replacement for our `$table` parameter. Within a plug-in method, `this` refers to the jQuery object that is being acted upon.

- Finally, we return `this` at the end of the function. The return value makes our new method chainable.

More information on writing jQuery plug-ins can be found in Chapter 10. There we will discuss making a plug-in ready for public consumption, as opposed to the small example here that is only to be used by our own code.

With our new plug-in defined, we can call `$table.alternateRowColors()`, which is a more natural jQuery syntax, intead of `alternateRowColors($table)`.

Performance Concerns

Our code works, but is quite slow. The culprit is the comparator function, which is performing a fair amount of work. This comparator will be called many times during the course of a sort, which means that every extra moment it spends on processing will be magnified.

The actual sort algorithm used by JavaScript is not defined by the standard. It may be a simple sort like a bubble sort (worst case of $\Theta(n^2)$ in computational complexity terms) or a more sophisticated approach like quick sort (which is $\Theta(n \log n)$ on average). In either case doubling the number of items increases the number of times the comparator function is called by more than double.

The remedy for our slow comparator is to pre-compute the keys for the comparison. We begin with the slow sort function:

```
rows.sort(function(a, b) {
  keyA = $(a).children('td').eq(column).text().toUpperCase();
  keyB = $(b).children('td').eq(column).text().toUpperCase();
  if (keyA < keyB) return -1;
  if (keyA > keyB) return 1;
  return 0;
});
$.each(rows, function(index, row) {
  $table.children('tbody').append(row);
});
```

We can pull out the key computation and do that in a separate loop:

```
$.each(rows, function(index, row) {
  row.sortKey = $(row).children('td').eq(column).text().toUpperCase();
});
rows.sort(function(a, b) {
  if (a.sortKey < b.sortKey) return -1;
  if (a.sortKey > b.sortKey) return 1;
  return 0;
});
$.each(rows, function(index, row) {
  $table.children('tbody').append(row);
  row.sortKey = null;
});
```

In the new loop, we are doing all of the expensive work and storing the result in a new property. This kind of property, attached to a DOM element but not a normal DOM attribute, is called an **expando**. This is a convenient place to store the key since we need one per table row element. Now we can examine this attribute within the comparator function, and our sort is markedly faster.

 We set the expando property to `null` after we're done with it to clean up after ourselves. This is not necessary in this case, but is a good habit to establish because expando properties left lying around can be the cause of memory leaks. For more information, see Appendix C.

Finessing the Sort Keys

Now we want to apply the same kind of sorting behavior to the **Author(s)** column of our table. By adding the `sort-alpha` class to its table header cell, the **Author(s)** column can be sorted with our existing code. But ideally authors should be sorted by last name, not first. Since some books have multiple authors, and some authors have middle names or initials listed, we need outside guidance to determine what part of the text to use as our sort key. We can supply this guidance by wrapping the relevant part of the cell in a tag:

```
<tr>
  <td>
    <img src="../covers/small/1847192386.png" width="49" height="61"
         alt="Building Websites with Joomla! 1.5 Beta 1" /></td>
  <td>Building Websites with Joomla! 1.5 Beta 1</td>
  <td>Hagen <span class="sort-key">Graf</span></td>
  <td>Feb 2007</td>
  <td>$40.49</td>
</tr>
<tr>
  <td>
    <img src="../covers/small/1904811620.png" width="49" height="61"
         alt="Learning Mambo: A Step-by-Step Tutorial to Building
                                          Your Website" /></td>
  <td>
    Learning Mambo: A Step-by-Step Tutorial to Building Your Website
  </td>
  <td>Douglas <span class="sort-key">Paterson</span></td>
  <td>Dec 2006</td>
  <td>$40.49</td>
</tr>
<tr>
  <td>
    <img src="../covers/small/1904811299.png" width="49" height="61"
         alt="Moodle E-Learning Course Development" /></td>
  <td>Moodle E-Learning Course Development</td>
  <td>William <span class="sort-key">Rice</span></td>
  <td>May 2006</td>
  <td>$35.99</td>
</tr>
```

Now we have to modify our sorting code to take this tag into account, without disturbing the existing behavior for the **Title** column, which is working well. By prepending the marked sort key to the key we have previously calculated, we can sort first on the last name if it is called out, but on the whole string as a fallback:

```
$.each(rows, function(index, row) {
  var $cell = $(row).children('td').eq(column);
  row.sortKey = $cell.find('.sort-key').text().toUpperCase()
                              + ' ' + $cell.text().toUpperCase();
});
```

Sorting by the **Author(s)** column now uses the last name:

	Title	Author(s)	Publish Date	Price
	Programming Windows Workflow Foundation: Practical WF Techniques and Examples using XAML and C#	K. Scott Allen	Dec 2006	$40.49
	Building Websites with XOOPS : A step-by-step tutorial	Steve Atwal	Oct 2006	$26.99
	Learn OpenOffice.org Spreadsheet Macro Programming: OOoBasic and Calc automation	Dr. Mark Alexander Bain	Dec 2006	$35.99
	UML 2.0 in Action: A project-based tutorial	Philippe Baumann, Henriette Baumann, Patrick Grassle	Sep 2005	$31.49

If two last names are identical, the sort uses the entire string as a tiebreaker for positioning.

Sorting Other Types of Data

Our sort routine should be able to handle not just the **Title** and **Author** columns, but the **Publish Dates** and **Price** as well. Since we streamlined our comparator function, it can handle all kinds of data, but the computed keys will need to be adjusted for other data types. For example, in the case of prices we need to strip off the leading $ character and parse the rest, then compare them:

```
var key = parseFloat($cell.text().replace(/^[^\d.]*/, ''));
row.sortKey = isNaN(key) ? 0 : key;
```

The result of `parseFloat()` needs to be checked, because if no number can be extracted from the text, NaN is returned, which can wreak havoc on `.sort()`. For the date cells, we can use the JavaScript `Date` object:

```
row.sortKey = Date.parse('1 ' + $cell.text());
```

The dates in this table contain a month and year only; Date.parse() requires a fully-specified date, so we prepend the string with 1. This provides a day to complement the month and year, and the combination is then converted into a timestamp, which can be sorted using our normal comparator.

We can apportion these expressions across separate functions, and call the appropriate one based on the class applied to the table header:

```
$.fn.alternateRowColors = function() {
  $('tbody tr:odd', this).removeClass('even').addClass('odd');
  $('tbody tr:even', this).removeClass('odd').addClass('even');
  return this;
};


$(document).ready(function() {
  var alternateRowColors = function($table) {
    $('tbody tr:odd', $table).removeClass('even').addClass('odd');
    $('tbody tr:even', $table).removeClass('odd').addClass('even');
  };

  $('table.sortable').each(function() {
    var $table = $(this);
    $table.alternateRowColors($table);
    $('th', $table).each(function(column) {
      var findSortKey;
      if ($(this).is('.sort-alpha')) {
        findSortKey = function($cell) {
          return $cell.find('.sort-key').text().toUpperCase()
                        + ' ' + $cell.text().toUpperCase();
        };
      }
      else if ($(this).is('.sort-numeric')) {
        findSortKey = function($cell) {
          var key = parseFloat($cell.text().replace(/^[^\d.]*/, ''));
          return isNaN(key) ? 0 : key;
        };
      }
      else if ($(this).is('.sort-date')) {
        findSortKey = function($cell) {
          return Date.parse('1 ' + $cell.text());
        };
      }
      if (findSortKey) {
        $(this).addClass('clickable').hover(function() {
          $(this).addClass('hover');
        }, function() {
          $(this).removeClass('hover');
```

```
    }).click(function() {
      var rows = $table.find('tbody > tr').get();
      $.each(rows, function(index, row) {
        row.sortKey =
                   findSortKey($(row).children('td').eq(column));
      });
      rows.sort(function(a, b) {
        if (a.sortKey < b.sortKey) return -1;
        if (a.sortKey > b.sortKey) return 1;
        return 0;
      });
      $.each(rows, function(index, row) {
        $table.children('tbody').append(row);
        row.sortKey = null;
      });
      $table.alternateRowColors($table);
    });
  }
 });
});
});
```

The `findSortKey` variable doubles as the function to calculate the key and a flag to indicate whether the column header is marked with a class making it sortable. We can now sort on date or price:

Title	Author(s)	Publish Date	Price
User Training for Busy Programmers	William Rice	Jun 2005	$11.69
Pluggable Authentication Modules: The Definitive Guide to PAM for Linux SysAdmins and C Developers	Kenneth Geisshirt	Jan 2007	$17.99
Creating your MySQL Database: Practical Design Tips and Techniques	Marc Delisle	Nov 2006	$17.99
The Microsoft Outlook Ideas Book	Barbara March	Mar 2006	$22.49

Column Highlighting

It can be a nice user interface enhancement to visually remind the user of what has been done in the past. By highlighting the column that was most recently used for sorting, we can focus the user's attention on the part of the table that is most likely to be relevant. Fortunately, since we've already determined how to select the table cells in the column, applying a class to those cells is simple:

```
$table.find('td').removeClass('sorted')
  .filter(':nth-child(' + (column + 1) + ')').addClass('sorted');
```

Note that we have to add one to the column index we found earlier, since the `:nth-child()` selector is *one-based* rather than *zero-based*. With this code in place, we get a highlighted column after any sort operation:

		Title	Author(s)	Publish Date	Price
		Building Websites with the ASP.NET Community Starter Kit	Cristian Darie, K. Scott Allen	May 2004	$40.49
		Building Websites with Plone	Cameron Cooper	Nov 2004	$44.99
		Windows Server 2003 Active Directory Design and Implementation: Creating, Migrating, and Merging Networks	John Savill	Jan 2005	$53.99
		SSL VPN: Understanding, evaluating and planning secure, web-based remote access	Tim Speed, Joseph Steinberg	Mar 2005	$44.99

Alternating Sort Directions

Our final sorting enhancement is to allow for both ascending and descending sort orders. When the user clicks on a column that is already sorted, we want to reverse the current sort order.

To reverse a sort, all we have to do is to invert the values returned by our comparator. We can do this with a simple variable:

```
if (a.sortKey < b.sortKey) return -newDirection;
if (a.sortKey > b.sortKey) return newDirection;
```

If newDirection equals 1, then the sort will be the same as before. If it equals -1, the sort will be reversed. We can use classes to keep track of the current sort order of a column:

```
$.fn.alternateRowColors = function() {
  $('tbody tr:odd', this).removeClass('even').addClass('odd');
  $('tbody tr:even', this).removeClass('odd').addClass('even');
  return this;
};

$(document).ready(function() {
  var alternateRowColors = function($table) {
    $('tbody tr:odd', $table).removeClass('even').addClass('odd');
    $('tbody tr:even', $table).removeClass('odd').addClass('even');
  };
  $('table.sortable').each(function() {
    var $table = $(this);
    $table.alternateRowColors($table);
    $('th', $table).each(function(column) {
      var findSortKey;
      if ($(this).is('.sort-alpha')) {
        findSortKey = function($cell) {
          return $cell.find('.sort-key').text().toUpperCase() + ' ' +
                                        $cell.text().toUpperCase();
        };
      }
      else if ($(this).is('.sort-numeric')) {
        findSortKey = function($cell) {
          var key = parseFloat($cell.text().replace(/^[^\d.]*/, ''));
          return isNaN(key) ? 0 : key;
        };
      }
      else if ($(this).is('.sort-date')) {
        findSortKey = function($cell) {
          return Date.parse('1 ' + $cell.text());
        };
      }
      if (findSortKey) {
        $(this).addClass('clickable').hover(function() {
          $(this).addClass('hover');
        }, function() {
          $(this).removeClass('hover');
        }).click(function() {
          var newDirection = 1;
```

```
    if ($(this).is('.sorted-asc')) {
      newDirection = -1;
    }
    var rows = $table.find('tbody > tr').get();

    $.each(rows, function(index, row) {
      row.sortKey =
                  findSortKey($(row).children('td').eq(column));
    });
    rows.sort(function(a, b) {
      if (a.sortKey < b.sortKey) return -newDirection;
      if (a.sortKey > b.sortKey) return newDirection;
      return 0;
    });
    $.each(rows, function(index, row) {
      $table.children('tbody').append(row);
      row.sortKey = null;
    });
  $table.find('th').removeClass('sorted-asc')
                                  .removeClass('sorted-desc');
   var $sortHead = $table.find('th').filter('
                           :nth-child(' + (column + 1) + ')');
   if (newDirection == 1) {
     $sortHead.addClass('sorted-asc');
   } else {
     $sortHead.addClass('sorted-desc');
   }
   $table.find('td').removeClass('sorted')
     .filter(':nth-child(' + (column + 1) + ')')
                                      .addClass('sorted');
  $table.alternateRowColors($table);
  });
 }
});
});
});
```

As a side benefit, since we use classes to store the sort direction we can style the columns headers to indicate the current order as well:

Title	Author(s)	Publish Date	Price
Enhancing Microsoft Content Management Server with ASP.NET 2.0	Lim Mei Ying, Spencer Harbar, Stefan Goßner	Aug 2006	$34.19
Openswan: Building and Integrating Virtual Private Networks	Paul Wouters, Ken Bantoft	Feb 2006	$53.99
Learning Jakarta Struts 1.2: a concise and practical tutorial	Stephan Wiesner	Aug 2005	$31.49
Implementing SugarCRM	Michael J.R. Whitehead	Feb 2006	$44.99

Pagination

Sorting is a great way to wade through a large amount of data to find information. We can also help the user focus on a portion of a large data set by paginating the data. Pagination can be done in two ways—Server-Side Pagination and JavaScript Pagination.

Server-Side Pagination

Much like sorting, **pagination** is often performed on the server. If the data to be displayed is stored in a database, it is easy to pull out one chunk of information at a time using MySQL's LIMIT clause, ROWNUM in Oracle, or equivalent methods in other database engines.

As with our initial sorting example, pagination can be triggered by sending information to the server in a query string, such as index.php?page=52. And again as before, we can perform this task either with a full page load or by using AJAX to pull in just one chunk of the table. This strategy is browser-independent, and can handle large data sets very well.

Sorting and Paging Go Together

Data that is long enough to benefit from sorting is likely long enough to be a candidate for paging. It is not unusual to wish to combine these two techniques for data presentation. Since they both affect the set of data that is present on a page, though, it is important to consider their interactions while implementing them.

Both sorting and pagination can be accomplished either on the server or in the web browser. However, we must keep the strategies for the two tasks in sync; otherwise, we can end up with confusing behavior. Suppose, for example, that both sorting and paging is done on the server:

When the table is re-sorted by number, a different set of rows is present on **Page 1** of the table. If paging is done by the server and sorting by the browser, the entire data set is not available for the sorting routine, making the results incorrect:

Only the data already present on the page can be displayed. To prevent this from being a problem, we must either perform both tasks on the server, or both in the browser.

JavaScript Pagination

So, let's examine how we would add JavaScript pagination to the table we have already made sortable in the browser. First, we'll focus on displaying a particular page of data, disregarding user interaction for now:

```
$(document).ready(function() {
  $('table.paginated').each(function() {
    var currentPage = 0;
    var numPerPage = 10;
    var $table = $(this);
    $table.find('tbody tr').show()
      .lt(currentPage * numPerPage)
        .hide()
      .end()
      .gt((currentPage + 1) * numPerPage - 1)
        .hide()
      .end();
  });
});
```

This code displays the first page—ten rows of data.

Once again we rely on the presence of a `<tbody>` element to separate data from headers; we don't want to have the headers or footers disappear when moving on to the second page. For selecting the rows containing data, we show all the rows first, then select the rows before and after the current page, hiding them. The method chaining supported by jQuery makes another appearance here when we filter the set of matched rows twice, using `.end()` in between to *pop* the current filter off the stack and start afresh with a new filter.

The most error-prone task in writing this code is formulating the expressions to use in the filters. To use the `.lt()` and `.gt()` methods, we need to find the indices of the rows at the beginning and end of the current page. For the beginning row, we just multiply the current page number by the number of rows on each page. Multiplying the number of rows by one more than the current page number gives us the *beginning* row of the *next* page; to find the *last* row of the *current* page, we must subtract one from this.

Displaying the Pager

To add user interaction to the mix, we need to place the **pager** itself next to the table. We could do this by simply inserting links for the pages in the HTML markup, but this would violate the progressive enhancement principle we've been espousing. Instead, we should add the links using JavaScript, so that users without scripting available are not misled by links that cannot work.

To display the links, we need to calculate the number of pages and create a corresponding number of DOM elements:

```
var numRows = $table.find('tbody tr').length;
var numPages = Math.ceil(numRows / numPerPage);

var $pager = $('<div class="pager"></div>');
for (var page = 0; page < numPages; page++) {
  $('<span class="page-number">' + (page + 1) + '</span>')
    .appendTo($pager).addClass('clickable');
}
$pager.insertBefore($table);
```

The number of pages can be found by dividing the number of data rows by the number of items we wish to display on each page. If the division does not yield an integer, we must round the result up using `Math.ceil()` to ensure that the final partial page will be accessible. Then, with this number in hand, we create buttons for each page and position the new pager before the table:

1 2 3 4 5 6 7				
Title	**Author(s)**		**Publish Date**	**Price**
Building Websites with Joomla! 1.5 Beta 1	Hagen Graf		Feb 2007	$40.49
Learning Mambo: A Step-by-Step Tutorial to Building Your Website	Douglas Paterson		Dec 2006	$40.49
Moodle E-Learning Course Development	William Rice		May 2006	$35.99
AJAX and PHP: Building Responsive Web Applications	Cristian Darie, Mihai Bucica, Filip Chereches-Toşa, Bogdan Brinzarea		Mar 2006	$31.49

Enabling the Pager Buttons

To make these new buttons actually work, we need to update the `currentPage` variable and then run our pagination routine. At first blush, it seems we should be able to do this by setting `currentPage` to `page`, which is the current value of the iterator that creates the buttons:

```
$(document).ready(function() {
  $('table.paginated').each(function() {
    var currentPage = 0;
    var numPerPage = 10;
    var $table = $(this);
```

```
var repaginate = function() {
  $table.find('tbody tr').show()
    .lt(currentPage * numPerPage)
      .hide()
    .end()
    .gt((currentPage + 1) * numPerPage - 1)
      .hide()
    .end();
};
var numRows = $table.find('tbody tr').length;
var numPages = Math.ceil(numRows / numPerPage);
var $pager = $('<div class="pager"></div>');
for (var page = 0; page < numPages; page++) {
  $('<span class="page-number">' + (page + 1) + '</span>')
    .click(function() {
      currentPage = page;
      repaginate();
    })
    .appendTo($pager).addClass('clickable');
}
$pager.insertBefore($table);
repaginate();
  });
});
```

This mostly works. The new `repaginate()` function is called when the page loads and when any button is clicked. All of the buttons take us to a page with no rows on it, though:

The problem is that in defining our click handler, we have created a **closure**. The click handler refers to the `page` variable, which is defined outside the function. When the variable changes the next time through the loop, this affects the click handlers that we have already set up for the earlier buttons. The net effect is that, for a pager with 7 pages, each button directs us to page 8 (the final value of `page`). More information on how closures work can be found in Appendix C, *JavaScript Closures*.

To correct this problem, we'll take advantage of one of the more advanced features of jQuery's event binding methods. We can add a set of data to the handler when we bind it that will still be available when the handler is eventually called. With this capability in our bag of tricks, we can write:

```
$('<span class="page-number">' + (page + 1) + '</span>')
  .bind('click', {'newPage': page}, function(event) {
    currentPage = event.data['newPage'];
    repaginate();
  })
  .appendTo($pager).addClass('clickable');
```

The new page number is passed into the handler by way of the event's `data` property. In this way the page number escapes the closure, and is frozen in time at the value it contained when the handler was bound. Now our pager buttons can correctly take us to different pages:

1 2 3 4 5 6 7

	Title	Author(s)	Publish Date	Price
	PHPEclipse: A User Guide	Shu-Wai Chow	Feb 2006	$31.49
	Alfresco Enterprise Content Management Implementation	Munwar Shariff	Jan 2007	$53.99
	Smarty PHP Template Programming and Applications	Joao Prado Maia, Hasin Hayder, Lucian Gheorghe	Apr 2006	$35.99
	JasperReports for Java Developers	David Heffelfinger	Aug 2006	$40.49

Marking the Current Page

Our pager can be made more user-friendly by highlighting the current page number. We just need to update the classes on the buttons every time one is clicked:

```
var $pager = $('<div class="pager"></div>');
for (var page = 0; page < numPages; page++) {
  $('<span class="page-number">' + (page + 1) + '</span>')
    .bind('click', {'newPage': page}, function(event) {
      currentPage = event.data['newPage'];
      repaginate();
      $(this).addClass('active').siblings().removeClass('active');
    })
    .appendTo($pager).addClass('clickable');
}
$pager.find('span.page-number:first').addClass('active');
$pager.insertBefore($table);
```

Now we have an indicator of the current status of the pager:

Title	Author(s)	Publish Date	Price
Linux Email: Set up and Run a Small Office Email Server	Patrick Ben Koetter, Carl Taylor, Ralf Hildebrandt, David Rusenko, Alistair McDonald, Magnus Back	Jul 2005	$35.99
Windows Small Business Server SBS 2003: A Clear and Concise Administrator's Reference and How-To	Stephanie Knecht-Thurmann	Aug 2005	$33.29
Creating your MySQL Database: Practical Design Tips and Techniques	Marc Delisle	Nov 2006	$17.99
Building Websites with VB.NET and DotNetNuke 4	Michael Washington, Steve Valenzuela, Daniel N. Egan	Oct 2006	$35.99

1 2 3 [4] 5 6 7

Paging with Sorting

We began this discussion by noting that sorting and paging controls needed to be aware of one another to avoid confusing results. Now that we have a working pager, we need to make sort operations respect the current page selection.

Doing this is as simple as calling our `repaginate()` function whenever a sort is performed. The scope of the function, though, makes this problematic. We can't reach `repaginate()` from our sorting routine because it is contained inside a different `$(document).ready()` handler. We could just consolidate the two pieces of code, but instead let's be a bit sneakier. We can decouple the behaviors, so that a sort calls the repaginate behavior if it exists, but ignores it otherwise. To accomplish this, we'll use a handler for a custom event.

In our earlier event handling discussion, we limited ourselves to event names that were triggered by the web browser, such as `click` and `mouseup`. The `.bind()` and `.trigger()` methods are not limited to these events, though; we can use any string as an event name. In this case, we can define a new event called `repaginate` as a stand-in for the function we've been calling:

```
$table.bind('repaginate', function() {
  $table.find('tbody tr').show()
    .lt(currentPage * numPerPage)
      .hide()
    .end()
```

```
        .gt((currentPage + 1) * numPerPage - 1)
          .hide()
        .end();
});
```

Now in places where we were calling `repaginate()`, we can call:

```
$table.trigger('repaginate');
```

We can issue this call in our sort code as well. It will do nothing if the table does not have a pager, so we can mix and match the two capabilities as desired.

The Finished Code

The completed sorting and paging code in its entirety follows:

```
$.fn.alternateRowColors = function() {
  $('tbody tr:odd', this).removeClass('even').addClass('odd');
  $('tbody tr:even', this).removeClass('odd').addClass('even');
  return this;
};

$(document).ready(function() {
  var alternateRowColors = function($table) {
    $('tbody tr:odd', $table).removeClass('even').addClass('odd');
    $('tbody tr:even', $table).removeClass('odd').addClass('even');
  };

  $('table.sortable').each(function() {
    var $table = $(this);
    $table.alternateRowColors($table);
    $table.find('th').each(function(column) {
      var findSortKey;

      if ($(this).is('.sort-alpha')) {
        findSortKey = function($cell) {
          return $cell.find('.sort-key').text().toUpperCase() +
                            ' ' + $cell.text().toUpperCase();
        };
      }
      else if ($(this).is('.sort-numeric')) {
        findSortKey = function($cell) {
          var key = parseFloat($cell.text().replace(/^[^\d.]*/, ''));
          return isNaN(key) ? 0 : key;
        };
```

```
    }
    else if ($(this).is('.sort-date')) {
      findSortKey = function($cell) {
        return Date.parse('1 ' + $cell.text());
      };
    }

    if (findSortKey) {
      $(this).addClass('clickable').hover(function() {
        $(this).addClass('hover');
      }, function() {
        $(this).removeClass('hover');
      }).click(function() {
        var newDirection = 1;
        if ($(this).is('.sorted-asc')) {
          newDirection = -1;
        }

        rows = $table.find('tbody > tr').get();

        $.each(rows, function(index, row) {
          row.sortKey =
                    findSortKey($(row).children('td').eq(column));
        });
        rows.sort(function(a, b) {
          if (a.sortKey < b.sortKey) return -newDirection;
          if (a.sortKey > b.sortKey) return newDirection;
          return 0;
        });
        $.each(rows, function(index, row) {
          $table.children('tbody').append(row);
          row.sortKey = null;
        });

        $table.find('th').removeClass('sorted-asc')
                                  .removeClass('sorted-desc');
        var $sortHead = $table.find('th').filter(':nth-child('
                                          + (column + 1) + ')');
        if (newDirection == 1) {
          $sortHead.addClass('sorted-asc');
        } else {
          $sortHead.addClass('sorted-desc');
        }
        $table.find('td').removeClass('sorted')
          .filter(':nth-child(' + (column + 1) + ')')
                                          .addClass('sorted');
```

```
            $table.alternateRowColors($table);
            $table.trigger('repaginate');
          });
        }
      });
    });
  });
  $(document).ready(function() {
    $('table.paginated').each(function() {
      var currentPage = 0;
      var numPerPage = 10;

      var $table = $(this);

      $table.bind('repaginate', function() {
        $table.find('tbody tr').show()
          .lt(currentPage * numPerPage)
            .hide()
          .end()
          .gt((currentPage + 1) * numPerPage - 1)
            .hide()
          .end();
      });

      var numRows = $table.find('tbody tr').length;
      var numPages = Math.ceil(numRows / numPerPage);

      var $pager = $('<div class="pager"></div>');
      for (var page = 0; page < numPages; page++) {
        $('<span class="page-number">' + (page + 1) + '</span>')
          .bind('click', {'newPage': page}, function(event) {
            currentPage = event.data['newPage'];
            $table.trigger('repaginate');
            $(this).addClass('active').siblings().removeClass('active');
          })
          .appendTo($pager).addClass('clickable');
      }
      $pager.find('span.page-number:first').addClass('active');
      $pager.insertBefore($table);

      $table.trigger('repaginate');
    });
  });
```

Advanced Row Striping

As we saw earlier in the chapter, row striping can be as simple as two lines of code to alternate the background color:

```
$(document).ready(function() {
  $('table.sortable tbody tr:odd').addClass('odd');
  $('table.sortable tbody tr:even').addClass('even');
});
```

If we declare background colors for the odd and even classes as follows, we can see the rows in alternating shades of gray:

```
tr.even {
  background-color: #eee;
}
tr.odd {
  background-color: #ddd;
}
```

While this code works fine for simple table structures, if we introduce non-standard rows into the table, such as sub-headings, the basic odd-even pattern no longer suffices. For example, suppose we have a table of news items grouped by year, with columns for date, headline, author, and topic. One way to express this information is to wrap each year's news items in a `<tbody>` element and use `<th colspan="4">` for the subheading. Such a table's HTML (in abridged form) would look like this:

```
<table class="striped">
  <thead>
    <tr>
      <th>Date</th>
      <th>Headline</th>
      <th>Author</th>
      <th class="filter-column">Topic</th>
    </tr>
  </thead>
  <tbody>
    <tr>
      <th colspan="4">2007</th>
    </tr>
    <tr>
      <td>Mar 11</td>
      <td>SXSWi jQuery Meetup</td>
      <td>John Resig</td>
```

```
      <td>conference</td>
    </tr>
    <tr>
      <td>Feb 28</td>
      <td>jQuery 1.1.2</td>
      <td>John Resig</td>
      <td>release</td>
    </tr>
    <tr>
      <td>Feb 21</td>
      <td>jQuery is OpenAjax Compliant</td>
      <td>John Resig</td>
      <td>standards</td>
    </tr>
    <tr>
      <td>Feb 20</td>
      <td>jQuery and Jack Slocum's Ext</td>
      <td>John Resig</td>
      <td>third-party</td>
    </tr>
  </tbody>
  <tbody>
    <tr>
      <th colspan="4">2006</th>
    </tr>
    <tr>
      <td>Dec 27</td>
      <td>The Path to 1.1</td>
      <td>John Resig</td>
      <td>source</td>
    </tr>
    <tr>
      <td>Dec 18</td>
      <td>Meet The People Behind jQuery</td>
      <td>John Resig</td>
      <td>announcement</td>
    </tr>
    <tr>
      <td>Dec 13</td>
      <td>Helping you understand jQuery</td>
      <td>John Resig</td>
      <td>tutorial</td>
    </tr>
```

```
    </tbody>
    <tbody>
      <tr>
        <th colspan="4">2005</th>
      </tr>
      <tr>
        <td>Dec 17</td>
        <td>JSON and RSS</td>
        <td>John Resig</td>
        <td>miscellaneous</td>
      </tr>
    </tbody>
</table>
```

With separate CSS styles applied to `<th>` elements within `<thead>` and `<tbody>`, a snippet of the table might look like this:

Date	Headline	Author	Topic
2007			
Mar 11	SXSWi jQuery Meetup	John Resig	conference
Feb 28	jQuery 1.1.2	John Resig	release
Feb 21	jQuery is OpenAjax Compliant	John Resig	standards
Feb 18	The jQuery IRC Channel	Yehuda Katz	announcement
Feb 14	jQuery Nightly Builds	Paul McLanahan	announcement
Feb 2	New jQuery Project Team Ms	ReyBango	announcement
Jan 15	Interface 1.1 Released	John Resig	Plug-in
Jan 14	jQuery Birthday: 1.1, New Site, New Docs	John Resig	announcement
Jan 13	jQuery wallpapers	Nate Cavanaugh	miscellaneous
Jan 11	Selector Speeds	John Resig	source
Jan 11	jQuery 1.1b	John Resig	release
2006			
Dec 27	The Path to 1.1	John Resig	source
Dec 18	Meet The People Behind jQuery	John Resig	announcement
Dec 13	Helping you understand jQuery	John Resig	tutorial
Dec 12	jQuery 1.0.4	John Resig	release

To ensure that the alternating gray rows do not override the color of the subheading rows, we need to adjust the selector expression:

```
$(document).ready(function() {
  $('table.striped tbody tr:not([th]):odd').addClass('odd');
  $('table.striped tbody tr:not([th]):even').addClass('even');
});
```

The added selector, :not([th]), removes any table row that contains a <th> from the matched set of elements. Now the table will look like this:

Date	Headline	Author	Topic
2007			
Mar 11	SXSWi jQuery Meetup	John Resig	conference
Feb 28	jQuery 1.1.2	John Resig	release
Feb 21	jQuery is OpenAjax Compliant	John Resig	standards
Feb 18	The jQuery IRC Channel	Yehuda Katz	announcement
Feb 14	jQuery Nightly Builds	Paul McLanahan	announcement
Feb 2	New jQuery Project Team Ms	ReyBango	announcement
Jan 15	Interface 1.1 Released	John Resig	Plug-in
Jan 14	jQuery Birthday: 1.1, New Site, New Docs	John Resig	announcement
Jan 13	jQuery wallpapers	Nate Cavanaugh	miscellaneous
Jan 11	Selector Speeds	John Resig	source
Jan 11	jQuery 1.1b	John Resig	release
2006			
Dec 27	The Path to 1.1	John Resig	source
Dec 18	Meet The People Behind jQuery	John Resig	announcement
Dec 13	Helping you understand jQuery	John Resig	tutorial
Dec 12	jQuery 1.0.4	John Resig	release

Three-color Alternating Pattern

There may be times when we want to apply more complex striping. For example, we can apply a pattern of three alternating row colors rather than just two. To do so, we first need to define another CSS rule for the third row. We'll also reuse the odd and even styles for the other two, but add more appropriate class names for them:

```
tr.even,
tr.first {
  background-color: #eee;
```

```
}
tr.odd,
tr.second {
  background-color: #ddd;
}
tr.third {
  background-color: #ccc;
}
```

To apply this pattern, we start the same way as the previous example—by selecting all rows that are descendants of a `<tbody>`, but filtering out the rows that contain a `<th>`. This time, however, we attach the `.each()` method so that we can use its built-in `index`:

```
$(document).ready(function() {
  $('table.striped tbody tr').not('[th]').each(function(index) {
    //Code to be applied to each element in the matched set.
  });
});
```

To make use of the index, we can assign our three classes to a numeric key: 0, 1, or 2. We'll do this by creating an object, or map:

```
$(document).ready(function() {
  var classNames = {
    0: 'first',
    1: 'second',
    2: 'third'
  };
  $('table.striped tbody tr').not('[th]').each(function(index) {
    // Code to be applied to each element in the matched set.
  });
});
```

Finally, we need to add the class that corresponds to those three numbers, sequentially, and then repeat the sequence. The modulus operator, designated by a %, is especially convenient for such calculations. A modulus returns the remainder of one number divided by another. This modulus, or remainder value, will always range between 0 and one less than the dividend. Using 3 as an example, we can see this pattern:

3/3 = 1, remainder 0.

4/3 = 1, remainder 1.

5/3 = 1, remainder 2.

6/3 = 2, remainder 0.

7/3 = 2, remainder 1.

8/3 = 3, remainder 2.

And so on. Since we want the remainder range to be 0 – 2, we can use 3 as the divisor (second number) and the value of index as the dividend (first number). Now we simply put that calculation in square brackets after classNames to retrieve the corresponding class from the object variable as the .each() method steps through the matched set of rows:

```
$(document).ready(function() {
  var classNames = {
    0: 'first',
    1: 'second',
    2: 'third'
  };
  $('table.striped tbody tr').not('[th]').each(function(index) {
    $(this).addClass(classNames[index % 3]);
  });
});
```

With this code in place, we now have the table striped with three alternating background colors:

Date	Headline	Author	Topic
2007			
Mar 11	SXSWi jQuery Meetup	John Resig	conference
Feb 28	jQuery 1.1.2	John Resig	release
Feb 21	jQuery is OpenAjax Compliant	John Resig	standards
Feb 18	The jQuery IRC Channel	Yehuda Katz	announcement
Feb 14	jQuery Nightly Builds	Paul McLanahan	announcement
Feb 2	New jQuery Project Team Ms	ReyBango	announcement
Jan 15	Interface 1.1 Released	John Resig	Plug-in
Jan 14	jQuery Birthday: 1.1, New Site, New Docs	John Resig	announcement
Jan 13	jQuery wallpapers	Nate Cavanaugh	miscellaneous
Jan 11	Selector Speeds	John Resig	source
Jan 11	jQuery 1.1b	John Resig	release
Jan 8	jQuery 1.1a	John Resig	release
2006			
Dec 27	The Path to 1.1	John Resig	source
Dec 18	Meet The People Behind jQuery	John Resig	announcement
Dec 13	Helping you understand jQuery	John Resig	tutorial

We could of course extend this pattern to four, five, six, or more background colors by adding key-value pairs to the object variable and increasing the value of the divisor in `classNames[index % n]`.

Alternating Triplets

Suppose we want to use two colors, but have each one display three rows at a time. For this, we can employ the `odd` and `even` classes again, as well as the modulus operator. But we'll also reset the class each time we're presented with a row containing `<th>` elements.

If we don't reset the alternating row class, we may be faced with unexpected colors after the first group of rows is striped. So far, our example table has avoided such problems because the first group consists of 12 rows, which, conveniently, is divisible by both 2 and 3. For the triplet striping scenario, we'll remove two rows, leaving us with 10 in the first group, to emphasize the class resetting.

We begin this striping technique by setting two variables, `rowClass` and `rowIndex`. We'll use the `.each()` method this time as well, but rather than relying on the built-in `index`, we'll use a custom `rowIndex` variable so that we can reset it on the rows with `<th>`:

```
$(document).ready(function() {
  var rowClass = 'even';
  var rowIndex = 0;
  $('table.striped tbody tr').each(function(index) {
    $(this).addClass(rowClass);
  });
});
```

Notice that since we have removed the `:not([th])` selector, we'll have to account for those subheading rows within the `.each()`. But first, let's get the triplet alternation working properly. So far, every `<tr>` will become `<tr class="even">`. For each row, we can check to see if the `rowIndex % 3` equals `0`. If it does, we toggle the value of `rowClass`. Then we increment the value of `rowIndex`:

```
$(document).ready(function() {
  var rowClass = 'even';
  var rowIndex = 0;
  $('table.striped tbody tr').each(function(index) {
    if (rowIndex % 3 == 0) {
      rowClass = (rowClass == 'even' ? 'odd' : 'even');
    };
    $(this).addClass(rowClass);
    rowIndex++;
  });
});
```

A **ternary**, or conditional, operator is used to set the changed value of rowClass because of its succinctness. That single line could be rewritten as:

```
if (rowClass == 'even') {
  rowClass = 'odd';
} else {
  rowClass = 'even';
}
```

In either case, the code now produces table striping that looks like this:

Date	Headline	Author	Topic
2007			
Mar 11	SXSWi jQuery Meetup	John Resig	conference
Feb 28	jQuery 1.1.2	John Resig	release
Feb 21	jQuery is OpenAjax Compliant	John Resig	standards
Feb 18	The jQuery IRC Channel	Yehuda Katz	announcement
Feb 14	jQuery Nightly Builds	Paul McLanahan	announcement
Feb 2	New jQuery Project Team Ms	ReyBango	announcement
Jan 15	Interface 1.1 Released	John Resig	Plug-in
Jan 14	jQuery Birthday: 1.1, New Site, New Docs	John Resig	announcement
Jan 13	jQuery wallpapers	Nate Cavanaugh	miscellaneous
Jan 11	Selector Speeds	John Resig	source
2006			
Dec 27	The Path to 1.1	John Resig	source
Dec 18	Meet The People Behind jQuery	John Resig	announcement
Dec 13	Helping you understand jQuery	John Resig	tutorial
Dec 12	jQuery 1.0.4	John Resig	release
Dec 12	jQuery v1.0.3 API docs on gotAPI.com	ReyBango	documentation

Perhaps surprisingly, the subheading rows have retained their proper formatting. But let's not be fooled by appearances. The **2007** subheading row is now set in the HTML as <tr class="odd"> and the **2006** row has <tr class="even">. In the stylesheet, however, the greater specificity of the element's rule outweighs that of the two classes:

```
#content tbody th {
  background-color: #6f93ce;
  padding left: 6px;
}
tr.even {
  background-color: #eee;
```

```
  }
tr.odd {
  background-color: #ddd;
}
```

Nevertheless, because the `rowIndex` numbering does not account for these subheading rows, we have mis-classed rows from the start; this is evident because the first striping color change occurs after two rows rather than three.

We need to include another condition, checking if the current row contains a `<th>`. If it does, we'll set the value of `rowClass` to `subhead` and set `rowIndex` to `-1`:

```
$(document).ready(function() {
  var rowClass = 'even';
  var rowIndex = 0;
  $('table.striped tbody tr').each(function(index) {
    if ($('th', this).length) {
      rowClass = 'subhead';
      rowIndex = -1;
    } else if (rowIndex % 3 == 0) {
      rowClass = (rowClass == 'even' ? 'odd' : 'even');
    };
    $(this).addClass(rowClass);
    rowIndex++;
  });
});
```

With `rowIndex` at `-1` for the subheading rows, the variable will be incremented to `0` for the next row — precisely where we want it to start for each group of striped rows. Now we can see the striping with each year's articles beginning with three light colored rows and alternating three at a time between lighter and darker:

Date	Headline	Author	Topic
2007			
Mar 11	SXSWi jQuery Meetup	John Resig	conference
Feb 28	jQuery 1.1.2	John Resig	release
Feb 21	jQuery Is OpenAjax Compliant	John Resig	standards
Feb 18	The jQuery IRC Channel	Yehuda Katz	announcement
Feb 14	jQuery Nightly Builds	Paul McLanahan	announcement
Feb 2	New jQuery Project Team Ms	ReyBango	announcement
Jan 15	Interface 1.1 Released	John Resig	Plug-in
Jan 14	jQuery Birthday: 1.1, New Site, New Docs	John Resig	announcement
Jan 13	jQuery wallpapers	Nate Cavanaugh	miscellaneous
Jan 11	Selector Speeds	John Resig	source
2006			
Dec 27	The Path to 1.1	John Resig	source
Dec 18	Meet The People Behind jQuery	John Resig	announcement
Dec 13	Helping you understand jQuery	John Resig	tutorial
Dec 12	jQuery 1.0.4	John Resig	release
Dec 12	jQuery v1.0.3 API docs on gotAPI.com	ReyBango	documentation

A final note about this striping code—while the ternary operator is indeed concise, it can get confusing when the conditions get more complex. The sophisticated striping variations can be more easily managed by using basic if-else conditions instead:

```
$(document).ready(function() {
  var rowIndex = 0;
  $('tbody tr').each(function(index) {
    if ($('th',this).length) {
      $(this).addClass('subhead');
      rowIndex = -1;
    } else {
      if (rowIndex % 6 < 3) {
        $(this).addClass('even');
      }
      else {
        $(this).addClass('odd');
      }
    };
    rowIndex++;
  });
});
```

Now we've achieved the same effect as before, but also made it easier to include additional `else if` conditions.

Row Highlighting

Another visual enhancement that we can apply to our news article table is row highlighting based on user interaction. Here we'll respond to clicking on an author's name by highlighting all rows that have the same name in their author cell. Just as we did with the row striping, we can modify the appearance of these highlighted rows by adding a class:

```
#content tr.highlight {
  background: #ff6;
}
```

It's important that we give this new `highlight` class adequate specificity for the background color to override that of the `even` and `odd` classes.

Now we need to select the appropriate cell and attach the `.click()` method to it:

```
$(document).ready(function() {
  var column = 3;
  $('table.striped td:nth-child(' + column + ')' )
  .click(function() {
    // Do something on click.
  });
});
```

Notice that we use the `:nth-child(n)` pseudo-class as part of the selector expression, but rather than simply including the number of the child element, we pass in the `column` variable. We'll need to refer to the same `nth-child` again, so using a variable allows us to change it in only one place if we later decide to highlight based on a different column.

 Unlike JavaScript indices, the CSS-based `:nth-child(n)` pseudo-class begins numbering at 1, not 0.

When the user clicks a cell in the third column, we want the cell's text to be compared to that of the same column's cell in every other row. If it matches, the `highlight` class will be toggled. In other words, the class will be added if it isn't already there and removed if it is. This way, we can click on an author cell to remove the row highlighting if that cell or one with the same author has already been clicked:

```
$(document).ready(function() {
  $('table.striped td:nth-child(' + column + ')' )
  .click(function() {
    var thisClicked = $(this).text();
    $('table.striped td:nth-child(' + column + ')')
                                  .each(function(index) {
      if (thisClicked == $(this).text()) {
        $(this).parent().toggleClass('highlight');
      };
    });
  });
})
```

The code is working well at this point, except when a user clicks on two authors'
names in succession. Rather than switching the highlighted rows from one author
to the next as we might expect, it adds the second clicked author's rows to the group
that has class="highlight". To avoid this behavior, we can add an else statement
to the code, removing the highlight class for any row that does not have the same
author name as the one clicked:

```
$(document).ready(function() {
  $('table.striped td:nth-child(' + column + ')' )
  .click(function() {
    var thisClicked = $(this).text();
    $('table.striped td:nth-child(' + column + ')' )
    .each(function(index) {
      if (thisClicked == $(this).text()) {
        $(this).parent().toggleClass('highlight');
      } else {
        $(this).parent().removeClass('highlight');
      };
    });
  });
})
```

Now when we click on **Rey Bango**, for example, we can see all of his articles much more easily:

Feb 28	jQuery 1.1.2	John Resig	release
Feb 21	jQuery is OpenAjax Compliant	John Resig	standards
Feb 18	The jQuery IRC Channel	Yehuda Katz	announcement
Feb 14	jQuery Nightly Builds	Paul McLanahan	announcement
Feb 2	New jQuery Project Team Members	Rey Bango	announcement
Jan 15	Interface 1.1 Released	John Resig	plug-in
Jan 14	jQuery Birthday: 1.1, New Site, New Docs	John Resig	announcement
Jan 13	jQuery wallpapers	Nate Cavanaugh	miscellaneous
Jan 11	Selector Speeds	John Resig	source
2006			
Dec 27	The Path to 1.1	John Resig	source
Dec 18	Meet The People Behind jQuery	John Resig	announcement
Dec 13	Helping you understand jQuery	John Resig	tutorial
Dec 12	jQuery 1.0.4	John Resig	release
Dec 12	jQuery v1.0.3 API docs on gotAPI.com	Rey Bango	documentation
Dec 12	jQuery Presentation in Phoenix on 11/28	Rey Bango	conference
Nov 28	jQuery at AZPhp	Rey Bango	conference
Nov 14	Expandable Sidebar Menu Screencast	John Resig	tutorial

If we then click on **John Resig**'s name in any one of the cells, the highlighting will be removed from **Rey Bango**'s rows and added to **John**'s.

Tooltips

Although the row highlighting might be a useful feature, so far it's not apparent to the user that the feature even exists. We can begin to remedy this situation by giving all author cells a `clickable` class, which will change the cursor to a pointer when a user hovers the mouse cursor over them:

```
$(document).ready(function() {
  $('table.striped td:nth-child(' + column + ')' )
  .addClass('clickable')
  .click(function() {
    var thisClicked = $(this).text();
    $('table.striped td:nth-child(' + column + ')' )
```

```
      .each(function(index) {
        if (thisClicked == $(this).text()) {
          $(this).parent().toggleClass('highlight');
        } else {
          $(this).parent().removeClass('highlight');
        };
      });
    })
  })
```

The `clickable` class is a step in the right direction, for sure, but it still doesn't tell the user what will happen when the cell is clicked. As far as anyone knows (without looking at the code, of course) that clicking could send the user to another page. Some further indication of what will happen upon clicking is in order.

Tooltips are a familiar feature of many software applications, including web browsers. We can simulate a tooltip with custom text, such as **Click to highlight all rows authored by Rey Bango**, when the mouse hovers over one of the author cells. This way, we can alert users to the effect their action will have.

We're going to create three functions—`showTooltip`, `hideTooltip`, and `positionTooltip`—outside any event handlers and then call or reference them as we need them. Let's start with `positionTooltip`, which we'll reference when the mouse moves over any of the author cells:

```
var positionTooltip = function(event) {
  var tPosX = event.pageX - 5;
  var tPosY = event.pageY + 20;
  $('div.tooltip').css({top: tPosY, left: tPosX});
};
```

Here we use the `pageX` and `pageY` properties of `event` to set the top and left positions of the tooltip. When we reference the function in the `.mousemove()` method, `tPosX` will refer to 5 pixels to the left of the mouse cursor while `tPosY` will refer to 20 pixels below the cursor. We can attach this method to the same chain as the one being used already for `.click()`:

```
$(document).ready(function() {
  var positionTooltip = function(event) {
    var tPosX = event.pageX - 5;
    var tPosY = event.pageY + 20;
    $('div.tooltip').css({top: tPosY, left: tPosX});
  };

  $('table.striped td:nth-child(' + column + ')' )
  .addClass('clickable')
```

```
    .click(function() {
// ...Code continues...
    })
    .mousemove(positionTooltip);
});
```

So, we've positioned the tooltip already, but we still haven't created it. That will be done in the showTooltip function.

The first thing that we do in the showTooltip function is remove all tooltips. This may seem counterintuitive, but if we are going to show the tooltip each time the mouse cursor hovers over an author cell; we don't want a proliferation of these tooltips appearing with each new cell hovered over:

```
var showTooltip = function(event) {
    $('div.tooltip').remove();
};
```

Now we're ready to create the tooltip. We can wrap the entire <div> and its contents in a $() function and then append it to the document's body:

```
var showTooltip = function(event) {
    $('div.tooltip').remove();
    var $thisAuthor = $(this).text();
    $('<div class="tooltip">Click to highlight all articles
                            written by ' + $thisAuthor + '</div>')
    .appendTo('body');
};
```

When the mouse cursor hovers over an author cell with **Rey Bango** in it, the tooltip will read, **Click to highlight all articles written by Rey Bango.** Unfortunately, the tooltip will appear at the bottom of the page. That's where the positionTooltip function comes in. We simply place that at the end of the showTooltip function:

```
var showTooltip = function(event) {
    $('div.tooltip').remove();
    var $thisAuthor = $(this).text();
    $('<div class="tooltip">Click to highlight all articles
                            written by ' + $thisAuthor + '</div>')
    .appendTo('body');
    positionTooltip(event);
};
```

The tooltip still won't be positioned correctly, though, unless we free it from its default `postion:static` property. We can do that in the stylesheet:

```
.tooltip {
  position: absolute;
  z-index: 2;
  background: #efd;
  border: 1px solid #ccc;
  padding: 3px;
}
```

The style rule also gives the tooltip a `z-index` higher than that of the surrounding elements to ensure that it is layered on top of them, as well as sprucing it up with a background color, a border, and some padding.

Finally, we write a simple `hideTooltip` function:

```
var hideTooltip = function() {
  $('div.tooltip').remove();
};
```

And now that we have functions for showing, hiding, and positioning the tooltip, we can reference them at the appropriate places in our code:

```
$(document).ready(function() {
  var column = 3;
  // Position the tooltip.
  var positionTooltip = function(event) {
    var tPosX = event.pageX - 5;
    var tPosY = event.pageY + 20;
    $('div.tooltip').css({top: tPosY, left: tPosX});
  };
  // Show (create) the tooltip.
  var showTooltip = function(event) {
    $('div.tooltip').remove();
    var $thisAuthor = $(this).text();
    $('<div class="tooltip">Click to highlight all articles written
                by ' + $thisAuthor + '</div>').appendTo('body');
    positionTooltip(event);
  };
  // Hide (remove) the tooltip.
  var hideTooltip = function() {
    $('div.tooltip').remove();
  },
  $('table.striped td:nth-child(' + column + ')' )
  .addClass('clickable')
  .click(function(event) {
```

```
    var thisClicked = $(this).text();
    $('table.striped td:nth-child(' + column + ')'
                                      ).each(function(index) {
      if (thisClicked == $(this).text()) {
        $(this).parent().toggleClass('highlight');
      } else {
        $(this).parent().removeClass('highlight');
      };
    });
  })
  .hover(showTooltip, hideTooltip)
  .mousemove(positionTooltip);
})
```

Note that the `.hover()` and `.mousemove()` methods are referencing functions that are defined elsewhere. As such, the functions take no parentheses. Also, because `positionTooltip(event)` is called inside `showTooltip`, the tooltip is immediately positioned on hover; it then continues to be referenced as the mouse cursor is moved over the cell due to the function's placement inside the `.mousemove()` method. The tooltip now looks like this:

Everything works fine now, with a tooltip that appears when we hover over an author cell, moves with the mouse movement, and disappears when we move the mouse cursor out of the cell. The only problem is that the tooltip continues to suggest clicking on a cell to highlight the articles even after those articles have been highlighted:

What we need is a way to change the tooltip if the row has the `highlight` class. Fortunately, we have the `showTooltip` function, in which we can place a conditional test to check for the class. If the current cell's parent `<tr>` has the `highlight` class, we add `un-` in front of the word `highlight` when we create the tooltip:

```
$(document).ready(function() {
  var highlighted = "";
  // Code continues...
  var showTooltip = function(event) {
    $('div.tooltip').remove();
    var $thisAuthor = $(this).text();
    if ($(this).parent().is('.highlight')) {
      highlighted = 'un-';
    } else {
      highlighted = '';
    };
    $('<div class="tooltip"> Click to '
              + highlighted + 'highlight all articles written by '
                    + $thisAuthor + '</div>').appendTo('body');
    positionTooltip(event);
  };
};
```

Our tooltip task would now be finished were it not for the need to trigger the tooltip-changing behavior when a cell is clicked as well. For that, we need to call the `showTooltip` function inside the `.click()` event handler:

```
$(document).ready(function() {
  // Code continues...
  .click(function(event) {
```

```
      var thisClicked = $(this).text();
      $('table.striped td:nth-child(' + column + ')'
   ).each(function(index) {
        if (thisClicked == $(this).text()) {
          $(this).parent().toggleClass('highlight');
        } else {
          $(this).parent().removeClass('highlight')
        };
      });
      showTooltip.call(this, event);
    })
    // Code continues...
  });
```

By using the JavaScript `call()` function, we can invoke `showTooltip` as if it were defined within the `.click()` handler. Therefore, `this` inherits the scope of `.click()`. Additionally, we pass in `event` so that we can use its `pageX` and `pageY` information for the positioning.

John Resig	standards
Yehuda Katz	announcement
Paul McLanahan	announcement
Rey Bango	announcement
John Resig	plug-in
John Resig	announcement
Nate Cavanaugh	miscellaneous
John Resig	source
John Resig	source

Click to un-highlight all articles written by Rey Bango

Now the tooltip offers a more intelligent suggestion when the hovered row is already highlighted.

Collapsing and Expanding

When large sets of data are grouped in tables, as each year's set of articles are in our News page, collapsing, or hiding, a section's contents can be a convenient way to get a broad view of all of the table's data without having to scroll so much.

To make the sections of the news article table collapsible, we first prepend a minus-symbol image to each subheading row's first cell. The image is inserted with JavaScript, because if JavaScript is not available for the row collapsing, the image might confuse those who expect clicking on it to actually trigger some kind of event:

```
$(document).ready(function() {
  var toggleMinus = '../icons/bullet_toggle_minus.png';
  var togglePlus = '../icons/bullet_toggle_plus.png';
  var $subHead = $('tbody th:first-child');
  $subHead.prepend('<img src="' + toggleMinus + '"
                              alt="collapse this section" />');
});
```

Note that we set variables for the location of both a minus-symbol and a plus-symbol image. This way we can change the image's `src` attribute when the image is clicked and the rows are collapsed or expanded.

Next we use the `.addClass()` method to make the newly created images appear clickable:

```
$(document).ready(function() {
  var toggleMinus = '../icons/bullet_toggle_minus.png';
  var togglePlus = '../icons/bullet_toggle_plus.png';
  var $subHead = $('tbody th:first-child');
  $subHead.prepend('<img src="' + toggleMinus + '"
                              alt="collapse this section" />');
  $('img', $subHead).addClass('clickable');
});
```

Finally, we can add code inside a `.click()` method to do the collapsing and expanding. A condition will check the current value of the clicked image's `src` attribute. If it equals the file path represented by the `toggleMinus` variable, then all of the other `<tr>` elements within the same `<tbody>` will be hidden, and the `src` attribute will be set to the value of the `togglePlus` variable. Otherwise, these `<tr>` elements will be shown and the `src` will change back to the value of `toggleMinus`:

```
$(document).ready(function() {
  var toggleMinus = '../icons/bullet_toggle_minus.png';
  var togglePlus = '../icons/bullet_toggle_plus.png';
  var $subHead = $('tbody th:first-child');
  $subHead.prepend('<img src="' + toggleMinus + '"
                              alt="collapse this section" />');
  $('img', $subHead).addClass('clickable')
  .click(function() {
    var toggleSrc = $(this).attr('src');
    if ( toggleSrc == toggleMinus ) {
```

```
        $(this).attr('src', togglePlus)
        .parents('tr').siblings().fadeOut('fast');
    } else{
        $(this).attr('src', toggleMinus)
        .parents('tr').siblings().fadeIn('fast');
    };
  });
})
```

With this code in place, clicking on the minus-symbol image next to **2007** makes the table look like this:

Date	Headline	Author	Topic
▪ 2007			
▪ 2006			
Dec 27	The Path to 1.1	John Resig	source
Dec 18	Meet The People Behind jQuery	John Resig	announcement
Dec 13	Helping you understand jQuery	John Resig	tutorial
Dec 12	jQuery 1.0.4	John Resig	release
Dec 12	jQuery v1.0.3 API docs on gotAPI.com	Rey Bango	documentation
Dec 12	jQuery Presentation in Phoenix on 11/28	Rey Bango	conference
Nov 28	jQuery at AZPhp	Rey Bango	conference

The **2007** news articles aren't removed; they are just hidden until we click the plus-symbol image that now appears in that row.

Table rows present particular obstacles to animation, since browsers use different values (`table-row` and `block`) for their visible `display` property. The `.hide()` and `.show()` methods, without animation, are always safe to use with table rows. As of jQuery version 1.1.3, `.fadeIn()` and `.fadeOut()` can be used as well.

Filtering

Earlier we examined sorting and paging as techniques for helping users focus on relevant portions of a table's data. We saw that both could be implemented either with server-side technology or with JavaScript. Filtering completes this arsenal of data arrangement strategies. By displaying to the user only the table rows that match a given criterion, we can strip away needless distractions.

We have already seen how to perform a type of filter, highlighting a set of rows. Now we will extend this idea to actually hiding rows that don't match the filter.

We can begin by creating a place to put our filter buttons. In typical fashion, we insert these controls using JavaScript so that people without scripting available do not see the options:

```
$(document).ready(function() {
  $('table.filterable').each(function() {
    var $table = $(this);
    $table.find('th').each(function (column) {
      if ($(this).is('.filter-column')) {
        var $filters = $('<div class="filters"><h3>Filter by '
                                  + $(this).text() + ':</h3></div>');
        $filters.insertBefore($table);
      }
    });
  });
});
```

We get the label for the filter box from the column headers, so that this code can be reused for other tables quite easily. Now we have a heading awaiting some buttons:

Date	Headline	Author	Topic	Filter by Topic:
2007				
Mar 11	SXSWi jQuery Meetup	John Resig	conference	
Feb 28	jQuery 1.1.2	John Resig	release	
Feb 21	jQuery is OpenAjax Compliant	John Resig	standards	
Feb 18	The jQuery IRC Channel	Yehuda Katz	announcement	
Feb 14	jQuery Nightly Builds	Paul McLanahan	announcement	
Feb 2	New jQuery Project Team Members	Rey Bango	announcement	
Jan 15	Interface 1.1 Released	John Resig	plug-in	
Jan 14	jQuery Birthday: 1.1, New Site, New Docs	John Resig	announcement	
Jan 13	jQuery wallpapers	Nate Cavanaugh	miscellaneous	
Jan 11	Selector Speeds	John Resig	source	
2006				
Dec 27	The Path to 1.1	John Resig	source	

Filter Options

Now we can move on to actually implementing a filter. To start with, we will add filters for a couple of known topics. The code for this is quite similar to the author highlighting example from before:

```
var keywords = ['conference', 'release'];
$.each(keywords, function (index, keyword) {
  $('<div class="filter"></div>').text(keyword).bind('click',
                         {'keyword': keyword}, function(event) {
```

```
$table.find('tbody tr').each(function() {
    if ($('td', this).filter(':nth-child(' + (column + 1) +
                            ')').text() == event.data['keyword']) {
        $(this).show();
    }
    else if ($('th',this).length == 0){
        $(this).hide();
    }
});


$(this).addClass('active').siblings().removeClass('active');
}).addClass('clickable').appendTo($filters);
});
```

Starting with a static array of keywords to filter by, we loop through and create a button for each. Just as in the paging example, we need to use the data parameter of `.bind()` to avoid accidental closure problems. Then, in the click handler, we compare each cell against the keyword and hide the row if there is no match. We must check whether the row is a subheader, to avoid hiding those in the process.

Both of the buttons now work as advertised:

Date	Headline	Author	Topic	Filter by Topic:
▼ 2007				conference
Feb 28	jQuery 1.1.2	John Resig	release	release
▼ 2006				
Dec 12	jQuery 1.0.4	John Resig	release	
Oct 27	jQuery 1.0.3	John Resig	release	
Oct 13	Minor API Change in 1.0.2	John Resig	release	
▼ 2005				

Collecting Filter Options from Content

Now we need to expand the filter options to cover the range of available topics in the table. Rather than hard-coding all of the topics, we can gather them from the text that has been entered in the table. We can change the definition of keywords to read:

```
var keywords = {};
$table.find('tbody tr td').filter(':nth-child(' + (column + 1) +
                                ')').each(function() {
    keywords[$(this).text()] = $(this).text();
});
```

This code relies on two tricks:

- By using a map rather than an array to hold the keywords as they are found, we eliminate duplicates automatically.

- jQuery's `$.each()` function lets us operate on arrays and maps identically, so no later code has to change. Now we have a full complement of filter options:

Reversing the Filters

For completeness, we need a way to get back to the full list after we have filtered it. Adding an option for all topics is pretty straightforward:

```
$('<div class="filter">all</div>').click(function() {
  $table.find('tbody tr').show();
  $(this).addClass('active').siblings().removeClass('active');
}).addClass('clickable active').appendTo($filters);
```

This gives us an **all** button that simply shows all rows of the table again. For good measure we mark it as active to begin with.

Interacting with Other Code

We learned with our sorting and paging code that we can't treat the various features we write as islands. The behaviors we build can interact in sometimes surprising ways; for this reason, it is worth revisiting our earlier efforts to examine how they coexist with the new filtering capabilities we have added.

Row Striping

The advanced row striping we put in place earlier is confused by our new filters. Since the tables are not re-striped after a filter is performed, rows retain their coloring as if the filtered rows were still present.

To account for the filtered rows, the striping code needs to be able to find them. We can add a class on the rows when they are filtered:

```
$(document).ready(function() {
  $('table.filterable').each(function() {
    var $table = $(this);

    $table.find('th').each(function (column) {
      if ($(this).is('.filter-column')) {
        var $filters = $('<div class="filters"><h3>Filter by ' +
                                  $(this).text() + ':</h3></div>');
        var keywords = {};

        $table.find('tbody tr td').filter(':nth-child(' + (column +
                                  1) + ')').each(function() {
          keywords[$(this).text()] = $(this).text();
        });

        $('<div class="filter">all</div>').click(function() {
          $table.find('tbody tr').show().removeClass('filtered');
          $(this).addClass('active').siblings().removeClass('active');
          $table.trigger('stripe');
        }).addClass('clickable active').appendTo($filters);

        $.each(keywords, function (index, keyword) {
          $('<div class="filter"></div>').text(keyword).bind('click',
                          {'keyword': keyword}, function(event) {
            $table.find('tbody tr').each(function() {
              if ($('td', this).filter(':nth-child(' + (column + 1) +
                          ')').text() == event.data['keyword']) {
                $(this).show().removeClass('filtered');
              }
              else if ($('th',this).length == 0) {
                $(this).hide().addClass('filtered');
              }
            });

            $(this).addClass('active').siblings().removeClass('active');
            $table.trigger('stripe');
          }).addClass('clickable').appendTo($filters);

        });
        $filters.insertBefore($table);
      }
    });
  });
});
```

Whenever the current filter changes, we trigger the `stripe` event. This uses the same trick we implemented when making our pager aware of sorting—adding a new custom event. We have to rewrite the striping code to define this event:

```
$(document).ready(function() {
  $('table.striped').each(function() {
    $(this).bind('stripe', function() {
      var rowIndex = 0;
      $('tbody tr:not(.filtered)', this).each(function(index) {
        if ($('th',this).length) {
          $(this).addClass('subhead');
          rowIndex = -1;
        } else {
          if (rowIndex % 6 < 3) {
            $(this).removeClass('odd').addClass('even');
          }
          else {
            $(this).removeClass('even').addClass('odd');
          }
        };
        rowIndex++;
      });
    });
    $(this).trigger('stripe');
  });
});
```

The selector to find table rows now skips filtered rows. We also must remove obsolete classes from rows, as this code may now be executed multiple times. With both the new event handler and its triggers in place, the filtering operation respects row striping:

Date	Headline	Author	Topic	Filter by Topic:
= 2007				conference
Feb 28	jQuery 1.1.2	John Resig	release	release
= 2006				standards
				announcement
Dec 12	jQuery 1.0.4	John Resig	release	plug-in
Oct 27	jQuery 1.0.3	John Resig	release	miscellaneous
Oct 13	Minor API Change in 1.0.2	John Resig	release	source
= 2005				tutorial
				documentation
				third-party

Expanding and Collapsing

The expanding and collapsing behavior added earlier also conflicts with our filters. If a section is collapsed and a new filter is chosen, then the matching items are displayed, even if in the collapsed section. Conversely, if the table is filtered and a section is expanded, then all items in the expanded section are displayed regardless of whether they match the filter.

Since we have added the `filtered` class to all rows when they are removed by a filter button, we can check for this class inside our collapser's click handler:

```
var toggleSrc = $(this).attr('src');
if ( toggleSrc == toggleMinus ) {
  $(this).attr('src', togglePlus)
  .parents('tr').siblings().addClass('collapsed').fadeOut('fast');
} else{
  $(this).attr('src', toggleMinus)
  .parents('tr').siblings().removeClass('collapsed')
                            .not('.filtered').fadeIn('fast');
};
```

While we are collapsing or expanding rows, we add or remove another new class on the rows. We need this class to solve the other half of the problem. The filtering code can use the class to ensure that a row should be shown when the filter changes:

```
$table.find('tbody tr').each(function() {
  if ($('td', this).filter(':nth-child(' + (column + 1) + ')').text()
                                    == e.data['keyword']) {
    $(this).removeClass('filtered').not('.collapsed').show();
  }
  else if ($('th',this).length == 0) {
    $(this).addClass('filtered').hide();
  }
});
```

Now our features play nicely, each able to hide and show the rows independently.

The Finished Code

Our second example page has demonstrated table row striping, highlighting, tooltips, collapsing/expanding, and filtering. Taken together, the JavaScript code for this page is:

```
$(document).ready(function() {
  var highlighted = "";
```

```
    var column = 3;

  var positionTooltip = function(event) {
    var tPosX = event.pageX;
    var tPosY = event.pageY + 20;
    $('div.tooltip').css({top: tPosY, left: tPosX});
  };
  var showTooltip = function(event) {
    $('div.tooltip').remove();
    var $thisAuthor = $(this).text();
    if ($(this).parent().is('.highlight')) {
      highlighted = 'un-';
    } else {
      highlighted = '';
    };
    $('<div class="tooltip">Click to ' + highlighted +
                'highlight all articles written by ' +
                    $thisAuthor + '</div>').appendTo('body');
    positionTooltip(event);
  };
  var hideTooltip = function() {
    $('div.tooltip').remove();
  };

  $('table.striped td:nth-child(' + column + ')' )
  .addClass('clickable')
  .click(function(event) {
    var thisClicked = $(this).text();
    $('table.striped td:nth-child(' + column + ')' )
      .each(function(index) {
        if (thisClicked == $(this).text()) {
          $(this).parent().toggleClass('highlight');
        } else {
          $(this).parent().removeClass('highlight');
        };
      })
    showTooltip.call(this, event);
  })
  .hover(showTooltip, hideTooltip)
  .mousemove(positionTooltip);
});

$(document).ready(function() {
  $('table.striped').each(function() {
```

```
    $(this).bind('stripe', function() {
      var rowIndex = 0;
      $('tbody tr:not(.filtered)', this).each(function(index) {
        if ($('th',this).length) {
          $(this).addClass('subhead');
          rowIndex = -1;
        } else {
          if (rowIndex % 6 < 3) {
            $(this).removeClass('odd').addClass('even');
          }
          else {
            $(this).removeClass('even').addClass('odd');
          }
        }
        rowIndex++;
      });
    });
    $(this).trigger('stripe');
  });
})


$(document).ready(function() {
  $('table.filterable').each(function() {
    var $table = $(this);

    $table.find('th').each(function (column) {
      if ($(this).is('.filter-column')) {
        var $filters = $('<div class="filters"><h3>Filter by ' +
                              $(this).text() + ':</h3></div>');
        var keywords = {};

        $table.find('tbody tr td').filter(':nth-child(' + (column +
                                1) + ')').each(function() {
          keywords[$(this).text()] = $(this).text();
        })

        $('<div class="filter">all</div>').click(function() {
          $table.find('tbody tr').removeClass('filtered')
                                      .not('.collapsed').show();
          $(this).addClass('active').siblings().removeClass('active');
          $table.trigger('stripe');
        }).addClass('clickable active').appendTo($filters);

        $.each(keywords, function (index, keyword) {
```

```
      $('<div class="filter"></div>').text(keyword).bind('click',
                          {'keyword': keyword}, function(event) {
        $table.find('tbody tr').each(function() {
          if ($('td', this).filter(':nth-child(' + (column + 1)
                      + ')').text() == event.data['keyword']) {
            $(this).removeClass('filtered').not('.collapsed')
                                                      .show();
          }
          else if ($('th',this).length == 0) {
            $(this).addClass('filtered').hide();
          }
        });

        $(this).addClass('active').siblings().removeClass(
                                  'active');
        $table.trigger('stripe');
      }).addClass('clickable').appendTo($filters);

    });
    $filters.insertBefore($table);
    }
  });
  });
});


$(document).ready(function() {
  var toggleMinus = '../icons/bullet_toggle_minus.png';
  var togglePlus = '../icons/bullet_toggle_plus.png';
  var $subHead = $('tbody th:first-child');
  $subHead.prepend('<img src="' + toggleMinus + '" alt="collapse
                                        this section" />');

  $('img', $subHead).addClass('clickable')
  .click(function() {
    var toggleSrc = $(this).attr('src');
    if ( toggleSrc == toggleMinus ) {
      $(this).attr('src', togglePlus)
      .parents('tr').siblings().addClass('collapsed').fadeOut('fast');
    } else {
      $(this).attr('src', toggleMinus)
      .parents('tr').siblings().removeClass('collapsed')
                          .not('.filtered').show().fadeIn('fast');
    };
  });
})
```

Summary

In this chapter, we have explored some of the ways to slice and dice the tables on our sites, reconfiguring them into beautiful and functional containers for our data. We have covered sorting data in tables, using different kinds of data (words, numbers, dates) as sort keys along with paginating tables into easily-viewed chunks. We have learned sophisticated row striping techniques and JavaScript-powered tooltips. We have also walked through expanding and collapsing as well as filtering and highlighting of rows that match the given criteria.

We've even touched briefly on some quite advanced topics, such as sorting and paging with server-side code and AJAX techniques, dynamically calculating page coordinates for elements, and writing a jQuery plug-in.

As we have seen, properly semantic HTML tables wrap a great deal of subtlety and complexity in a small package. Fortunately, jQuery can help us easily tame these creatures, allowing the full power of tabular data to come to the surface.

8
Forms with Function

I'm shoutin'
We're waiting for a reply
     — Devo,
      "Shout"

Nearly every website that requires feedback from the user will employ a form in one capacity or another. Throughout the life of the Internet, forms have played the role of pack mule, carrying information from the end user back to the website's publisher—dependably, reliably, but with very little grace or style. Perhaps this lack of flair was caused by the repetitious, arduous journey to the server and back; or perhaps it had something to do with the intransigent elements the form had to work with and their unwillingness to follow the latest fashion. Whatever the reason, it wasn't until recently, with the resurgence of client-side scripting, that forms found new vigor, purpose, and style. In this chapter, we will look at ways in which we can breathe new life into forms. We'll enhance their style, create validation routines for them, use them for calculations, and send their results to the server while nobody is watching.

Progressively Enhanced Form Styling

As we apply jQuery to websites, we must always ask ourselves how pages will look and function when visitors have JavaScript disabled (unless, of course, we know exactly who every visitor will be and how their browsers will be configured). This is not to say, though, that we can't create a *more* beautiful or feature-full site for visitors with JavaScript turned on. The principle of **progressive enhancement** is popular among JavaScript developers because it respects the needs of all users while providing something extra to most of them.

Let us create a form, a contact form, that demonstrates progressive enhancement in both its appearance and its behavior. Without JavaScript enabled, the form's first `fieldset` looks like this:

While it certainly appears functional, with plenty of information to guide the user through each field, it could definitely stand some improvement. Let's progressively enhance this group in three ways:

1. Modify the DOM to allow for flexible styling of the `<legend>`.

2. Change the required field messages to an asterisk (*) and the special field (required only when the corresponding checkbox is checked) message to a double asterisk (**). Bold the label for each required field and place a key at the top of the form explaining what the asterisk and double asterisk mean.

3. Hide each checkbox's corresponding text input on page load, and then toggle them, visible and hidden, when the user checks and unchecks the boxes.

We start with the `<fieldset>`'s HTML:

```
<fieldset>
  <legend>Personal Info</legend>
  <ol>
    <li><label for="first-name">First Name</label><input
                  class="required" type="text" name="first-name"
                    id="first-name" /> <span>(required)</span></li>
    <li><label for="last-name">Last Name</label><input
                  class="required" type="text" name="last-name"
                    id="last-name" /> <span>(required)</span></li>
    <li>How would you like to be contacted? (choose at least one
method)
      <ul>
        <li><label for="by-email"><input type="checkbox"
              name="by-contact-type" value="E-mail" id="by-email" />
                                    by E-Mail</label>
```

```
<input class="conditional" type="text" name="email"
        id="email" /> <span>(required when corresponding
                             checkbox checked)</span></li>
<li><label for="by-phone"><input type="checkbox" name="by-
        contact-type" value="Phone" id="by-phone" />
                                      by Phone</label>
<input class="conditional" type="text" name="phone"
        id="phone" /> <span>(required when corresponding
                             checkbox checked)</span></li>
<li><label for="by-fax"><input type="checkbox" name="by-
        contact-type" value="Fax" id="by-fax" /> by Fax</label>
<input class="conditional" type="text" name="fax" id="fax"
        /> <span>(required when corresponding checkbox
                             checked)</span></li>
        </ul>
      </li>
    </ol>
  </fieldset>
```

One thing to note here is that each element or pair of elements is considered a list item (`<li>`). All elements are placed within an ordered list (`<ol>`), and the checkboxes (along with their text fields) are placed within a nested unordered list (`<ul>`). Furthermore, we use the `<label>` element to indicate the name of each field. For text fields, the `<label>` precedes the `<input>`; for checkboxes, it encloses the `<input>`.

With our HTML in place, we're now ready to use jQuery for the progressive enhancement.

The Legend

The form's `legend` is a notoriously difficult element to style with CSS. Browser inconsistencies and positioning limitations make working with it an exercise in frustration. Yet, if we're concerned about using meaningful, well-structured page elements, the `legend` is an attractive, if not visually appealing, choice for displaying a title in our form's `<fieldset>`.

Left with only HTML and CSS, we're forced to compromise either semantic markup or flexible design choices. However, we can change the HTML as the page loads, turning each `<legend>` into an `<h3>` for people viewing the page, while machines reading the page—and those with JavaScript disabled—will still see the `<legend>`.

For each `<fieldset>`, we want to get the text inside the `<legend>` element, store it in a variable, and then remove the `<legend>`:

```
$(document).ready(function() {
  $('fieldset').each(function() {
    var heading = $('legend', this).remove().text();
  });
});
```

We use the `.each()` method here because the contact form has three `<fieldset>` elements. If we were working with a single-fieldset form, we could simply rely on jQuery's implicit iteration. Also, notice the selector expression we use for the `heading` variable: `$('legend', this)`. Since `heading` is being set each time we iterate over a `<fieldset>`, we need to use `this` as a contextual selector for `<legend>` to ensure that the text is being taken from only one `<legend>` at a time. Otherwise, the first iteration would get the text from all three `<legend>`s, leaving the second and third with nothing.

Next, we create the `<h3>` element, insert it at the beginning of each `<fieldset>`, and fill it with the text stored in the `heading` variable:

```
$(document).ready(function() {
  $('fieldset').each(function() {
    var heading = $('legend', this).remove().text();
    $('<h3></h3>')
    .text(heading)
    .prependTo( this );
  });
});
```

Note here that we've created and inserted a new element the long way — first creating the element, then inserting the text, and finally prepending it — on three separate lines. We could have accomplished the same task in one line, like so:

```
$(this).prepend('<h3>' + heading + '</h3>');
```

However, the three-line version is less error-prone: the use of the `.text` method ensures that any special HTML characters are properly escaped.

Now, when we apply a blue background and white text color to the `<h3>` in the stylesheet, the form's first fieldset looks like this:

Personal Info

First Name	(required)
Last Name	(required)

How would you like to be contacted? (choose at least one method)

☐ by E-Mail	(required when corresponding checkbox checked)
☐ by Phone	(required when corresponding checkbox checked)
☐ by Fax	(required when corresponding checkbox checked)

The form's `legend` elements are now sufficiently styled for our purposes; it's time to clean up the required field messages.

Required Field Messages

In our contact form, required fields have `class="required"` to allow for styling as well as response to user input; the input fields for each type of contact have `class="conditional"` applied to them. We're going to use these classes to change the instructions printed within parentheses to the right of each `input`.

We start by setting variables for `requiredFlag` and `conditionalFlag`, and then we fill the `<span>` element next to each required and conditional field with the text stored in those variables:

```
$(document).ready(function() {
  var requiredFlag = ' * ';
  var conditionalFlag = ' ** ';

  $('form :input').filter('.required')
  .next('span').text(requiredFlag);

  $('form :input').filter('.conditional')
  .next('span').text(conditionalFlag);
});
```

Since a single asterisk (*) may not immediately capture the user's attention, we'll also add `class="req-label"` to the `<label>` for each required field and apply `font-weight:bold` to that class:

```
$(document).ready(function() {
  var requiredFlag = ' * ';
```

```
var conditionalFlag = ' ** ';

$('form :input').filter('.required')
.next('span').text(requiredFlag).end()
.prev('label').addClass('req-label');

$('form :input').filter('.conditional')
.next('span').text(conditionalFlag);
});
```

In order to select the `label` properly, we had to add `.end()` to the previous line. The chain had already selected all form inputs, filtered those to include only fields with `class="required"`, and then selected the `<span>` elements immediately following those filtered inputs. Adding `.end()` to the chain takes the selector expression back one step; in this case, to all form inputs with `class="required"`. So, following that with `.prev('label')` will work as expected. The fieldset with the modified text and the added `class` now looks like this:

Not bad. Still, the `required` and `conditional` field messages really weren't so bad after all; they were just too repetitive. Lets take the first instance of each message and display it above the form next to the *flag* we're using to symbolize it.

Before we populate the `<span>` elements holding the messages with their respective flags, we need to store the initial messages in a couple of variables. Then we can strip out the parentheses by using a regular expression:

```
$(document).ready(function() {
    var requiredFlag = ' * ';
    var requiredKey = $('input.required:first').next('span').text();
    requiredKey = requiredFlag + requiredKey
                                    .replace(/^\((.+)\)$/,"$1");
    var conditionalFlag = ' ** ';
    var conditionalKey = $('input.conditional:first').next(
                                            'span').text();
```

```
conditionalKey = conditionalFlag + conditionalKey
                              .replace(/^\((.+)\)$/,"$1");

  $('form :input').filter('.required')
  .next('span').text(requiredFlag).end()
  .prev('label').addClass('req-label');

  $('form :input').filter('.conditional')
  .next('span').text(conditionalFlag);
});
```

The first line of each addition to the code simply sets the variable as the text of the message. The second line then concatenates each flag and its respective message, minus the parentheses. Perhaps the regular expression, along with its .replace method, warrants further explanation.

A Regular Expression Digression

The regular expression is contained within the two forward slashes, and looks like this: /^\((.+)\)$/. The first character, ^, indicates that what follows needs to appear at the beginning of the string. It's followed by two characters, \(, which look for an opening parenthesis. The back-slash is used as an **escape** that tells the regular-expression parser to treat the following character literally. This is necessary because parentheses are among the characters that have special meaning in regular expressions, as we'll see next. The next four characters, (.+) look for one or more (+) characters of any kind within the same line (.) and put them in a group by use of the parentheses. The final three characters, \)$, look for a closing parenthesis at the end of the string. So, all together the regular expression is selecting an opening parenthesis, followed by a group of characters, and ending with a closing parenthesis.

The .replace() method looks within a particular context for a string represented by a regular expression and replaces it with another string. The syntax looks like this:

```
context-string.replace(/regular-expression/, "replacement-string")
```

The context strings of our two .replace() methods are the variables requiredKey and conditionalKey. We've already looked at the regular expression part of this, contained within the two slashes. A comma separates the regular expression and the replacement string, which in our two cases is "$1". The $1 placeholder represents the first group in the regular expression. Since, again, our regular expression has one group of one or more characters, with a parenthesis on either side, the replacement string will be everything inside, and not including, the parentheses.

Inserting the Field-Message Legend

Now that we've retrieved the field messages without the parentheses, we can insert them, along with their corresponding flags, above the form:

```
$(document).ready(function() {
  var requiredFlag = ' * ';
  var requiredKey = $('input.required:first').next('span').text();
  requiredKey = requiredFlag + requiredKey.replace(/^\((.+)\)$/,"$1");

  var conditionalFlag = ' ** ';
  var conditionalKey =
                $('input.conditional:first').next('span').text();
  conditionalKey = conditionalFlag +
                conditionalKey.replace(/\((.+)\)/,"$1");

  $('form :input').filter('.required')
  .next('span').text(requiredFlag).end()
  .prev('label').addClass('req-label');

  $('form :input').filter('.conditional')
  .next('span').text(conditionalFlag);

  $('<p></p>')
  .addClass('field-keys')
  .append(requiredKey + '<br />')
  .append(conditionalKey)
  .insertBefore('#contact');
});
```

The five new lines should look relatively familiar now. Here is what they do:

1. Create a new paragraph element
2. Give the paragraph a class of `field-keys`
3. Append `requiredKey` and a line break to the paragraph
4. Append `conditionalKey` to the paragraph
5. Insert the paragraph and everything we've appended inside it before the contact form

When using `.append()` with an HTML string, as we do here, we need to be careful that any special HTML characters are properly escaped. In this case, the `.text` method has done this for us.

When we define some styles for `.field-keys` in the stylesheet, the result looks like this:

```
* required
** required when corresponding checkbox checked
```

Personal Info

First Name [   ] *

Last Name [   ] *

How would you like to be contacted? (choose at least one method)

☐ by E-Mail [   ] **

☐ by Phone [   ] **

☐ by Fax   [   ] **

Our jQuery work for the first `fieldset` is almost complete.

Conditionally Displayed Fields

Let's further improve the group of fields that ask visitors how they would like to be contacted. Since the text inputs need to be entered only if their corresponding checkboxes are checked, we can hide them when the document is initially loaded:

```
$(document).ready(function() {
  $('input.conditional').hide().next('span').hide();
});
```

The `fieldset` now has its streamlined interface:

Personal Info

First Name [   ] *

Last Name [   ] *

How would you like to be contacted? (choose at least one method)

☐ by E-Mail

☐ by Phone

☐ by Fax

To make the text inputs and flags appear, we can attach the `.click` method to each checkbox. We'll do so within the context of each conditional text input so that we can set a couple of variables for reuse:

```
$(document).ready(function() {
  $('input.conditional').hide().next('span').hide();
  $('input.conditional').each(function() {
    var $thisInput = $(this);
    var $thisFlag = $thisInput.next('span').hide();
    $thisInput.prev('label').find(':checkbox').click(function() {
      // code continues . . .
    });
  });
});
```

Now we have a variable for the current text input and the current flag. When the user clicks the checkbox, we see if it is checked; if it is, we show the text input, show the flag, and add the `req-label` class to the parent `<label>` element:

```
$(document).ready(function() {
  $('input.conditional').hide().next('span').hide();
  $('input.conditional').each(function() {
    var $thisInput = $(this);
    var $thisFlag = $thisInput.next('span').hide();
    $thisInput.prev('label').find(':checkbox').click(function() {
      if (this.checked) {
        $thisInput.show();
        $thisFlag.show();
        $(this).parent('label').addClass('req-label');
      };
    });
  });
});
```

For testing whether a box is checked here, `this.checked` is preferred because we have direct access to the DOM node via the `this` keyword. When the DOM node is not so accessible, we can use `$('selector').is(':checked')` instead, since `.is()` returns a Boolean (`true` or `false`).

All we need now is to add an `else` condition that hides the conditional elements and removes the `req-label` class when the checkbox is not checked:

```
$(document).ready(function() {
  $('input.conditional').hide().next('span').hide();
  $('input.conditional').each(function() {
```

```
    var $thisInput = $(this);
    var $thisFlag = $thisInput.next('span').hide();
    $thisInput.prev('label').find(':checkbox').click(function() {
      if (this.checked) {
        $thisInput.show();
        $thisFlag.show();
        $(this).parent('label').addClass('req-label');
      } else {
        $thisInput.hide();
        $thisFlag.hide();
        $(this).parent('label').removeClass('req-label');
      };
    });
  });
});
```

And that concludes the styling portion of this form makeover. Next, we'll add some client-side validation.

Form Validation

Before we add validation to any form with jQuery, we need to remember one important rule: *client-side validation is not a substitute for server-side validation*. Again, we cannot rely on users to have JavaScript enabled. If we truly require certain fields to be entered, or to be entered in a particular format, JavaScript alone can't guarantee the result we demand. Some users prefer not to enable JavaScript, some devices simply don't support it, and a few users could intentionally submit malicious data by circumventing JavaScript restrictions.

Immediate Feedback

Why then should we bother implementing validation with jQuery? Client-side form validation using jQuery can offer one advantage over server-side validation: **immediate feedback**. Server-side code, whether it's ASP, PHP, or any other fancy acronym, needs the page to be reloaded to take effect (unless it is accessed asynchronously, of course, which in any case requires JavaScript). With jQuery, we can capitalize on the peppy response of client-side code by applying validation to each required field when it loses focus (on blur) or when a key is pressed (on keyup).

Required Fields

For our contact form, we'll check for the required class on each input when the user tabs or clicks out of it. Before we begin with this code, however, we should make a quick trip back to our conditional text fields. To simplify our validation routine, we'll add the required class to the <input> when it is shown, and remove the class when the <input> is subsequently hidden. This portion of the code now looks like this:

```
$thisInput.prev('label').find(':checkbox').click(function() {
  if (this.checked) {
    $thisInput.show().addClass('required');
    $thisFlag.show();
    $(this).parent('label').addClass('req-label');
  } else {
    $thisInput.hide().removeClass('required');
    $thisFlag.hide();
    $(this).parent('label').removeClass('req-label');
  };
});
```

With all of the required classes in place, we're ready to respond when the user leaves one of these fields empty. A message will be placed after the required flag, and the field's <li> element will receive styles to alert the user through class="warning":

```
$(document).ready(function() {
  $('form :input').blur(function() {
    if ($(this).is('.required')) {
      var $listItem = $(this).parents('li:first');
      if (this.value == '') {
        var errorMessage = 'This is a required field';
        $('<span></span>')
          .addClass('error-message')
          .text(errorMessage)
          .appendTo($listItem);
        $listItem.addClass('warning');
      };
    };
  });
});
```

The code has two if statements for each form input on blur: the first checks for the required class, and the second checks for an empty string. If both conditions are met, we construct an error message, put it in <span class="error-message">, and append it all to the parent <li>.

We want to give a slightly different message if the field is one of the `conditional` text fields—only required when its corresponding checkbox is checked. We'll concatenate a qualifier message to the standard error message. To do so, we can nest one more `if` statement that checks for the `conditional` class only after the first two `if` conditions have been met:

```
$(document).ready(function() {
  $('form :input').blur(function() {
    if ($(this).is('.required')) {
      var $listItem = $(this).parents('li:first');
      if (this.value == '') {
        var errorMessage = 'This is a required field';
        if ($(this).is('.conditional')) {
          errorMessage += ', when its related checkbox is checked';
        };
        $('<span></span>')
          .addClass('error-message')
          .text(errorMessage)
          .appendTo($listItem);
        $listItem.addClass('warning');
      };
    };
  });
});
```

Our code works great the first time the user leaves a field blank; however, two problems with the code are evident when the user subsequently enters and leaves the field:

If the field remains blank, the error message is repeated as many times as the user leaves the field. If the field has text entered, the `class="warning"` is not removed. Obviously, we want only one message per field, and we want the message to be removed if the user fixes the error. We can fix both problems by removing `class="warning"` from the current field's parent `<li>` and any `<span class="error-message>` within the same `<li>` every time the field is blurred, before running through the validation checks:

```
$(document).ready(function() {
  $('form :input').blur(function() {
    $(this).parents('li:first').removeClass('warning')
    .find('span.error-message').remove();
    if ($(this).is('.required')) {
      var $listItem = $(this).parents('li:first');
      if (this.value == '') {
        var errorMessage = 'This is a required field';
        if ($(this).is('.conditional')) {
          errorMessage += ', when its related checkbox is checked';
        };
        $('<span></span>')
          .addClass('error-message')
          .text(errorMessage)
          .appendTo($listItem);
        $listItem.addClass('warning');
      };
    };
  });
});
```

Finally, we have a functioning validation script for required and conditionally required fields. Even after repeatedly entering and leaving required fields, our error messages now display correctly:

Personal Info

First Name Karl   *

Last Name Swedberg   *

How would you like to be contacted? (choose at least one method)

☑ by E-Mail   ** This is a required field, when its related checkbox is checked

☑ by Phone   ** This is a required field, when its related checkbox is checked

☐ by Fax

But wait! We want to remove the `<li>`'s warning class and its `<span class="error-message">` elements when the user unchecks a checkbox too! We can do that by visiting our previous checkbox code once more and getting it to trigger `blur` on the corresponding text field when its checkbox is unchecked:

```
if (this.checked) {
  $thisInput.show().addClass('required');
  $thisFlag.show();
  $(this).parent('label').addClass('req-label');
} else {
  $thisInput.hide().removeClass('required').blur();
  $thisFlag.hide();
  $(this).parent('label').removeClass('req-label');
};
```

Now when a checkbox is unchecked, the related warning styles and error messages will be out of sight and out of mind.

Required Formats

There is one further type of validation to implement in our contact form—correct input formats. Sometimes it can be helpful to provide a warning if text is entered into a field incorrectly (rather than simply having it blank). Prime candidates for this type of warning are email, phone, and credit-card fields. For our demonstration, we will put in place a relatively simple regular-expression test for the email field. Let's take a look at the full code for the email validation before we dig into the regular expression in particular:

```
$(document).ready(function() {
// . . . code continues . . .

   if ($(this).is('#email')) {
     var $listItem = $(this).parents('li:first');
     if (this.value != '' && !/.+@.+\.[a-zA-Z]{2,4}$/
                                        .test(this.value)) {
       var errorMessage = 'Please use proper e-mail format'
                               + (e.g. joe@example.com)';
       $('<span></span>')
         .addClass('error-message')
         .text(errorMessage)
         .appendTo($listItem);
       $listItem.addClass('warning');
     };
   };
// . . . code continues . . .
});
```

The code performs the following tasks:

- Tests for the `id` of the email field; if the test is successful:
  - Sets a variable for the parent list item
  - Tests for two more conditions in the email field—value is not an empty string and does not match the regular expression; if the two tests are successful:
    - Creates an error message
    - Inserts the message in `<span class="error-message">`
    - Appends the `<span class="error-message">` element and its contents to the parent list item
    - Adds the `warning` class to the parent list item

Now let's take a look at the regular expression in isolation:

```
!/.+@.+\.[a-zA-Z]{2,4}$/.test(this.value)
```

Although this regular expression is similar to the one we created earlier in the chapter, it uses the `.test` method rather than the `.replace` method, since we only need it to return `true` or `false`. As before, the regular expression goes inside the two forward slashes. It is then tested against a string that is placed inside the parentheses of `.test()`, in this case the value of the email field.

In this regular expression we look for a group of one or more non-linefeed characters (`.+`), followed by an `@` symbol, and then followed by another group of one or more non-linefeed characters. So far, a string such as `lucia@example` would pass the test, as would millions of other permutations. Notice, though, that this is not a valid email address.

We can make the test more precise by looking for a `.` character, followed by two through four letters between `a` and `z` at the end of the string. And that is exactly what the remaining portion of the regular expression does. It first looks for a character between `a` and `z` or `A` and `Z`— `[a-zA-Z]`. It then says that a letter in that range can appear two through four times only— `{2,4}`. Finally, it insists that those two through four letters appear at the end of the string: `$`. Now a string such as `lucia@example.com` would return `true`, whereas `lucia@example.2fn` or `lucia@example.example` or `lucia-example.com` would not.

But we want `true` returned (and the error message, etc., created) only if the proper email address format is not entered. That's why we precede the regular expression with the exclamation mark (*not* operator):

```
!/.+@.+\.[a-zA-Z]{2,4}$/.test(this.value)
```

A Final Check

The validation code is now almost complete for the contact form. We can validate the form's fields one more time when the user attempts to submit it, this time all at once. Using the `.submit()` event handler on the form, not the **Send** button, we trigger `blur` on all of the required fields:

```
$(document).ready(function() {
  $('form').submit(function() {
    $('#submit-message').remove();
    $(':input.required').trigger('blur');
  });
});
```

Note here that we've sneaked in a line to remove an element that does not yet exist. We'll add this element in the next step. We're just preemptively removing it here because we already know that we'll need to do it based on the problems we encountered with creating multiple error messages earlier in the chapter.

After triggering `blur`, we get the total number of `warning` classes in the current form. If there are any at all, we create a new `submit-message` `<div>` and insert it before the **Send** button where the user is most likely to see it. We also stop the form from actually being submitted:

```
$(document).ready(function() {
  $('form').submit(function() {
    $('#submit-message').remove();
    $(':input.required').trigger('blur');
    var numWarnings = $('.warning', this).length;
    if (numWarnings) {
      $('<div></div>').attr({'id': 'submit-message',
                                          'class': 'warning'})
      .append('Please correct errors with ' + numWarnings
                                          + ' fields')
      .insertBefore('#send');
      return false;
    };
  });
});
```

In addition to providing a generic request to fix errors, the message indicates the number of fields that need to be fixed:

```
Please correct errors with 3 fields
Send
```

We can do better than that, though; rather than just showing the number of errors, we can list the names of the fields that contain errors:

```
$(document).ready(function() {
  $('form').submit(function() {
    $('#submit-message').remove();
    $(':input.required').trigger('blur');
    var numWarnings = $('.warning', this).length;
    if (numWarnings) {
      var fieldList = [];
      $('.warning label').each(function() {
        fieldList.push($(this).text());
      });
      $('<div></div>')
      .attr({'id': 'submit-message','class': 'warning'})
      .append('Please correct errors with the following ' +
                                    numWarnings + ' fields:<br />')
      .append('&bull; ' + fieldList.join('<br />&bull; '))
      .insertBefore('#send');
      return false;
    };
  });
});
```

The first change to the code is the `fieldList` variable set to an empty array. Then we get each label that is a descendant of an element with the `warning` class and *push* its text into the `fieldList` array (with the native JavaScript `push` function). Now the text of each of these labels constitutes a separate element in the `fieldList` array.

We modify our first version of the `submit-message` a bit and append our `fieldList` array to it. We use the native JavaScript `join` function to convert the array into a string, joining each of the array's elements with a line break and a bullet:

```
Please correct errors with the following 3 fields:
• First Name
• Last Name
• by E-Mail
Send
```

Admittedly, the HTML for the field list is presentational rather than semantic. However, for an ephemeral list—one that is generated by JavaScript as a last step and meant to be discarded as soon as possible—we'll forgive this quick and dirty code for the sake of ease and brevity.

Checkbox Manipulation

To round out our enhancements to the contact form, we'll help the user manage the list of checkboxes in the **Miscellaneous** section. A group of 10 checkboxes can be daunting, especially if the user wishes to click most or all of them, as seen with the following group of ways the user may have discovered us:

An option to check or uncheck all of the checkboxes would certainly come in handy in this type of situation. So, let's create one.

To begin, we create a new `<li>` element, fill it with a `<label>`, inside which we place `<input type="checkbox" id="discover-all">` and some text, and prepend it all to the `<ul>` element inside `<li class="discover">`:

```
$(document).ready(function() {
  $('<li></li>')
  .html('<label><input type="checkbox" id="discover-all" />'
                        + '<em>check all</em></label>')
  .prependTo('li.discover > ul');
});
```

Now we have a new checkbox with a label that reads **check all**. But it doesn't do anything yet. We need to attach the `.click()` method to it:

```
$(document).ready(function() {
  $('<li></li>')
  .html('<label><input type="checkbox" id="discover-all" />
                        <em>check all</em></label>')
  .prependTo('li.discover > ul');
```

```
$('#discover-all').click(function() {
  var $checkboxes = $(this).parents('ul:first').find(':checkbox');
  if (this.checked) {
    $checkboxes.attr('checked', 'true');
  } else {
    $checkboxes.attr('checked', '');
  };
});
});
```

Inside this event handler, we first set the $checkboxes variable, which consists of a jQuery object containing every checkbox within the current list. With the variable set, manipulating the checkboxes becomes a matter of checking them if the **check all** checkbox is checked and unchecking them if the **check all** one is unchecked.

These finishing touches can be applied to this checkbox feature by adding a few CSS properties to the **check all** checkbox's label and changing its text to **un-check all** after it has been checked by the user:

```
$(document).ready(function() {
  $('<li></li>')
  .html('<label><input type="checkbox" id="discover-all" /> <em>check
all</em></label>')
  .prependTo('li.discover > ul');
  $('#discover-all').click(function() {
    var $checkboxes = $(this).parents('ul:first').find(':checkbox');
    if (this.checked) {
      $(this).next().text(' un-check all');
      $checkboxes.attr('checked', 'true');
    } else {
      $(this).next().text(' check all');
      $checkboxes.attr('checked', '');
    };
  })
  .parent('label')
  .css({
    borderBottom: '1px solid #ccc',
    color: '#777',
    lineHeight: 2
  });
});
```

The group of checkboxes, along with the **check all** box, now looks like this:

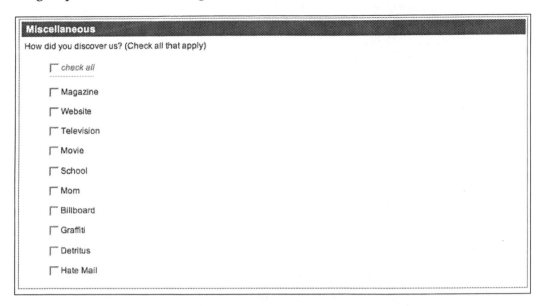

And with the **check all** box checked, looks like this:

The Finished Code

Here it is, the finished code for the contact form:

```
$(document).ready(function() {

  // enhance style of form elements

  $('fieldset').each(function(index) {
    var heading = $('legend', this).remove().text();
    $('<h3></h3>')
    .text(heading)
    .prependTo(this);
  });
```

```
var requiredFlag = ' * ';
var requiredKey = $('input.required:first').next('span').text();
requiredKey = requiredFlag + requiredKey.replace(/^\((.+)\)$/,"$1");
var conditionalFlag = ' ** ';
var conditionalKey =
                    $('input.conditional:first').next('span').text();
conditionalKey = conditionalFlag +
                    conditionalKey.replace(/\((.+)\)/,"$1");

$('form :input').filter('.required')
.next('span').text(requiredFlag).end()
.prev('label').addClass('req-label');

$('form :input').filter('.conditional')
.next('span').text(conditionalFlag);

$('<p></p>')
.addClass('field-keys')
.append(requiredKey + '<br />')
.append(conditionalKey)
.insertBefore('#contact');

// conditional text inputs, checkbox toggle

$('input.conditional').hide().each(function() {
  var $thisInput = $(this);
  var $thisFlag = $thisInput.next('span').hide();
  $thisInput.prev('label').find(':checkbox').click(function() {
    if (this.checked) {
      $thisInput.show().addClass('required');
      $thisFlag.show();
      $(this).parent('label').addClass('req-label');
    } else {
      $thisInput.hide().removeClass('required').blur();
      $thisFlag.hide();
      $(this).parent('label').removeClass('req-label');
    };
  });
});

//validate fields on blur

$('form :input').blur(function() {
  $(this).parents('li:first').removeClass('warning')
```

```
        .find('span.error-message').remove();

    if ($(this).is('.required')) {
      var $listItem = $(this).parents('li:first');
      if (this.value == '') {
        var errorMessage = 'This is a required field';
        if ($(this).is('.conditional')) {
          errorMessage += ', when its related checkbox is checked';
        };
        $('<span></span>')
          .addClass('error-message')
          .text(errorMessage)
          .appendTo($listItem);
        $listItem.addClass('warning');
      };
    };

    if ($(this).is('#email')) {
      var $listItem = $(this).parents('li:first');
      if (this.value != '' && !/.+@.+\.[a-zA-Z]{2,4}$/
                                          .test(this.value)) {
        var errorMessage = 'Please use proper e-mail format'
                              + '(e.g. joe@example.com)';
        $('<span></span>')
          .addClass('error-message')
          .text(errorMessage)
          .appendTo($listItem);
        $listItem.addClass('warning');
      };
    };
  });

//validate form on submit

  $('form').submit(function() {
    $('#submit-message').remove();
    $(':input.required').trigger('blur');
    var numWarnings = $('.warning', this).length;
    if (numWarnings) {
      var fieldList = [];
      $('.warning label').each(function() {
        fieldList.push($(this).text());
      });
      $('<div></div>')
      .attr({
```

```
                'id': 'submit-message',
                'class': 'warning'
            })
            .append('Please correct errors with the following ' +
                                        numWarnings + ' fields:<br />')
            .append('&bull; ' + fieldList.join('<br />&bull; '))
            .insertBefore('#send');
            return false;
        };
    });

    //checkboxes

    $('form :checkbox').removeAttr('checked');

    //checkboxes with (un)check all
    $('<li></li>').html('<label><input type="checkbox" '
                    + ' id="discover-all" /> <em>check all</em>'
                        + '</label>').prependTo('li.discover > ul');
    $('#discover-all')
    .click(function() {
      var $checkboxes = $(this).parents('ul:first').find(':checkbox');
      if (this.checked) {
        $(this).next().text(' un-check all');
        $checkboxes.attr('checked', 'true');
      } else {
        $(this).next().text(' check all');
        $checkboxes.attr('checked', '');
      };
    })
    .parent('label')
    .css({
      borderBottom: '1px solid #ccc',
      color: '#777',
      lineHeight: 2
    });
  });
```

Although we've made significant improvements to the contact form, there is still much that could be done. Validation, for example, comes in a number of varieties. For a flexible validation plug-in, visit the jQuery Plugin Repository at `http://jquery.com/Plugins/`.

Placeholder Text for Fields

Some forms are much simpler than contact forms. In fact, many sites incorporate a single-field form on every single page—a search function for the site. The usual trappings of a form—field labels, submit buttons, and the text—are cumbersome for such a small, single-purpose part of the page. We can use jQuery to help us slim down the form while retaining its functionalities.

The label element for a form field is an essential component of accessible websites. Every field should be labeled, so that screen readers and other assistive devices can identify which field is used for which purpose. Even in the HTML source, the label helps describe the field:

```
<form id="search" action="search/index.php" method="get">
  <label for="search-text">search the site</label>
  <input type="text" name="search-text" id="search-text" />
</form>
```

Without styling, we see the label right before the field:

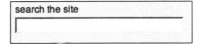

While this doesn't take up much room, in some site layouts even this single line of text might be too much. We could hide the text with CSS, but this then provides the user with no way to know what the field is for. Instead, we can use jQuery to transform this label into placeholder text within the field itself.

To achieve this, when the DOM has loaded, we'll remove the label and use its text to populate the field:

```
$(document).ready(function() {
  var searchLabel = $('#search label').remove().text();
  $('#search-text').addClass('placeholder').val(searchLabel);
});
```

We can remove the label before we retrieve its text, because .remove() yanks an element from the DOM tree without deleting it. This text is then set as the value of the field. The class grays out the text to distinguish it as a placeholder:

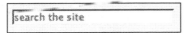

This is a nice effect, but it has an adverse interaction with the search field itself. Since the value of the field has changed, clicking in the field allows the user to append to this value rather than replace it. This could make the search do something unexpected:

To avoid this problem, we need to remove the text when the field gets focus, and replace it when the focus is lost. This is simple enough:

```
$(document).ready(function() {
  var searchLabel = $('#search label').remove().text();
  $('#search-text').addClass('placeholder').val(searchLabel)
                                            .focus(function() {
    if (this.value == searchLabel) {
      $(this).removeClass('placeholder').val('');
    };
  }).blur(function() {
    if (this.value == '') {
      $(this).addClass('placeholder').val(searchLabel);
    };
  });
});
```

When the field gets focus, we test whether the value of the field is still equal to the placeholder text we inserted earlier. If so, we remove the text. This check is important because we don't want to lose any text the user has typed earlier.

When the field loses focus, we perform the opposite procedure. If the user hasn't typed anything, the value of the field will be empty. In this case, we restore the placeholder text that had been present before.

We also remove and add the `placeholder` CSS class, so the text in the field is styled appropriately when the user is typing:

One glitch caused by our enhancement remains; if the form is submitted without user input, the field could still contain the placeholder text. To avoid this, we can remove it when the form is submitted:

```
$('#search').submit(function() {
  if ($('#search-text').val() == searchLabel) {
    $('#search-text').val('');
  }
});
```

Unknown to the server that has provided the initial search interface, we have provided a visual enhancement for users with JavaScript enabled.

AJAX Auto-Completion

We can further spruce up our search field by offering auto-completion of its contents. This feature will allow users to type the beginning of a search term and see all of the possible terms that begin with the typed string. Since the list of terms can be drawn from a database that is driving the site, the user can know that search results are forthcoming if the typed term is used. Also, if the database provides the terms in order of popularity or number of results, the user can be guided to more appropriate searches.

Auto-completion is a very complicated subject, with subtleties introduced by different kinds of user interaction. We will craft a working example here, but cannot in this space explore all of the advanced concepts such as limiting the rate of requests or multi-term completion. The auto-complete plug-in for jQuery is recommended for simple, real-world implementations, and as a starting point for more complex ones. More information on plug-ins can be found in Chapter 10.

The basic idea behind an auto-completion routine is to react to a keystroke, and to send an AJAX request to the server containing the contents of the field in the request. The results will contain a list of possible completions for the field. The script then presents this list as a dropdown below the field.

On the Server

We need some server-side code to handle requests. While a real-world implementation will usually rely on a database to produce a list of possible completions, for this example we can use a simple PHP script with the results built in:

```
<?php
  if (strlen($_REQUEST['search-text']) < 1) {
    print '[]';
```

```
      exit;
    }
    $terms = array(
      'access',
      'action',
      // List continues...
      'xaml',
      'xoops',
    );
    $possibilities = array();
    foreach ($terms as $term) {
      if (strpos($term, strtolower($_REQUEST['search-text'])) === 0) {
        $possibilities[] = "'". str_replace("'", "\\'", $term) ."'";
      }
    }
    print ('['. implode(', ', $possibilities) .']');
```

The page compares the provided string against the beginning of each term, and composes a JSON array of matches.

In the Browser

Now we can make a request to this PHP script from our JavaScript code:

```
$(document).ready(function() {
  var $autocomplete = $('<ul class="autocomplete"></ul>').hide().
insertAfter('#search-text');

  $('#search-text').keyup(function() {
    $.ajax({
      'url': '/bookstore/search/autocomplete.php',
      'data': {'search-text': $('#search-text').val()},
      'dataType': 'json',
      'type': 'POST',
      'success': function(data) {
        if (data.length) {
          $autocomplete.empty();
          $.each(data, function(index, term) {
            $('<li></li>').text(term).appendTo($autocomplete);
          });
          $autocomplete.show();
        }
      }
    });
  });
});
```

We need to use `keyup`, *not* `keydown` or `keypress`, as the event that triggers the AJAX request. The latter two events occur during the process of the key press, before the character has actually been entered in the field. If we attempt to act on these events and issue the request, the suggestion list will lag behind the search text. When the third character is entered, for example, the AJAX request will be made using just the first two characters. By acting on `keyup`, we avoid this problem.

In our stylesheet, we position this list of suggestions absolutely, so that it overlaps the text underneath. Now when we type in the search field, we see our possible terms presented to us:

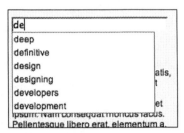

To properly display our list of suggestions, we have to take into account the built-in auto-completion mechanism of some web browsers. Browsers will often remember what users have typed in a form field, and suggest these entries the next time the form is used. This can look confusing when in conjunction with our custom auto-complete suggestions:

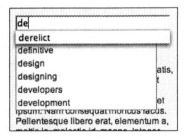

Fortunately, this can be disabled in the browsers that perform auto-completion by setting the `autocomplete` attribute of the form field to `off`. We could do this right in the HTML, but this would not be in keeping with the principle of progressive enhancement. Instead, we can add this attribute from our script:

```
$('#search-text').attr('autocomplete', 'off')
```

Populating the Search Field

Our list of suggestions doesn't do us much good if we can't place them in the search box. To begin with, we'll allow a mouse click to confirm a suggestion:

```
'success': function(data) {
  if (data.length) {
    $autocomplete.empty();
    $.each(data, function(index, term) {
      $('<li></li>').text(term)
      .appendTo($autocomplete).click(function() {
        $('#search-text').val(term);
        $autocomplete.hide();
      });
    });
    $autocomplete.show();
  }
}
```

This modification sets the text of the search box to whatever list item was clicked. We also hide the suggestions after this, since we are done with them.

Keyboard Navigation

Since the user is already at the keyboard typing in the search term, it is very convenient to allow the keyboard to control selection from the suggestion list as well. We'll need to keep track of the currently selected item to enable this. First we can add a helper function that will store the index of the item, and perform the necessary visual effects to reveal which item is currently selected:

```
var selectedItem = null;
var setSelectedItem = function(item) {
  selectedItem = item;
  if (selectedItem === null) {
    $autocomplete.hide();
    return;
  }
  if (selectedItem < 0) {
    selectedItem = 0;
  }
  if (selectedItem >= $autocomplete.find('li').length) {
    selectedItem = $autocomplete.find('li').length - 1;
  }
  $autocomplete.find('li').removeClass('selected')
    .eq(selectedItem).addClass('selected');
  $autocomplete.show();
};
```

The `selectedItem` variable will be set to `null` whenever no item is selected. By always calling `setSelectedItem()` to change the value of the variable, we can be sure that the suggestion list is only visible when there is a selected item.

The two tests for the numeric value of `selectedItem` are present to *clamp* the results to the appropriate range. Without these tests, `selectedItem` could end up with any value, even negative ones. This function ensures that the current value of `selectedItem` is always a valid index in the list of suggestions.

We can now revise our existing code to use the new function:

```
$('#search-text').attr('autocomplete', 'off').keyup(function() {
  $.ajax({
    'url': '/bookstore/search/autocomplete.php',
    'data': {'search-text': $('#search-text').val()},
    'dataType': 'json',
    'type': 'POST',
    'success': function(data) {
      if (data.length) {
        $autocomplete.empty();
        $.each(data, function(index, term) {
          $('<li></li>').text(term)
          .appendTo($autocomplete).mouseover(function() {
            setSelectedItem(index);
          }).click(function() {
            $('#search-text').val(term);
            $autocomplete.hide();
          });
        });

        setSelectedItem(0);
      }
      else {
        setSelectedItem(null);
      }
    }
  });
});
```

This revision has several immediate benefits. First, the suggestion list is hidden when there are no results for a given search. Second, we are able to add a `mouseover` handler that highlights the item under the mouse cursor. Third, the first item is highlighted immediately when the suggestion list is shown:

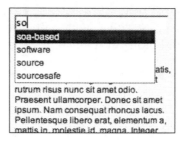

Now we need to allow the keyboard keys to change which item is currently active in the list.

Handling the Arrow Keys

We can use the `keyCode` attribute of the event object to determine which key was pressed. This will allow us to watch for codes 38 and 40, corresponding to the up and down arrow keys, and react accordingly:

```
$('#search-text').attr('autocomplete', 'off').keyup(function(event) {
  if (event.keyCode > 40 || event.keyCode == 8) {
    // Keys with codes 40 and below are special
    //   (enter, arrow keys, escape, etc.).
    // Key code 8 is backspace.
    $.ajax({
      'url': '/bookstore/search/autocomplete.php',
      'data': {'search-text': $('#search-text').val()},
      'dataType': 'json',
      'type': 'POST',
      'success': function(data) {
        if (data.length) {
          $autocomplete.empty();
          $.each(data, function(index, term) {
            $('<li></li>').text(term)
            .appendTo($autocomplete).mouseover(function() {
              setSelectedItem(index);
            }).click(function() {
              $('#search-text').val(term);
              $autocomplete.hide();
            });
```

```
      });

        setSelectedItem(0);
      }
      else {
        setSelectedItem(null);
      }
    }
  });
}
else if (event.keyCode == 38 && selectedItem !== null) {
  // User pressed up arrow.
  setSelectedItem(selectedItem - 1);
  event.preventDefault();
}
else if (event.keyCode == 40 && selectedItem !== null) {
  // User pressed down arrow.
  setSelectedItem(selectedItem + 1);
  event.preventDefault();
}
});
```

Our `keyup` handler now checks the `keyCode` that was sent, and performs the corresponding action. The AJAX requests are now skipped if the pressed key was special, such as an *arrow* key or *escape* key. If an arrow key is detected and the suggestion list is currently displayed, the handler changes the selected item by 1 in the appropriate direction. Since we wrote `setSelectedItem()` to clamp the values to the range of indices possible for the list, we don't have to worry about the user *stepping off* of either end of the list.

Inserting Suggestions in the Field

Next we need to handle the *Enter* key. When the suggestion list is displayed, a press of the *Enter* key should populate the field with the currently selected item. Since we are now going to be doing this in two places, we should factor-out the field population we coded earlier for the mouse button into a separate function:

```
var populateSearchField = function() {
  $('#search-text').val($autocomplete
    .find('li').eq(selectedItem).text());
  setSelectedItem(null);
};
```

Now our `click` handler can be a simple call to this function. We can call this function when handling the *Enter* key as well:

```
$('#search-text').keypress(function(event) {
  if (event.keyCode == 13 && selectedItem !== null) {
    // User pressed enter key.
    populateSearchField();
    event.preventDefault();
  }
});
```

This handler is attached to the `keypress` event, rather than `keyup` as before. We have to make this alteration so that we can prevent the keystroke from submitting the form. If we wait until the `keyup` event is triggered, the submission will already be underway.

Removing the Suggestion List

There's one final tweak we will make to our auto-complete behavior. We should hide the suggestion list when the user decides to do something else on the page. First of all, we can react to the escape key in our `keyup` handler, and let the user dismiss the list that way:

```
else if (event.keyCode == 27 && selectedItem !== null) {
  // User pressed escape key.
  setSelectedItem(null);
}
```

More importantly, we should hide the list when the search field loses focus. A first attempt at this is quite simple:

```
$('#search-text').blur(function(event) {
  setSelectedItem(null);
});
```

However, this causes an unintended side effect. Since a mouse click on the list removes focus from the field, this handler is called and the list is hidden. That means that our `click` handler defined earlier never gets called, and it becomes impossible to interact with the list using the mouse.

There is no easy solution to this problem. The `blur` handler will always be called before the `click` handler. A workaround is to hide the list when the focus is lost, but to wait a fraction of a second first:

```
$('#search-text').blur(function(event) {
  setTimeout(function() {
```

```
      setSelectedItem(null);
   }, 250);
});
```

This gives a chance for the `click` event to get triggered on the list item before the list item is hidden.

Auto-Completion versus Live Search

The earlier example focused on auto-completion of the text field, as it is a technique that applies to many forms. However, for searches in particular an alternative called **live search** is preferred. This feature actually performs the content searches as the user types.

Functionally, auto-completion and live search are very similar. In both cases, key presses initiate an AJAX submission to the server, passing the current field contents along with the request. The results are then placed in a drop-down box below the field. In the case of auto-completion, as we have seen, the results are possible search terms to use. With live search, the results are the actual pages that contain the search terms that have been typed.

On the JavaScript end, the code to build these two features is nearly identical, so we won't go into detail here. Deciding which to use is a matter of tradeoffs; live search provides more information to the user with less effort, but is typically more resource intensive.

The Finished Code

Our completed code for the search field's presentation and auto-complete behaviors is as follows:

```
$(document).ready(function() {
  var searchLabel = $('#search label').remove().text();
  $('#search-text').addClass('placeholder').val(searchLabel)
                                           .focus(function() {
    if (this.value == searchLabel) {
      $(this).removeClass('placeholder').val('');
    };
  }).blur(function() {
    if (this.value == '') {
      $(this).addClass('placeholder').val(searchLabel);
    };
  });
  $('#search').submit(function() {
```

```
      if ($('#search-text').val() == searchLabel) {
        $('#search-text').val('');
      }
    });

  var $autocomplete = $('<ul class="autocomplete"></ul>').hide().
insertAfter('#search-text');
  var selectedItem = null;

  var setSelectedItem = function(item) {
    selectedItem = item;
    if (selectedItem === null) {
      $autocomplete.hide();
      return;
    }
    if (selectedItem < 0) {
      selectedItem = 0;
    }
    if (selectedItem >= $autocomplete.find('li').length) {
      selectedItem = $autocomplete.find('li').length - 1;
    }
    $autocomplete.find('li').removeClass('selected').eq(selectedItem)
                                              .addClass('selected');
    $autocomplete.show();
  };
  var populateSearchField = function() {
    $('#search-text').val($autocomplete.find('li').eq(selectedItem)
                                              .text());
    setSelectedItem(null);
  };
  $('#search-text').attr('autocomplete', 'off').keyup(function(event)
{
    if (event.keyCode > 40 || event.keyCode == 8) {
     // Keys with codes 40 and below are special
     //   (enter, arrow keys, escape, etc.).
     // Key code 8 is backspace.

       $.ajax({
         'url': '/bookstore/search/autocomplete.php',
         'data': {'search-text': $('#search-text').val()},
         'dataType': 'json',
         'type': 'POST',
```

```
          'success': function(data) {
            if (data.length) {
              $autocomplete.empty();
              $.each(data, function(index, term) {
                $('<li></li>').text(term).appendTo($autocomplete)
                                          .mouseover(function() {
                  setSelectedItem(index);
                }).click(populateSearchField);
              });

              setSelectedItem(0);
            }
            else {
              setSelectedItem(null);
            }
          }
        });
    }
    else if (event.keyCode == 38 && selectedItem !== null) {
      // User pressed up arrow.
      setSelectedItem(selectedItem - 1);
      event.preventDefault();
    }
    else if (event.keyCode == 40 && selectedItem !== null) {
      // User pressed down arrow.
      setSelectedItem(selectedItem + 1);
      event.preventDefault();
    }
    else if (event.keyCode == 27 && selectedItem !== null) {
      // User pressed escape key.
      setSelectedItem(null);
    }
  }).keypress(function(event) {
    if (event.keyCode == 13 && selectedItem !== null) {
      // User pressed enter key.
      populateSearchField();
      event.preventDefault();
    }
  }).blur(function(event) {
    setTimeout(function() {
      setSelectedItem(null);
    }, 250);
  });
});
```

Input Masking

We've now looked at several form features that apply to textual inputs from the user. Often, though, our forms are primarily numeric in content. There are several more form enhancements we can make when we are dealing with numbers as form values.

In our bookstore site, a prime candidate for a numeric form is the shopping cart. We need to allow the user to update quantities of items being purchased, and we also need to present numeric data back to the user for prices and totals.

Shopping Cart Table Structure

The HTML for the shopping cart will describe one of the more involved table structures we have seen so far:

```html
<form action="checkout.php" method="post">
  <table id="cart">
    <thead>
      <tr>
        <th class="item">Item</th>
        <th class="quantity">Quantity</th>
        <th class="price">Price</th>
        <th class="cost">Total</th>
      </tr>
    </thead>
    <tfoot>
      <tr class="subtotal">
        <td class="item">Subtotal</td>
        <td class="quantity"></td>
        <td class="price"></td>
        <td class="cost">$152.95</td>
      </tr>
      <tr class="tax">
        <td class="item">Tax</td>
        <td class="quantity"></td>
        <td class="price">6%</td>
        <td class="cost">$9.18</td>
      </tr>
      <tr class="shipping">
        <td class="item">Shipping</td>
        <td class="quantity">5</td>
        <td class="price">$2 per item</td>
        <td class="cost">$10.00</td>
      </tr>
      <tr class="total">
```

```
          <td class="item">Total</td>
          <td class="quantity"></td>
          <td class="price"></td>
          <td class="cost">$172.13</td>
        </tr>
        <tr class="actions">
          <td></td>
          <td><input type="button" name="recalculate"
                        value="Recalculate" id="recalculate" /></td>
          <td></td>
          <td><input type="submit" name="submit"
                        value="Place Order" id="submit" /></td>
        </tr>
      </tfoot>
      <tbody>
        <tr>
          <td class="item">Building Telephony Systems With Asterisk</td>
          <td class="quantity"><input type="text" name="quantity-2"
                        value="1" id="quantity-2" maxlength="3" /></td>
          <td class="price">$26.99</td>
          <td class="cost">$26.99</td>
        </tr>
        <tr>
          <td class="item">Smarty PHP Template Programming and
                                                Applications</td>
          <td class="quantity"><input type="text" name="quantity-1"
                        value="2" id="quantity-1" maxlength="3" /></td>
          <td class="price">$35.99</td>
          <td class="cost">$71.98</td>
        </tr>
        <tr>
          <td class="item">Creating your MySQL Database: Practical
                                        Design Tips and Techniques</td>
          <td class="quantity"><input type="text" name="quantity-3"
                        value="1" id="quantity-3" maxlength="3" /></td>
          <td class="price">$17.99</td>
          <td class="cost">$17.99</td>
        </tr>
        <tr>
          <td class="item">Drupal: Creating Blogs, Forums, Portals, and
                                        Community Websites</td>
          <td class="quantity"><input type="text" name="quantity-4"
                        value="1" id="quantity-4" maxlength="3" /></td>
          <td class="price">$35.99</td>
          <td class="cost">$35.99</td>
        </tr>
      </tbody>
    </table>
  </form>
```

This table introduces another element rarely seen in the world, `<tfoot>`. Like `<thead>`, this element groups a set of table rows. Note that though the element comes before the table body, it is presented after the body when the page is rendered:

Item	Quantity	Price	Total
Building Telephony Systems With Asterisk	1	$26.99	$26.99
Smarty PHP Template Programming and Applications	2	$35.99	$71.98
Creating your MySQL Database: Practical Design Tips and Techniques	1	$17.99	$17.99
Drupal: Creating Blogs, Forums, Portals, and Community Websites	1	$35.99	$35.99
Subtotal			$152.95
Tax		6%	$9.18
Shipping	5	$2 per item	$10.00
Total			$172.13
		Recalculate	Place Order

This source code ordering, while non-intuitive to designers thinking visually about the table rendering, is useful to those with visual impairments. When the table is read aloud by assistive devices, the footer is read before the potentially long content, allowing the user to get a summary of what is to come.

We've also placed a class on each cell of the table, identifying which column of the table contains that cell. In the previous chapter, we demonstrated some ways to find cells in a column by looking at the index of the cell within its row. Here, we'll make a tradeoff and allow the JavaScript code to be simpler by making the HTML source a bit more complex. With a class identifying the column of each cell, our selectors can become a bit more straightforward.

Before we proceed with manipulating the form fields, we will apply our standard row striping code to spruce up the table's appearance:

```
$(document).ready(function() {
  $('#cart tbody tr:even').addClass('even');
  $('#cart tbody tr:odd').addClass('odd');
});
```

Once again, we make sure to only select rows to color if they are in the body of
the table:

Item	Quantity	Price	Total
Building Telephony Systems With Asterisk	1	$26.99	$26.99
Smarty PHP Template Programming and Applications	2	$35.99	$71.98
Creating your MySQL Database: Practical Design Tips and Techniques	1	$17.99	$17.99
Drupal: Creating Blogs, Forums, Portals, and Community Websites	1	$35.99	$35.99
Subtotal			$152.95
Tax		6%	$9.18
Shipping	5	$2 per item	$10.00
Total			$172.13
		Recalculate	Place Order

Rejecting Non-numeric Input

When improving the contact form, we discussed some input validation techniques.
With JavaScript, we verified that what the user typed matched what we were
expecting, so that we could provide feedback before the form was even sent to the
server. Now we'll examine the counterpart to input validation, called **input masking**.

Input validation checks what the user has typed against some criteria for valid
inputs. Input masking applies criteria to the entries while they are being typed in
the first place, and simply disallows invalid keystrokes. In the example of our
shopping-cart form, for example, the input fields must contain only numbers. Input
masking code can cause any key that is not a number to do nothing when one of
these fields is in focus:

```
$('.quantity input').keypress(function(event) {
  if (event.charCode && (event.charCode < 48 || event.charCode > 57))
  {
    event.preventDefault();
  }
});
```

When catching keystrokes for our search field's auto-completion function, we
watched the `keyup` event. This allowed us to examine the `.keyCode` property of the
event, which told us which key on the keyboard was pressed. Here, we observe the
`keypress` event instead. This event does not have a `.keyCode` property, but instead
offers the `.charCode` property. This property reports the actual ASCII character that
is represented by the keystroke that just occurred.

If the keystroke results in a character (that is, it is not an arrow key, delete, or some other editing function) and that character is not in the range of ASCII codes that represent numerals, then we call `.preventDefault()` on the event. As we have seen before, this stops the browser from acting on the event; in this case, that means that the character is never inserted into the field. Now every one of the **quantity** fields can accept only numbers.

Numeric Calculations

Now we'll move on to some manipulation of the actual numbers the user will enter in the shopping cart form. We have a **Recalculate** button on the form, which would cause the form to be submitted to the server, where new totals can be calculated and the form can be presented again to the user. This requires a round trip that is not necessary, though; all of this work can be done on the browser side using jQuery.

The simplest calculation on this form is for the cell in the **Shipping** row that displays the total quantity of items ordered. When the user modifies a quantity in one of the rows, we want to add up all of the entered values to produce a new total and display this total in the cell:

```
$('.quantity input').change(function() {
  var totalQuantity = 0;
  $('.quantity input').each(function() {
    var quantity = parseInt(this.value);
    totalQuantity += quantity;
  });
  $('.shipping .quantity').text(String(totalQuantity));
});
```

We have several choices for which event to watch for this recalculation operation. We could observe the `keyup` event, and fire the recalculation with each keystroke. We could also observe the `blur` event, which is triggered each time the user leaves the field. Here we can be a little more conservative with CPU usage, though, and only perform our calculations when the `change` event is triggered. This way we recalculate the totals only if the user leaves the field with a different value than it had before.

The total quantity is calculated using a simple `.each` loop. The `.value` property of a field will report the string representation of the field's value, so we use the built-in `parseInt` function to convert this into an integer for our calculation. This practice can avoid strange situations in which addition is interpreted as string concatenation, since the two operations use the same symbol. Conversely, we need a string to pass to jQuery's `.text` method when displaying the calculation's result, so we use the `String` function to build a new one using our calculated total quantity.

Changing a quantity now updates the total automatically:

Item	Quantity	Price	Total
Building Telephony Systems With Asterisk	11	$26.99	$26.99
Smarty PHP Template Programming and Applications	2	$35.99	$71.98
Creating your MySQL Database: Practical Design Tips and Techniques	1	$17.99	$17.99
Drupal: Creating Blogs, Forums, Portals, and Community Websites	1	$35.99	$35.99
Subtotal			$152.95
Tax		6%	$9.18
Shipping	15	$2 per item	$10.00
Total			$172.13

Recalculate   Place Order

Parsing and Formatting Currency

Now we can move on to the totals in the right-hand column. Each row's total cost should be calculated by multiplying the quantity entered by the price of that item. Since we're now performing multiple tasks for each row, we can begin by refactoring the quantity calculations a bit to be row-based rather than field-based:

```
$('#cart tbody tr').each(function() {
  var quantity = parseInt($('.quantity input', this).val());
  totalQuantity += quantity;
});
```

This produces the same result as before, but we now have a convenient place to insert our total cost calculation for each row:

```
$('.quantity input').change(function() {
  var totalQuantity = 0;
  $('#cart tbody tr').each(function() {
    var price = parseFloat($('.price', this).text()
                                    .replace(/^[^\d.]*/, ''));
    price = isNaN(price) ? 0 : price;
    var quantity = parseInt($('.quantity input', this).val());
    var cost = quantity * price;
    $('.cost', this).text('$' + cost);
    totalQuantity += quantity;
  });
  $('.shipping .quantity').text(String(totalQuantity));
});
```

We fetch the price of each item out of the table using the same technique we needed when sorting tables by price earlier. The regular expression first strips the currency symbols off from the front of the value, and the resulting string is then sent to `parseFloat()`, which interprets the value as a floating-point number. Since we will be doing calculations with the result, we need to check that a number was found, and set the price to `0` if not. Finally, we multiply the cost by the quantity, and place the result in the total column with a `$` preceding it. We can now see our total calculations in action:

Item	Quantity	Price	Total
Building Telephony Systems With Asterisk	11	$26.99	$296.89
Smarty PHP Template Programming and Applications	3	$35.99	$107.97
Creating your MySQL Database: Practical Design Tips and Techniques	1	$17.99	$17.99
Drupal: Creating Blogs, Forums, Portals, and Community Websites	1	$35.99	$35.99
Subtotal			$152.95
Tax		6%	$9.18
Shipping	16	$2 per item	$10.00
Total			$172.13
	Recalculate		Place Order

Dealing with Decimal Places

Though we have placed dollar signs in front of our totals, JavaScript is not aware that we are dealing with monetary values. As far as the computer is concerned, these are just numbers, and should be displayed as such. This means that if the total ends in a zero after the decimal point, this will be chopped off:

Item	Quantity	Price	Total
Building Telephony Systems With Asterisk	11	$26.99	$296.89
Smarty PHP Template Programming and Applications	30	$35.99	$1079.7
Creating your MySQL Database: Practical Design Tips and Techniques	1	$17.99	$17.99
Drupal: Creating Blogs, Forums, Portals, and Community Websites	1	$35.99	$35.99
Subtotal			$152.95
Tax		6%	$9.18
Shipping	43	$2 per item	$10.00
Total			$172.13
	Recalculate		Place Order

Even worse, the precision limitations of JavaScript can sometimes lead to rounding errors. These can make the calculations appear to be completely broken:

Item	Quantity	Price	Total
Building Telephony Systems With Asterisk	11	$26.99	$296.89
Smarty PHP Template Programming and Applications	30	$35.99	$1079.7
Creating your MySQL Database: Practical Design Tips and Techniques	10	$17.99	$179.89999999999998
Drupal: Creating Blogs, Forums, Portals, and Community Websites	1	$35.99	$35.99
Subtotal			$152.95
Tax		6%	$9.18
Shipping	52	$2 per item	$10.00
Total			$172.13
	Recalculate		Place Order

Fortunately, the fix for both problems is simple. JavaScript's Number class has several methods to deal with this sort of issue, and .toFixed() fits the bill here. This method takes a number of decimal places as a parameter, and returns a string representing the floating-point number rounded to that many decimal places:

```
$('#cart tbody tr').each(function() {
  var price = parseFloat($('.price', this).text()
                                    .replace(/^[^\d.]*/, ''));
  price = isNaN(price) ? 0 : price;
  var quantity = parseInt($('.quantity input', this).val());
  var cost = quantity * price;
  $('.cost', this).text('$' + cost.toFixed(2));
  totalQuantity += quantity;
});
```

Now our totals all look like normal monetary values:

Item	Quantity	Price	Total
Building Telephony Systems With Asterisk	11	$26.99	$296.89
Smarty PHP Template Programming and Applications	30	$35.99	$1079.70
Creating your MySQL Database: Practical Design Tips and Techniques	10	$17.99	$179.90
Drupal: Creating Blogs, Forums, Portals, and Community Websites	1	$35.99	$35.99
Subtotal			$152.95
Tax		6%	$9.18
Shipping	52	$2 per item	$10.00
Total			$172.13

Recalculate   Place Order

Other Calculations

The rest of the calculations on the page follow a similar pattern. For the subtotal, we can add up our totals for each row as they are calculated, and display the result using the same currency formatting as before:

```
$('.quantity input').change(function() {
  var totalQuantity = 0;
  var totalCost = 0;
  $('#cart tbody tr').each(function() {
    var price = parseFloat($('.price', this).text()
                                  .replace(/^[^\d.*/, ''));
    price = isNaN(price) ? 0 : price;
    var quantity = parseInt($('.quantity input', this).val());
    var cost = quantity * price;
    $('.cost', this).text('$' + cost.toFixed(2));
    totalQuantity += quantity;
    totalCost += cost;
  });
  $('.shipping .quantity').text(String(totalQuantity));
  $('.subtotal .cost').text('$' + totalCost.toFixed(2));
});
```

Item	Quantity	Price	Total
Building Telephony Systems With Asterisk	11	$26.99	$296.89
Smarty PHP Template Programming and Applications	1	$35.99	$35.99
Creating your MySQL Database: Practical Design Tips and Techniques	10	$17.99	$179.90
Drupal: Creating Blogs, Forums, Portals, and Community Websites	1	$35.99	$35.99
Subtotal			$548.77
Tax		6%	$9.18
Shipping	23	$2 per item	$10.00
Total			$172.13
	Recalculate		Place Order

Rounding Values

To calculate `tax`, we need to divide the figure given by 100 and then multiply the `taxRate` by the subtotal. Tax is always rounded up, however, so we must ensure that the correct value is used both for display and for later calculations. JavaScript's `Math.ceil` function can round a number up to the nearest integer, but since we are dealing with dollars and cents we need to be a bit trickier:

```
var taxRate = parseFloat($('.tax .price').text()) / 100;
var tax = Math.ceil(totalCost * taxRate * 100) / 100;
$('.tax .cost').text('$' + tax.toFixed(2));
totalCost += tax;
```

The tax is multiplied by 100 first so that it becomes a value in cents, not dollars. This can then be rounded safely by `Math.ceil()` and then divided by 100 to convert it back into dollars. Finally `.toFixed()` is called as before to produce the correct result:

Item	Quantity	Price	Total
Building Telephony Systems With Asterisk	3	$26.99	$80.97
Smarty PHP Template Programming and Applications	1	$35.99	$35.99
Creating your MySQL Database: Practical Design Tips and Techniques	2	$17.99	$35.98
Drupal: Creating Blogs, Forums, Portals, and Community Websites	1	$35.99	$35.99
Subtotal			$188.93
Tax		6%	$11.34
Shipping	7	$2 per item	$10.00
Total			$172.13
	Recalculate		Place Order

Finishing Touches

The shipping calculation is simpler than tax, since no rounding is involved. The shipping rate is just multiplied by the number of items to determine the total:

```
$('.shipping .quantity').text(String(totalQuantity));
var shippingRate = parseFloat($('.shipping .price')
  .text().replace(/^[^\d.]*/, ''));
var shipping = totalQuantity * shippingRate;
$('.shipping .cost').text('$' + shipping.toFixed(2));
totalCost += shipping;
```

Item	Quantity	Price	Total
Building Telephony Systems With Asterisk	3	$26.99	$80.97
Smarty PHP Template Programming and Applications	1	$35.99	$35.99
Creating your MySQL Database: Practical Design Tips and Techniques	2	$17.99	$35.98
Drupal: Creating Blogs, Forums, Portals, and Community Websites	2	$35.99	$71.98
Subtotal			$224.92
Tax		6%	$13.50
Shipping	8	$2 per item	$16.00
Total			$172.13
	Recalculate		Place Order

We have been keeping track of the grand total as we have gone along, so all we need to do for this last cell is to format totalCost appropriately:

```
$('.total .cost').text('$' + totalCost.toFixed(2));
```

Item	Quantity	Price	Total
Building Telephony Systems With Asterisk	1	$26.99	$26.99
Smarty PHP Template Programming and Applications	2	$35.99	$71.98
Creating your MySQL Database: Practical Design Tips and Techniques	2	$17.99	$35.98
Drupal: Creating Blogs, Forums, Portals, and Community Websites	2	$35.99	$71.98
Subtotal			$206.93
Tax		6%	$12.42
Shipping	7	$2 per item	$14.00
Total			$233.35
	Recalculate		Place Order

Now we have completely replicated any server-side calculations that would occur, so we can safely hide the **Recalculate** button:

```
$('#recalculate').hide();
```

Item	Quantity	Price	Total
Building Telephony Systems With Asterisk	1	$26.99	$26.99
Smarty PHP Template Programming and Applications	2	$35.99	$71.98
Creating your MySQL Database: Practical Design Tips and Techniques	1	$17.99	$17.99
Drupal: Creating Blogs, Forums, Portals, and Community Websites	2	$35.99	$71.98
Subtotal			$188.94
Tax		6%	$11.34
Shipping	6	$2 per item	$12.00
Total			$212.28
			Place Order

This change once again echoes our **progressive enhancement** principle: Ensure that the page works properly without JavaScript first, then use jQuery to perform the same task more elegantly when possible.

Deleting Items

If shoppers on our site change their minds about items they have added to their carts, they can change the **Quantity** field for those items to 0. We can provide a more reassuring behavior, though, by adding explicit **Delete** buttons for each item. The actual effect of the button can be the same as changing the **Quantity** field, but the visual feedback can reinforce the fact that the item will not be purchased.

First, we need to add the new buttons. Since they won't function without JavaScript, we won't put them in the HTML. Instead, we'll let jQuery add them to each row:

```
$('<th> </th>').insertAfter('#cart thead th:nth-child(2)');
$('#cart tbody tr').each(function() {
  $deleteButton = $('<img />').attr({
    'width': '16',
    'height': '16',
    'src': '../icons/cross.png',
    'alt': 'remove from cart',
    'title': 'remove from cart',
    'class': 'clickable'
  });
```

```
    $('<td></td>').insertAfter($('td:nth-child(2)', this))
      .append($deleteButton);
});
$('<td> </td>').insertAfter('#cart tfoot td:nth-child(2)');
```

We need to create empty cells in the header and footer rows as placeholders so that the columns of the table still line up correctly. The buttons are created and added on the body rows only:

Item	Quantity		Price	Total
Building Telephony Systems With Asterisk	3	✖	$26.99	$80.97
Smarty PHP Template Programming and Applications	2	✖	$35.99	$71.98
Creating your MySQL Database: Practical Design Tips and Techniques	1	✖	$17.99	$17.99
Drupal: Creating Blogs, Forums, Portals, and Community Websites	1	✖	$35.99	$35.99
Subtotal				$206.93
Tax			6%	$12.42
Shipping	7		$2 per item	$14.00
Total				$233.35
				Place Order

Now we need to make the buttons do something. We can change the button definition to add a click handler:

```
$deleteButton = $('<img />').attr({
  'width': '16',
  'height': '16',
  'src': '../icons/cross.png',
  'alt': 'remove from cart',
  'title': 'remove from cart',
  'class': 'clickable'
}).click(function() {
  $(this).parents('tr').find('.quantity input').val(0);
});
```

The handler finds the quantity field in the same row as the button, and sets the value to 0. Now the field is updated, but the calculations are out of sync:

Item	Quantity		Price	Total
Building Telephony Systems With Asterisk	3	✗	$26.99	$80.97
Smarty PHP Template Programming and Applications	0	✗	$35.99	$71.98
Creating your MySQL Database: Practical Design Tips and Techniques	1	✗	$17.99	$17.99
Drupal: Creating Blogs, Forums, Portals, and Community Websites	1	✗	$35.99	$35.99
Subtotal				$206.93
Tax			6%	$12.42
Shipping	7		$2 per item	$14.00
Total				$233.35
				Place Order

We need to trigger the calculation as if the user had manually changed the field value:

```
$deleteButton = $('<img />').attr({
  'width': '16',
  'height': '16',
  'src': '../icons/cross.png',
  'alt': 'remove from cart',
  'title': 'remove from cart',
  'class': 'clickable'
}).click(function() {
  $(this).parents('tr').find('.quantity input')
    .val(0).trigger('change');
});
```

Now the totals update when the button is clicked:

Item	Quantity		Price	Total
Building Telephony Systems With Asterisk	3	✕	$26.99	$80.97
Smarty PHP Template Programming and Applications	0	✕	$35.99	$0.00
Creating your MySQL Database: Practical Design Tips and Techniques	1	✕	$17.99	$17.99
Drupal: Creating Blogs, Forums, Portals, and Community Websites	1	✕	$35.99	$35.99
Subtotal				$134.95
Tax			6%	$8.10
Shipping	5		$2 per item	$10.00
Total				**$153.05**
				Place Order

Now for the visual feedback. We'll hide the row that was just clicked, so that the item is clearly removed from the cart:

```
$deleteButton = $('<img />').attr({
  'width': '16',
  'height': '16',
  'src': '../icons/cross.png',
  'alt': 'remove from cart',
  'title': 'remove from cart',
  'class': 'clickable'
}).click(function() {
  $(this).parents('tr').find('.quantity input')
    .val(0).trigger('change')
  .end().hide();
});
```

Item	Quantity		Price	Total
Building Telephony Systems With Asterisk	3	✕	$26.99	$80.97
Creating your MySQL Database: Practical Design Tips and Techniques	1	✕	$17.99	$17.99
Drupal: Creating Blogs, Forums, Portals, and Community Websites	1	✕	$35.99	$35.99
Subtotal				$134.95
Tax			6%	$8.10
Shipping	5		$2 per item	$10.00
Total				**$153.05**
				Place Order

While the row is hidden, the field is still present on the form. This means it will be submitted with the rest of the form, and the item will be removed on the server side at that time.

Our row striping has been disturbed by the removal of this row. To correct this, we can first move our existing striping code into a function so that we can call it again later:

```
var stripe = function() {
  $('#cart tbody tr:visible:even').removeClass('odd')
                                        .addClass('even');
  $('#cart tbody tr:visible:odd').removeClass('even')
                                      .addClass('odd');
};
stripe();
```

At the same time, we have modified the code to exclude invisible rows from the calculation of odd and even row numbers, and have made sure to remove the odd class when applying even and vice versa. Now we can call this function again after removing a row:

```
$deleteButton = $('<img />').attr({
  'width': '16',
  'height': '16',
  'src': '../icons/cross.png',
  'alt': 'remove from cart',
  'title': 'remove from cart',
  'class': 'clickable'
}).click(function() {
  $(this).parents('tr').find('.quantity input')
    .val(0).trigger('change')
  .end().hide();
  stripe();
});
```

The deleted row has now seamlessly disappeared:

Item	Quantity		Price	Total
Building Telephony Systems With Asterisk	3	✕	$26.99	$80.97
Creating your MySQL Database: Practical Design Tips and Techniques	1	✕	$17.99	$17.99
Drupal: Creating Blogs, Forums, Portals, and Community Websites	1	✕	$35.99	$35.99
Subtotal				$134.95
Tax			6%	$8.10
Shipping		5	$2 per item	$10.00
Total				$153.05
				Place Order

This completes yet another enhancement using jQuery that is completely transparent to the code on the server. As far as the server is concerned, the user just typed a **0** in the input field, but to the user this is a distinct *remove* operation that is different than changing a quantity.

Editing Shipping Information

The shopping cart page also has a form for shipping information. Actually, it isn't a form at all when the page loads, and without JavaScript enabled, it remains a little box tucked away on the right side of the content area, containing a link to a page where the user can edit the shipping information:

But with JavaScript turned on, and with the power of jQuery at our disposal, we can turn this little link into a full-fledged form. We'll do this by requesting the form from a PHP page. Typically the data populating the form would be stored in a database of some sort, but for the purpose of this demonstration, we'll just keep some static data in a PHP array.

To retrieve the form and make it appear inside the **Shipping to** box, we use the `$.get` method inside the `.click` event handler:

```
$(document).ready(function() {
  $('#shipping-name').click(function() {
```

```
    $.get('shipping.php', function(data) {
      $('#shipping-name').remove();
      $(data).hide().appendTo('#shipping').slideDown();
    });
    return false;
  });
});
```

In the callback of the `$.get` method we remove the name that was just clicked and in its place append the form and its data from `shipping.php`. We then add `return false` so that the default event for the clicked link (loading the page indicated in the `href` attribute) does not occur. Now the **Shipping to** box is an editable form:

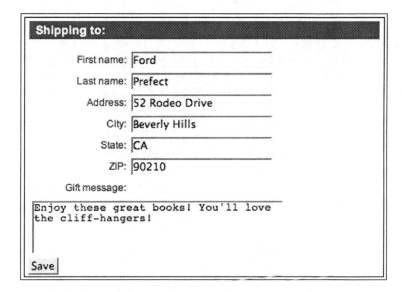

The user can now edit the shipping information without leaving the page.

The next step is to *hijack* the form submission and post the edited data back to the server with jQuery. We start by serializing the data in the form and storing it in a `postData` variable. Then we post the data back to the server using `shipping.php` once again:

```
$(document).ready(function() {
  $('shipping form').submit(function() {
    var postData = $('#shipping :input').serialize();
    $.post('shipping.php', postData);
    return false;
  };
});
```

It makes sense for the form to be removed at this point and for the **Shipping to** box to return to its original state. We can achieve this in the callback of the $.post method that we just used:

```
$(document).ready(function() {
  $('#shipping form').submit(function() {
    var postData = $('#shipping :input').serialize();
    $.post('shipping.php', postData, function(data) {
      $('#shipping form').remove();
      $(data).appendTo('#shipping');
    });
    return false;
  };
});
```

The only problem is that this is not going to work. The way we have it set up now, the .submit event handler is being bound to the **Shipping to** form as soon as the DOM is loaded, but the form is not in the DOM until the user clicks on the **Shipping to** name. The event can't be bound to something that doesn't exist.

To overcome this problem, we can put the form-creation code into a function called editShipping and the form-submission or form-removal code into a function called saveShipping. Then we can bind the saveShipping function in the callback of $.get(), after the form has been created. Likewise, we can bind the editShipping function both when the DOM is ready and when the **Edit shipping** link is re-created in the callback of $.post():

```
$(document).ready(function() {
  var editShipping = function() {
    $.get('shipping.php', function(data) {
      $('#shipping-name').remove();
      $(data).hide().appendTo('#shipping').slideDown();
      $('#shipping form').submit(saveShipping);
    });
    return false;
  };
  var saveShipping = function() {
    var postData = $('#shipping :input').serialize();
    $.post('shipping.php', postData, function(data) {
      $('#shipping form').remove();
      $(data).appendTo('#shipping');
      $('#shipping-name').click(editShipping);
    });
    return false;
  };
  $('#shipping-name').click(editShipping);
});
```

The code has formed a circular pattern of sorts, in which one function allows for the other by rebinding their respective event handlers.

The Finished Code

Taken together, the code for the shopping cart page is a mere 79 lines—quite small considering the functionality it accomplishes, but especially so when we take into account the breezy style that the code has acquired for optimum readability. Because of jQuery's chainability, many of the lines could have been merged were we particularly concerned with number of lines. At any rate, here is the finished code for the shopping cart page, which concludes this chapter on forms:

```
$(document).ready(function() {
  // shopping cart
  var stripe = function() {
    $('#cart tbody tr:visible:even').removeClass('odd')
                                    .addClass('even');
    $('#cart tbody tr:visible:odd').removeClass('even')
                                   .addClass('odd');
  };
  stripe();
  $('#recalculate').hide();
  $('.quantity input').keypress(function(event) {
    if (event.charCode && (event.charCode < 48 ||
                                 event.charCode > 57)) {
      event.preventDefault();
    }
  }).change(function() {
    var totalQuantity = 0;
    var totalCost = 0;
    $('#cart tbody tr').each(function() {
      var price = parseFloat($('.price', this).text()
                                     .replace(/^[^\d.]*/, ''));
      price = isNaN(price) ? 0 : price;
      var quantity = parseInt($('.quantity input', this).val());
      var cost = quantity * price;
      $('.cost', this).text('$' + cost.toFixed(2));
      totalQuantity += quantity;
      totalCost += cost;
    });
    $('.subtotal .cost').text('$' + totalCost.toFixed(2));
    var taxRate = parseFloat($('.tax .price').text()) / 100;
    var tax = Math.ceil(totalCost * taxRate * 100) / 100;
    $('.tax .cost').text('$' + tax.toFixed(2));
```

```
      totalCost += tax;
      $('.shipping .quantity').text(String(totalQuantity));
      var shippingRate = parseFloat($('.shipping .price').text()
                                     .replace(/^[^\d.]*/, ''));
      var shipping = totalQuantity * shippingRate;
      $('.shipping .cost').text('$' + shipping.toFixed(2));
      totalCost += shipping;
      $('.total .cost').text('$' + totalCost.toFixed(2));
    });


    $('<th> </th>').insertAfter('#cart thead th:nth-child(2)');
    $('#cart tbody tr').each(function() {
      $deleteButton = $('<img />').attr({
        'width': '16',
        'height': '16',
        'src': '../icons/cross.png',
        'alt': 'remove from cart',
        'title': 'remove from cart',
        'class': 'clickable'
      }).click(function() {
        $(this).parents('tr').find('.quantity input')
          .val(0).trigger('change')
        .end().hide();
        stripe();
      });
      $('<td></td>').insertAfter($('td:nth-child(2)', this))
                                        .append($deleteButton);
    });
    $('<td> </td>').insertAfter('#cart tfoot td:nth-child(2)');
  });


  //edit shipping information

  $(document).ready(function() {
    var editShipping = function() {
      $.get('shipping.php', function(data) {
        $('#shipping-name').remove();
        $(data).hide().appendTo('#shipping').slideDown();
        $('#shipping form').submit(saveShipping);
      });
      return false;
    };
    var saveShipping = function() {
      var postData = $('#shipping :input').serialize();
```

```
    $.post('shipping.php', postData, function(data) {
      $('#shipping form').remove();
      $(data).appendTo('#shipping');
      $('#shipping-name').click(editShipping);
    });
    return false;
  };
  $('#shipping-name').click(editShipping);
});
```

Summary

In this chapter we have investigated ways to improve the appearance and behavior of common HTML form elements. We have learned about enhancing the styling of forms while leaving the original markup semantic, conditionally hiding and showing fields based on other field values, and validating field contents both before submission and during data entry. We have covered features like AJAX auto-completion for text fields, allowing only specific characters to be entered in a field, and performing calculations on numeric values in fields. We have also learned to submit forms using AJAX rather than a page refresh.

The form element is often the glue that holds an interactive site together. With jQuery, we can easily improve the user's experience in filling out forms while still preserving their utility and flexibility.

9

Shufflers and Rotators

Spin that wheel
Go along for the ride
— Devo,
"Spin the Wheel"

It's not enough anymore to craft literary masterpieces on the web. People clamor for more. They want the words to move. They want pretty pictures on demand. They want **Shufflers** and **Rotators**! In this third and final how-to chapter, we'll use advanced animations, ultra-hip AJAX, and superfluous eye candy in an attempt to give the people what they want and really shuffle things around.

Headline Rotator

For our first rotator example, we'll take a news feed and scroll the headlines, along with an excerpt of the article, one at a time into view. Unlike with the typical news ticker, however, each news item will scroll up, not across. Then it will pause for a few seconds before it continues up and out of sight while the next one scrolls into view.

Setting Up the Page

At its most basic level, this feature is not very difficult to implement. But as we will soon see, making it production-ready requires a bit of finesse.

We begin, as usual, with a chunk of HTML. We'll place the news feed in the sidebar of the page:

```
<div id="sidebar">

  <!-- Code continues... -->
```

```
      <h3>Recent News</h3>
      <div id="news-feed">
       <a href=news/index.html>News Releases</a>
      </div>
    </div>
```

So far, the news-feed `<div>` contains only a single link to the main news page. This is our **fall back** position, in case the user does not have JavaScript enabled. The content we'll be working with will come from an actual RSS feed instead.

The CSS for this `<div>` is important, as it will determine not only how much of each news item will be shown at a time, but also where on the page the news items will appear. Together with the style rule for the individual news items, the CSS looks like this:

```
#news-feed {
  position: relative;
  height: 200px;
  width: 17em;
  overflow: hidden;
}
.headline {
  position: absolute;
  height: 200px;
  top: 210px;
  overflow: hidden;
}
```

Notice here that the `height` of both the individual news items (represented by the `headline` class) and their container is `200px`. Also, since `.headline` is absolutely positioned relative to `#news-feed`, we're able to set the top of the news items just below the bottom edge of their container. That way, when we set `#news-feed` to `overflow:hidden`, we effectively hide the news items in their initial position.

Setting the news items to `position:absolute` is necessary for another reason as well; for any element to have its position animated on the page, it must have either `absolute` or `relative` positioning, rather than the default static positioning.

Now that we have the HTML and CSS in place, we can inject the news items from an RSS feed. To start, we'll wrap the code in a `.each()` method, which will act as an `if` statement of sorts and contain the code inside a private namespace:

```
$(document).ready(function() {
  $('#news-feed').each(function() {
    $(this).empty();
  });
});
```

There are two possible results when we use the selector #news-feed to create a jQuery object. The factory function could make a jQuery object matching one unique element with the news-feed ID, or it could find no elements on the page with that ID and produce an empty jQuery object. The .each() call takes care of executing the contained code only if the jQuery object is non-empty.

Immediately following the .each(), the news feed <div> is emptied to make it ready for its new content.

Retrieving the Feed

To retrieve the feed, we'll use the $.get() method, one of jQuery's many utility functions for communicating with the server. For more information on $.get() and other AJAX methods, see Chapter 6.

The content of the feed is passed in the first argument (data) as an XML structure, which, in turn, is used as the context for a selector:

```
$(document).ready(function() {
  $('#news-feed').each(function() {
    $(this).empty();

    $.get('news/feed.xml', function(data) {
      $('/rss//item', data).each(function() {

      // Code continues...

      });
    });
  });
});
```

We can use another .each() method for the items in the feed to combine the parts of each item into a usable block of HTML markup. To start, we build the links:

```
$(document).ready(function() {
  $('#news-feed').each(function() {
    $(this).empty();

    $.get('news/feed.xml', function(data) {
      $('/rss//item', data).each(function() {
        var title = $('title', this).text();
        var linkText = $('link', this).text();
        var $link = $('<a></a>')
          .attr('href', linkText)
```

```
        .text(title);
    $link = $('<h3></h3>').html($link);
      });
    });
  });
});
```

We get the text of the each item's `<title>` and `<link>` elements, and then construct the `<a>` element, setting our `linkText` variable as the `href` attribute and the `title` variable as the text to appear between the `<a>` and `</a>` tags. We finish by wrapping an `<h3>` element around each `<a>`.

In addition to the links, we reformat and insert each item's publication date and append the HTML of each summary, wrapping everything in its own `<div>`:

```
$(document).ready(function() {
  $('#news-feed').each(function() {
    $(this).empty();

    $.get('news/feed.xml', function(data) {
      $('/rss//item', data).each(function() {
        var title = $('title', this).text();
        var linkText = $('link', this).text();
        var $link = $('<a></a>')
          .attr('href', linkText)
          .text(title);
        $link = $('<h3></h3>').html($link);

        var pubDate = new Date($('pubDate', this).text());
        var pubMonth = pubDate.getMonth() + 1;
        var pubDay = pubDate.getDate();
        var pubYear = pubDate.getFullYear();
        var $pubDiv = $('<div></div>')
          .addClass('publication-date')
          .text(pubMonth + '/' + pubDay + '/' + pubYear;);

        var summaryText = $('description', this).text();
        var $summary = $('<div></div>')
          .addClass('summary')
          .html(summaryText);
      });
    });
  });
});
```

The last step for getting the feed items onto the page involves creating one more
<div>, adding a class of headline to it, appending $link, $pubDiv, and $summary
to it, and then appending all of that together to <div id="news-feed">, which is
already part of the HTML:

```
$(document).ready(function() {
  $('#news-feed').each(function() {
    $(this).empty();

    $.get('news/feed.xml', function(data) {
      $('/rss//item', data).each(function() {
        var title = $('title', this).text();
        var linkText = $('link', this).text();
        var $link = $('<a></a>')
          .attr('href', linkText)
          .text(title);
        $link = $('<h3></h3>').html($link);

        var pubDate = new Date($('pubDate', this).text());
        var pubMonth = pubDate.getMonth() + 1;
        var pubDay = pubDate.getDate();
        var pubYear = pubDate.getFullYear();
        var $pubDiv = $('<div></div>')
          .addClass('publication-date')
          .text(pubMonth + '/' + pubDay + '/' + pubYear);
        var summaryText = $('description', this).text();
        var $summary = $('<div></div>')
          .addClass('summary')
          .html(summaryText);

        $('<div></div>')
          .addClass('headline')
          .append($link)
          .append($pubDiv)
          .append($summary)
          .appendTo('#news-feed');
      });
    });
  });
});
```

So, now we have multiple <div class="headline"> elements—each with a title,
date, link, and summary—ready to be shown.

Setting Up the Rotator

Before we dive into the heart of the headline rotator code, we have a few more things to set up. First, we'll set two variables, one for the currently visible headline and one for the headline that has just scrolled out of view. Initially, both values will be 0:

```
var currentHeadline = 0, oldHeadline = 0;
```

Next, we'll take care of some initial positioning of the headlines. Recall that in the stylesheet we have already set the `top` property of the headlines to be 10 pixels greater than their container's `height` so that they can be hidden. It'll be helpful later on if we store that property in a variable so that we can reset a headline's hidden position after it is scrolled out of the visible area. We also want the first headline to be visible immediately upon page load, so we can set its `top` property to 0:

```
var hiddenPosition = $('#news-feed').height() + 10;
$('div.headline:eq(' + currentHeadline + ')').css('top','0');
```

The rotator area of the page is beginning to shape up:

Recent News

Google Groups and Amazon S3
4/2/2007

Two new improvements have just gone into place to help improve the quality of the jQuery site. The jQuery Mailing List is now hosted with Google Groups. This move is going to help provide huge increases in the overall speed, and quality, of the jQuery mailing list. At the time of the move we were sending out, ...

Finally, we'll store the total number of headlines and define a time out variable to be used for the pause mechanism between each rotation.

```
var headlineCount = $('div.headline').length;
var headlineTimeout;
```

There is no need yet to give `headlineTimeout` a value; it will be set each time the rotation occurs. Nevertheless, we must always declare variables using `var` to avoid the risk of collisions with global variables of the same name.

The Headline Rotate Function

Now we're ready to rotate the headlines, their corresponding dates, and summaries. We'll define a function for this task so that we can reuse the code. The first line inside this function changes the value of currentHeadline by adding 1 to it and then using the modulus operator with headlineCount. This way, currentHeadline will equal oldHeadline + 1 until the latter value matches the value of headlineCount, at which point it will be reset to 0. For a more detailed discussion of the modulus operator, see the *Three-color Alternating Pattern* section of Chapter 7.

The last line inside the function, after the rotation has occurred, sets the oldHeadline value to the currentHeadline value. Now, with these two lines book-ending our function, we can use the two variables as indexes of the currently and previously visible headlines:

```
var headlineRotate = function() {
  currentHeadline = (oldHeadline + 1) % headlineCount;

  // Headline rotation will occur here...

  oldHeadline = currentHeadline;
};
```

In between these two lines we have the code that actually moves the headlines. It starts by animating the top property of the <div class="headline"> element with an index of oldHeadline, moving it up until it's no longer visible, and then, as soon as the animation is complete, setting the top property back to its original hiddenPosition:

```
var headlineRotate = function() {
  currentHeadline = (oldHeadline + 1) % headlineCount;
  $('div.headline:eq(' + oldHeadline + ')')
    .animate({top: -hiddenPosition}, 'slow', function() {
      $(this).css('top',hiddenPosition);
  });
  oldHeadline = currentHeadline;
};
```

Notice here that since hiddenPosition is greater than the height of <div id="news-feed">, animating the top of the headline to -headlinePosition moves it up until it is entirely hidden above its containing element. Using the .animate method's callback then ensures that headline is not repositioned in its original location until after the animation occurs.

The current headline slides up into view simultaneously. Then, when its animation is complete, we use the `setTimeout` function to call `headlineRotate` again after a pause of 5 seconds (5000 milliseconds):

```javascript
var headlineRotate = function() {
  currentHeadline = (oldHeadline + 1) % headlineCount;
  $('div.headline:eq(' + oldHeadline + ')')
    .animate({top: -hiddenPosition}, 'slow', function() {
      $(this).css('top',hiddenPosition);
    });
  $('div.headline:eq(' + currentHeadline + ')')
    .animate({top: 0},'slow', function() {
      headlineTimeout = setTimeout(headlineRotate, 5000);
    });
  oldHeadline = currentHeadline;
};
```

Now that we have the `headlineRotate` function completed, we still have to call it. Although it is called inside of itself, after the animations run, it still needs to be called initially so that it will start when the document is ready. All we need to do for that is to repeat the `headlineTimeout` line after the function. With the repeated line, our full code so far looks like this:

```javascript
$(document).ready(function() {
  $('#news-feed').each(function() {
    $(this).empty();

    // Retrieve the news feed.
    $.get('news/feed.xml', function(data) {
      $('/rss//item', data).each(function() {
        var title = $('title', this).text();
        var linkText = $('link', this).text();
        var $link = $('<a></a>')
          .attr('href', linkText)
          .text(title);
        $link = $('<h3></h3>').html($link);

        var pubDate = new Date($('pubDate', this).text());
        var pubMonth = pubDate.getMonth() + 1;
        var pubDay = pubDate.getDate();
        var pubYear = pubDate.getFullYear();
        var $pubDiv = $('<div></div>')
          .addClass('publication-date')
          .text(pubMonth + '/' + pubDay + '/' + pubYear);
        var summaryText = $('description', this).text();
        var $summary = $('<div></div>')
```

```
        .addClass('summary')
        .html(summaryText);
    $('<div></div>')
        .append($link)
        .append($pubDiv)
        .append($summary)
        .appendTo('#news-feed');
    });

    // Set up the rotator.
    var currentHeadline = 0, oldHeadline = 0;
    var hiddenPosition = ($('#news-feed').height() + 10);
    $('div.headline:eq(' + currentHeadline + ')').css('top','0');

    var headlineCount = $('div.headline').length;
    var headlineTimeout;

    // Perform the rotation.
    var headlineRotate = function() {
      currentHeadline = (oldHeadline + 1) % headlineCount;
      $('div.headline:eq(' + oldHeadline + ')')
        .animate({top: -hiddenPosition}, 'slow', function() {
          $(this).css('top',hiddenPosition);
        });
      $('div.headline:eq(' + currentHeadline + ')')
        .animate({top: 0},'slow', function() {
          headlineTimeout = setTimeout(headlineRotate, 5000);
        });
      oldHeadline = currentHeadline;
    };
    headlineTimeout = setTimeout(headlineRotate,5000);
  }); // End $.get()
}); // End .each() for #news-feed
});
```

Pause on Hover

Even though the headline rotator is now fully functioning, there is one usability issue that we should address—a headline might scroll out of the viewable area before a user is able to click on one of its links, forcing the user to wait until the scroller has cycled through the full set of headlines again. We can reduce the likelihood of this problem by having the scroller pause when the user's mouse cursor hovers anywhere within the headline.

```
$('#news-feed').hover(function() {
  clearTimeout(headlineTimeout);
```

```
}, function() {
  headlineTimeout = setTimeout(headlineRotate, 250);
});
```

The code within the `.hover` method calls JavaScript's `clearTimeout` function on mouseover of `<div id="news-feed">`, effectively preventing our `headlineRotate` function from being called again. On `mouseout`, `headlineRotate()` is called once more, set to begin after a short 250-millisecond delay.

This simple code works fine most of the time. However, if the user mouses over and back out of the `<div>` quickly and repeatedly, a very undesirable effect can occur: Multiple headlines layering on top of each other in the visible area:

Unfortunately, we need to perform some serious surgery to remove this cancer.

Before the `headlineRotate` function, we'll introduce one more variable:

```
var rotateInProgress = false;
```

Now, on the very first line of our function, we can check if a rotation is currently in progress. Only if the value of `rotateInProgress` is `false` do we want the code to run again. Therefore, we wrap everything within the function in an `if` statement. Immediately after this statement, we set the variable to `true`, and then in the callback of the second `.animate` method, we set it back to `false`:

```
var headlineRotate = function() {
  if (!rotateInProgress) {
    rotateInProgress = true;
    currentHeadline = (oldHeadline + 1) % headlineCount;
    $('div.headline:eq(' + oldHeadline + ')')
    .animate({top: -hiddenPosition}, 'slow', function() {
      $(this).css('top',hiddenPosition);
    });
```

```
    $('div.headline:eq(' + currentHeadline + ')')
    .animate({top: 0},'slow', function() {
      rotateInProgress = false;
      headlineTimeout = setTimeout(headlineRotate, 5000);
    });
    oldHeadline = currentHeadline;
  }
};
```

These few additional lines improve our headline rotator substantially. The repeated mouseover-mouseout behavior no longer causes the headlines to pile up on top of each other. Yet this repeated behavior still leaves us with one nagging problem: Subsequent headlines appear to come on a different timetable, two or three immediately following each other rather than all evenly spaced out at five-second intervals.

The problem is that more than one timer can become active concurrently if a user mouses out of the <div> before the existing timer completes. We therefore need to put one more safeguard into place, setting our headlineTimeout variable to false at the top of the function and immediately after the clearTimeout() within the .hover(). Then, in the two places where we use headlineTimeout to call the headlineRotate function, we check first to make sure that the value is false. This way we ensure that a new timer is not set until all existing timers have ended:

```
var headlineRotate = function() {
  if (!rotateInProgress) {
    rotateInProgress = true;
    headlineTimeout = false;
    currentHeadline = (oldHeadline + 1) % headlineCount;
    $('div.headline:eq(' + oldHeadline + ')')
      .animate({top: -hiddenPosition}, 'slow', function() {
        $(this).css('top',hiddenPosition);
    });
    $('div.headline:eq(' + currentHeadline + ')')
      .animate({top: 0},'slow', function() {
      rotateInProgress = false;
      if (!headlineTimeout) {
        headlineTimeout = setTimeout(headlineRotate, 5000);
      }
    });
    oldHeadline = currentHeadline;
  }
};

headlineTimeout = setTimeout(headlineRotate,5000);
```

```
$('#news-feed').hover(function() {
  clearTimeout(headlineTimeout);
  headlineTimeout = false;
}, function() {
  if (!headlineTimeout) {
    headlineTimeout = setTimeout(headlineRotate, 250);
  }
});
```

At last, our headline rotator can withstand all manner of mousing escapades.

Retrieving a Feed from a Different Domain

The news feed that we've been using for our example is a local file, but we might want to retrieve a feed from another site altogether. Although there are a number of solutions for cross-site data retrieval, we'll just look at one using PHP. We create a new file called `feed.php` (rather than `feed.xml`) and refer to it in our `$.get` method:

```
$.get('news/feed.php', function(data) {
  // Code continues...
}
```

Inside the `feed.php` file, we pull in the content of the cross-site news feed, like so:

```
<?php
  header('Content-Type: text/xml');
  print file_get_contents('http://jquery.com/blog/feed');
?>
```

Note here that we need to explicitly set the `Content-Type` of the page to `text/xml` so that jQuery can fetch it and parse it. Some web-hosting providers may not allow the use of the PHP `file_get_contents` function because of security concerns.

Pulling in a remote file like this might take some time, depending on a number of factors, so we can indicate to the user that the headlines are being loaded by appending an image when the `$.get()` request starts and removing it when the request stops:

```
$(document).ready(function() {
  $('#news-feed').each(function() {
    $(this).empty();

    var $newsLoading = $('<img/>')
      .attr({
        'src': '/cookbook/images/loading.gif',
        'alt': 'loading. please wait'
      })
```

```
      .addClass('news-wait');
      $(this).ajaxStart(function() {
        $(this).append($newsLoading);
      }).ajaxStop(function() {
        $newsLoading.remove();
      });
    // Code continues...
    });
  });
```

Now, when the page first loads, if there is a delay in retrieving the headline content, we'll see a **loading** image rather than an empty area:

This image is an animated GIF, so it will obviously look a little more interesting on the web page than it does in print.

Gratuitous Inner-fade Effect

Before we finish the headline rotator, let's give it a finishing touch, making the headline text appear as if it is fading in from the background. To accomplish this bit of visual flair, we can create a series of <div> elements, each given an incrementally greater opacity and top value than the one before it. All of the div *slices* have a few style properties in common, which we can declare in our stylesheet:

```
.fade-slice {
  position: absolute;
  width: 20em;
  height: 2px;
  background: #efd;
  z-index: 3;
}
```

They all have the same `width` and `background-color` property as their containing element `<div id="news-feed">`. Now we can determine the number of `<div class="fade-slice">` elements to be created by first setting a height for all of the `<div>`s together, in this case, 25 percent of the `<div id="news-feed">` height, and then running a `for` loop, incrementing from 0 to the combined fade height by twos:

```
$(document).ready(function() {
  $('#news-feed').each(function() {
    var $this = $(this);
    $this.empty();

    var totalheight = $this.height();
    var fadeHeight = $('#news-feed').height() / 4;
    for (var i = 0; i < fadeHeight; i+=2) {
      $('<div></div>')
      .addClass('fade-slice')
      .appendTo(this);
    }
    // Code continues...
  });
});
```

Since we're beginning to make fairly heavy use of the `$(this)` jQuery object, we've declared a variable `$this` for it so that we can reuse it with impunity.

Rather than using the standard `i++` incrementing in the `for` loop, we've used `i+=2` to increment by 2 because of the slices' 2-pixel height. Given that the height of `<div id="news-feed">` is set at 200 pixels, we arrive at a `fadeHeight` value of 50, which in turn produces 25 `<div class="fade-slice">` elements, each one 2 pixels tall as indicated in the stylesheet.

Now we just have to mathematically determine each element's `opacity` and `top` properties:

```
$(document).ready(function() {
  $('#news-feed').each(function() {
    var $this = $(this);
    $this.empty();

    var totalheight = $this.height();
    var fadeHeight = $totalheight() / 4;
    for (var i = 0; i < fadeHeight; i+=2) {
      $('<div></div>')
      .css({
        opacity: i / fadeHeight,
        top: $totalHeight - fadeHeight + i
      })
```

```
      .addClass('fade-slice')
      .appendTo(this);
    }

    // Code continues...

  });
});
```

As we can see in the table below, the `opacity` values start at `0`, step up to `.04`, and continue incrementally until they reach `.96`, nearly full opacity. Meanwhile, the `top` values begin at `150` and increase by 2 until they reach `198`:

	i	/	fadeHeight	=	opacity	totalHeight	-	fadeHeight	+	i	=	top
1	0	/	50	=	0.00	200	-	50	+	0	=	150
2	2	/	50	=	0.04	200	-	50	+	2	=	152
3	4	/	50	=	0.08	200	-	50	+	4	=	154
4	6	/	50	=	0.12	200	-	50	+	6	=	156
5	8	/	50	=	0.16	200	-	50	+	8	=	158
6	10	/	50	=	0.20	200	-	50	+	10	=	160
7	12	/	50	=	0.24	200	-	50	+	12	=	162
8	14	/	50	=	0.28	200	-	50	+	14	=	164
9	16	/	50	=	0.32	200	-	50	+	16	=	166
10	18	/	50	=	0.36	200	-	50	+	18	=	168
11	20	/	50	=	0.40	200	-	50	+	20	=	170
12	22	/	50	=	0.44	200	-	50	+	22	=	172
13	24	/	50	=	0.48	200	-	50	+	24	=	174
14	26	/	50	=	0.52	200	-	50	+	26	=	176
15	28	/	50	=	0.56	200	-	50	+	28	=	178
16	30	/	50	=	0.60	200	-	50	+	30	=	180
17	32	/	50	=	0.64	200	-	50	+	32	=	182
18	34	/	50	=	0.68	200	-	50	+	34	=	184
19	36	/	50	=	0.72	200	-	50	+	36	=	186
20	38	/	50	=	0.76	200	-	50	+	38	=	188
21	40	/	50	=	0.80	200	-	50	+	40	=	190
22	42	/	50	=	0.84	200	-	50	+	42	=	192
23	44	/	50	=	0.88	200	-	50	+	44	=	194
24	46	/	50	=	0.92	200	-	50	+	46	=	196
25	48	/	50	=	0.96	200	-	50	+	48	=	198

Keep in mind that since the top position of the final `<div class="fade-slice">` is `198`, its 2-pixel height will neatly overlay the bottom two pixels of the 200-pixel-tall containing `<div>`.

With our code in place, the text in the headline area of the page now blends beautifully from transparent to opaque as it scrolls up from the bottom of the `<div>`:

> With a little bit of nice theming, the Fisheye component from Interface has been adapted to build a beautiful "CSS dock menu". It's currently making all the rounds on design blogs and on Digg. Some more information about what this menu was designed for can be found on the developer's site: If you are a big Mac
> ...
>
> **Learning jQuery Book Details**
> 4/18/2007

An Image Carousel

As another example of shuffling around page content, we'll implement an image gallery for the front page of the bookstore site. The gallery will present a few featured books for sale, with links to larger cover art for each. Unlike the previous example, where the headlines in our news ticker moved on a set schedule, here we'll use jQuery to slide the images across the screen when the user clicks on a cover.

An alternative mechanism for scrolling through a set of images is implemented by the **jCarousel** plug-in for jQuery. While not identical to the result we'll achieve here, this plug-in can produce high-quality shuffling effects with very little code. More information on using plug-ins can be found in Chapter 10.

Setting Up the Page

As always, we begin by crafting the HTML and CSS so that users without JavaScript available receive an appealing and functional representation of the information:

```
<div id="featured-books">
  <div class="covers">
    <a href="covers/large/1847190871.jpg"
                              title="Community Server Quickly">
      <img src="covers/medium/1847190871.jpg" width="120" height="148"
                              alt="Community Server Quickly" />
      <span class="price">$35.99</span>
    </a>
    <a href="covers/large/1847190901.jpg"
                    title="Deep Inside osCommerce: The Cookbook">
```

```
        <img src="covers/medium/1847190901.jpg" width="120" height="148"
                        alt="Deep Inside osCommerce: The Cookbook" />
        <span class="price">$44.99</span>
    </a>
    <a href="covers/large/1847190979.jpg" title="Learn OpenOffice.org
        Spreadsheet Macro Programming: OOoBasic and Calc automation">
        <img src="covers/medium/1847190979.jpg" width="120" height="148"
                alt="Learn OpenOffice.org Spreadsheet Macro Programming:
                                OOoBasic and Calc automation" />
        <span class="price">$35.99</span>
    </a>
    <a href="covers/large/1847190987.jpg" title="Microsoft AJAX C#
            Essentials: Building Responsive ASP.NET 2.0 Applications">
        <img src="covers/medium/1847190987.jpg" width="120" height="148"
                alt="Microsoft AJAX C# Essentials: Building Responsive
                                ASP.NET 2.0 Applications" />
        <span class="price">$31.99</span>
    </a>
    <a href="covers/large/1847191002.jpg"
                title="Google Web Toolkit GWT Java AJAX Programming">
        <img src="covers/medium/1847191002.jpg" width="120" height="148"
                alt="Google Web Toolkit GWT Java AJAX Programming" />
        <span class="price">$40.49</span>
    </a>
    <a href="covers/large/1847192386.jpg"
                title="Building Websites with Joomla! 1.5 Beta 1">
        <img src="covers/medium/1847192386.jpg" width="120" height="148"
                alt="Building Websites with Joomla! 1.5 Beta 1" />
        <span class="price">$40.49</span>
    </a>
  </div>
</div>
```

Each image is contained within an anchor tag, pointing to the larger version of the cover. We also have prices given for each cover; these will be hidden for now, and we'll use JavaScript to display them later at an appropriate time.

To save space on the front page, we want to show only three covers at a time. Without JavaScript, we can accomplish this by setting the overflow property of the container to scroll, and adjusting the width appropriately:

```
#featured-books {
    position: relative;
    background: #ddd;
    width: 440px;
    height: 186px;
```

```
    overflow: scroll;
    margin: 1em auto;
    padding: 0;
    text-align: center;
    z-index: 2;
}
#featured-books .covers {
    position: relative;
    width: 840px;
    z-index: 1;
}
#featured-books a {
    float: left;
    margin: 10px;
    height: 146px;
}
#featured-books .price {
    display: none;
}
```

These styles bear a bit of discussion. The outermost element needs to have a larger z-index property than the one inside it; this allows Internet Explorer to hide the part of the inner element that stretches beyond its container. We set the width of the outer element to 440px, which accommodates three images, the 10px margin around each, and an extra 20px for the scroll bar.

With these styles in place, the images can be browsed using a standard system scroll bar:

Revising the Styles with JavaScript

Now that we have gone to the work of making the image gallery usable without JavaScript, we need to undo some of the niceties. The scroll bar will be redundant when we implement our own scrolling mechanism, and the automatic layout of the covers using the `float` property will get in the way of the positioning we need to do to animate the covers. So our first order of business will be overriding some styles:

```javascript
$(document).ready(function() {
  var spacing = 140;

  $('#featured-books').css({
    'width': spacing * 3,
    'height': '166px',
    'overflow': 'hidden'
  }).find('.covers a').css({
    'float': 'none',
    'position': 'absolute',
    'left': 1000
  });

  var $covers = $('#featured-books .covers a');

  $covers.eq(0).css('left', 0);
  $covers.eq(1).css('left', spacing);
  $covers.eq(2).css('left', spacing * 2);
});
```

The spacing variable is going to come in handy throughout many of our calculations. It represents the width of one of the cover images, plus the padding on either side of it. The width of the containing element can now be set to exactly what is necessary to contain three of the cover images since we don't need space for the scroll bar anymore. Indeed, we change the `overflow` property to `hidden`, and bye-bye scroll bar.

The cover images all get positioned absolutely, and start with a left coordinate of 1000. This places them out of the visible area. Then we move the first three covers into position, one at a time. The `$covers` variable holding all of the anchor elements will also come in handy later.

Now the first three covers are visible, with no scrolling mechanism available:

Shuffling Images when Clicked

Now we need to add code to respond to a click on either of the end images, and
reorder the covers as necessary. When the left cover is clicked, this means the user
wants to see more images to the left, which in turn means we need to *shift* the covers
to the right. Similarly, when the right cover is clicked we will have to *shift* the covers
to the left. We want the carousel to wrap around, so when images fall off the left side
they get appended to the right. To begin, we will just change the image positions
without animation:

```
$(document).ready(function() {
  var spacing = 140;

  $('#featured-books').css({
    'width': spacing * 3,
    'height': '166px',
    'overflow': 'hidden'
  }).find('.covers a').css({
    'float': 'none',
    'position': 'absolute',
    'left': 1000
  });

  var setUpCovers = function() {
    var $covers = $('#featured-books .covers a');

    $covers.unbind('click');

    // Left image; scroll right (to view images on left) when clicked.
    $covers.eq(0).css('left', 0).click(function(event) {
      $covers.eq(2).css('left', 1000);
      $covers.eq($covers.length - 1).prependTo(
                                  '#featured-books .covers');
```

```
    setUpCovers();

    event.preventDefault();
  });

  // Right image; scroll left (to view images on right) when clicked.
  $covers.eq(2).css('left', spacing * 2).click(function(event) {
    $covers.eq(0).css('left', 1000);
    $covers.eq(0).appendTo('#featured-books .covers');
    setUpCovers();

    event.preventDefault();
  });

  // Center image.
  $covers.eq(1).css('left', spacing);
};

setUpCovers();
});
```

The new `setUpCovers` function incorporates the image positioning code that we wrote earlier. By encapsulating this in a function, we can repeat the image positioning after the elements have been reordered.

In our example, there are six images in total (which JavaScript will reference with the numbers 0 through 5), and numbers 0, 1, and 2 are visible. When image #0 is clicked, we want to shift all the images to the right by one position. We first move image #2 out of the viewable area, since it will not be visible after the shift. Then we move the image at the end of the line (#5) to the front of the queue. This reorders all of the images, so when `setUpCovers()` is called again the former #5 is now #0, #0 has become #1, and #1 has become #2. The existing positioning code is therefore sufficient to move the covers to their new locations:

Clicking on image #2 performs the process in reverse. This time it is #0 that gets hidden from view, and then moved to the end of the queue. This shifts #1 to the #0 spot, #2 to #1, and #3 to #2.

There are a couple of details that we have to take care of to avoid user interaction anomalies:

1. We need to call .preventDefault() within our click handler, since we have made the covers into links to the large version. Without this call, the link will be followed and we would never see our shuffle effect.

2. We need to unbind all of the click handlers at the beginning of the setUpCovers() function, or we could end up with multiple handlers bound to the same image as the carousel rotates.

Adding Sliding Animation

It can be difficult to understand what just happened when an image is clicked; since the covers move instantaneously, they can appear to have just changed rather than moved. To mitigate this issue, we can add an animation that causes the covers to slide into place rather than just appearing in their new positions. This requires a revision of the setUpCovers function:

```
var setUpCovers = function() {
  var $covers = $('#featured-books .covers a');

  $covers.unbind('click');

  // Left image; scroll right (to view images on left) when clicked.
  $covers.eq(0).css('left', 0).click(function(event) {
    $covers.eq(0).animate({'left': spacing}, 'fast');
    $covers.eq(1).animate({'left': spacing * 2}, 'fast');
    $covers.eq(2).animate({'left': spacing * 3}, 'fast');
    $covers.eq($covers.length - 1).css('left', -spacing).animate({
                                  'left': 0}, 'fast', function() {
      $(this).prependTo('#featured-books .covers');
      setUpCovers();
    });

    event.preventDefault();
  });

  // Right image; scroll left (to view images on right) when clicked.
  $covers.eq(2).css('left', spacing * 2).click(function(event) {
```

```
    $covers.eq(0).animate({'left': -spacing}, 'fast', function() {
      $(this).appendTo('#featured-books .covers');
      setUpCovers();
    });
    $covers.eq(1).animate({'left': 0}, 'fast');
    $covers.eq(2).animate({'left': spacing}, 'fast');
    $covers.eq(3).css('left', spacing * 3).animate({
                        'left': spacing * 2}, 'fast');

    event.preventDefault();
  });

  // Center image.
  $covers.eq(1).css('left', spacing);
};
```

When the left image is clicked, we can move all three visible images to the right by one image width (reusing the `spacing` variable we defined earlier). This part is straightforward, but we also have to make the new image slide into view. To do this, we grab the image from the end of the queue, and first set its screen position to be just offscreen on the left side. Then we slide it into view along with the other items:

Even though the animation takes care of the initial move, we still need to change the cover order by calling `setUpCovers()` again. If we don't, the next click won't work correctly. Since `setUpCovers()` changes the cover positions, we must defer the call until after the animation completes, so we place the call in the animation's callback.

Displaying Action Icons

Our image carousel now rotates smoothly, but we haven't provided any hint to the user that clicking on the covers will cause them to scroll. We can assist the user by displaying appropriate icons when the mouse hovers over the images.

In this case, we'll place the icons on top of the existing images. By using the opacity property, we can continue to see the cover underneath when the icon is displayed. We'll use simple monochrome icons so that the cover is not too obscured:

We'll need three icons, one each for scrolling left and right and one for the middle cover, which the user can click for an enlarged version. We can create the icons and store them in variables for later use:

```
var $leftRollover = $('<img/>')
  .attr('src', 'images/left.gif')
  .addClass('control')
  .css('opacity', 0.6)
  .hide();
var $rightRollover = $('<img/>')
  .attr('src', 'images/right.gif')
  .addClass('control')
  .css('opacity', 0.6)
  .hide();
var $enlargeRollover = $('<img/>')
  .attr('src', 'images/enlarge.gif')
  .addClass('control')
  .css('opacity', 0.6)
  .hide();
```

But we've got a fair amount of repetition here. Instead, we can pull this work out into a function that we call for each icon that needs to be created:

```
function createControl(src) {
  return $('<img/>')
    .attr('src', src)
    .addClass('control')
    .css('opacity', 0.6)
    .hide();
}

var $leftRollover = createControl('images/left.gif');
var $rightRollover = createControl('images/right.gif');
var $enlargeRollover = createControl('images/enlarge.gif');
```

In the CSS for the page, we set the z-index of these controls to be higher than the images', and then position them absolutely so that they can overlap the covers:

```
#featured-books .control {
  position: absolute;
  z-index: 3;
  left: 0;
  top: 0;
}
```

The rollover icons all share the same control class so one might be tempted to place the opacity style in the CSS stylesheet. However, element opacity is not handled consistently between browsers; in Internet Explorer, the syntax for 60% opacity is filter: alpha(opacity=60). Rather than wrestle with these distinctions, we set the opacity style using jQuery's .css method, which abstracts away these browser inconsistencies.

Now all we have to do in our hover handlers is to place the images in the right DOM location:

```
var setUpCovers = function() {
  var $covers = $('#featured-books .covers a');

  $covers.unbind('click').unbind('mouseover').unbind('mouseout');

  // Left image; scroll right (to view images on left) when clicked.
  $covers.eq(0).css('left', 0).click(function(event) {
    $covers.eq(0).animate({'left': spacing}, 'fast');
    $covers.eq(1).animate({'left': spacing * 2}, 'fast');
    $covers.eq(2).animate({'left': spacing * 3}, 'fast');
    $covers.eq($covers.length - 1).css('left', -spacing).
animate({'left': 0}, 'fast', function() {
      $(this).prependTo('#featured-books .covers');
      setUpCovers();
    });

    event.preventDefault();
  }).hover(function() {
    $leftRollover.appendTo(this).show();
  }, function() {
    $leftRollover.hide();
  });

  // Right image; scroll left (to view images on right) when clicked.
  $covers.eq(2).css('left', spacing * 2).click(function(event) {
    $covers.eq(0).animate({'left': -spacing}, 'fast', function() {
      $(this).appendTo('#featured-books .covers');
      setUpCovers();
```

```
    });
    $covers.eq(1).animate({'left': 0}, 'fast');
    $covers.eq(2).animate({'left': spacing}, 'fast');
    $covers.eq(3).css('left', spacing * 3).animate(
                                    {'left': spacing * 2}, 'fast');

    event.preventDefault();
  }).hover(function() {
    $rightRollover.appendTo(this).show();
  }, function() {
    $rightRollover.hide();
  });

  // Center image; enlarge cover when clicked.
  $covers.eq(1).css('left', spacing).hover(function() {
    $enlargeRollover.appendTo(this).show();
  }, function() {
    $enlargeRollover.hide();
  });
};
```

Just as we did with `click` earlier, we unbind `mouseover` and `mouseout` handlers at the beginning of `setUpCovers()` so that the hover behaviors do not accumulate.

Now when the mouse cursor is over a cover, the appropriate rollover image is overlaid on top of the cover:

Image Enlargement

Our image gallery is fully functional, with a carousel that allows the user to navigate to a desired image. A click on the center image leads to an enlarged view of the cover in question. But there is more we can do with this image enlargement functionality.

Rather than lead the user to a separate URL when the center image is clicked, we can overlay the enlarged book cover on the page itself. The **Thickbox** plug-in for jQuery provides a different way to display information overlaid on the page. We will develop the feature without plug-ins here. More information on using plug-ins can be found in Chapter 10.

This larger cover image will require a new image element, which we can create at the same time that the hover images are instantiated:

```
var $enlargedCover = $('<img/>')
  .addClass('enlarged')
  .hide()
  .appendTo('body');
```

We will apply a set of style rules to this new class that are similar to the ones we have seen before:

```
img.enlarged {
  position: absolute;
  z-index: 5;
  cursor: pointer;
}
```

This absolute positioning will allow the cover to float above the other images we have positioned, because the z-index is higher than the ones we have already used. Now we need to actually position the enlarged image when the center image in the carousel is clicked:

```
// Center image; enlarge cover when clicked.
$covers.eq(1).css('left', spacing).click(function(event) {
  $enlargedCover.attr('src', $(this).attr('href')).css({
    'left': ($('body').width() - 360) / 2,
    'top' : 100,
    'width': 360,
    'height': 444
  }).show();

  event.preventDefault();
}).hover(function() {
  $enlargeRollover.appendTo(this).show();
}, function() {
  $enlargeRollover.hide();
});
```

We can take advantage of the links already present in the HTML source to know where the larger cover's image file resides on the server. We pluck this from the `href` attribute of the link, and set it as the `src` attribute of the enlarged cover image.

Now we must position the image. The top, width, and height are hard-coded for now, but the left requires a little calculation. We want the enlarged image to be centered on the page, but we can't know in advance what the appropriate coordinate is to achieve this positioning. We can find the halfway mark across the page by measuring the width of the body element and dividing this by two. Half of our enlarged image will be on either side of this point, so the left coordinate of the image will be `($('body').width() - 360) / 2`, where `360` is the width of the enlarged cover. The cover is now positioned appropriately, centered horizontally across the page:

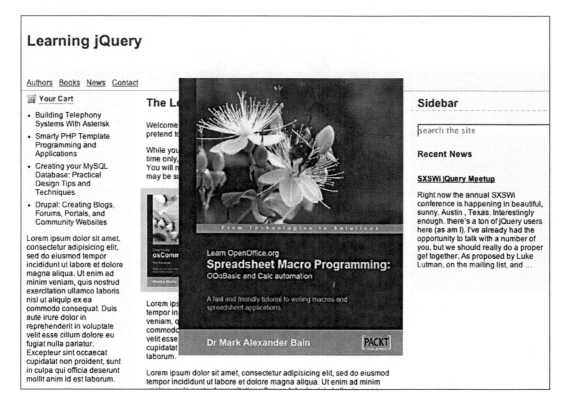

Hiding the Enlarged Cover

We need a mechanism for dismissing the cover once it has been enlarged. The simplest way to do this is by making a click event on the cover fade it out:

```
// Center image; enlarge cover when clicked.
$covers.eq(1).css('left', spacing).click(function(event) {
  $enlargedCover.attr('src', $(this).attr('href')).css({
    'left': ($('body').width() - 360) / 2,
    'top' : 100,
```

```
    'width': 360,
    'height': 444
  }).show()
  .one('click', function() {
    $enlargedCover.fadeOut();
  });

  event.preventDefault();
}).hover(function() {
  $enlargeRollover.appendTo(this).show();
}, function() {
  $enlargeRollover.hide();
});
```

We use the .one method to bind this click handler, which sidesteps a couple of potential problems. With a regular .bind() of the handler, the user could click on the image again as it was fading out. This would cause the handler to fire again. Also, since we are reusing the same image element every time the cover is enlarged, the bind will happen again for each enlargement. If we do nothing to unbind the handler, they will stack up over time. Using .one() ensures that the handlers are removed once used.

Displaying a Close Button

This behavior is sufficient for removing the large cover, but we've given no indication to the user that clicking the cover will make it go away. We can provide this assistance by *badging* the enlarged image with a close button. Creating the button is similar to defining the other singleton elements we've used, and we can call the utility function that we created earlier:

```
var $closeButton = createControl('images/close.gif')
  .addClass('enlarged-control')
  .appendTo('body');
```

When the center cover is clicked and the enlarged cover is displayed, we need to position and show the button:

```
$closeButton.css({
  'left': ($('body').width() - 360) / 2,
  'top' : 100
}).show();
```

The coordinates of the close button are identical to the enlarged cover, so their top-left corners are aligned:

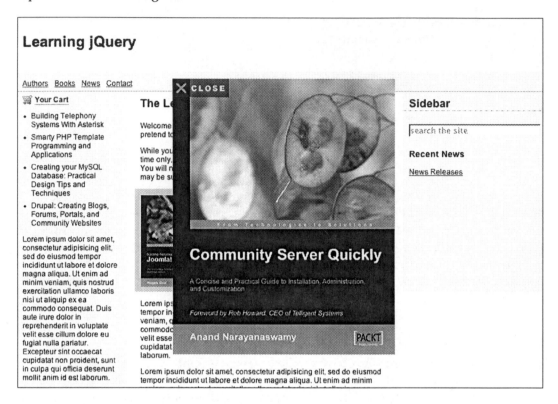

We already have a behavior bound to the image that hides it when the image is clicked, so typically in this situation we could rely on event bubbling to cause a click on the close button to have the same behavior. In this case, however, the close button is not a descendant element of the cover, despite appearances. We've absolutely positioned the close button on top of the cover, which means that clicks on the button do not get passed to the enlarged image. Instead, we must handle clicks on the close button ourselves:

```
// Center image; enlarge cover when clicked.
$covers.eq(1).css('left', spacing).click(function(event) {
  $enlargedCover.attr('src', $(this).attr('href')).css({
    'left': ($('body').width() - 360) / 2,
    'top' : 100,
    'width': 360,
    'height': 444
  }).show()
  .one('click', function() {
```

```
    $closeButton.unbind('click').hide();
    $enlargedCover.fadeOut();
  });

  $closeButton.css({
    'left': ($('body').width() - 360) / 2,
    'top' : 100
  }).click(function() {
    $enlargedCover.click();
  }).show();

  event.preventDefault();
}).hover(function() {
  $enlargeRollover.appendTo(this).show();
}, function() {
  $enlargeRollover.hide();
});
```

When we show the close button, we bind a click event handler for it. All this handler needs to do, though, is to trigger the click handler we've already bound to the enlarged cover. We do need to modify that handler, though, and hide the close button there. While we're at it, we unbind the click handler to prevent handlers from accumulating over time.

More Fun with Badging

Since we have the prices for the books available to us in the HTML source, we can display this as additional information when the book cover is enlarged. This time we'll apply the technique we just developed for the close button to textual content rather than an image.

Once again, we create a singleton element at the beginning of our JavaScript code:

```
var $priceBadge = $('<div/>')
  .addClass('enlarged-price')
  .css('opacity', 0.6)
  .css('display', 'none')
  .appendTo('body');
```

Since the price will be partially transparent, a high contrast between font color and background will work best:

```
.enlarged-price {
  background-color: #373c40;
  color: #fff;
  width: 80px;
  padding: 5px;
```

```
        font-size: 18px;
        font-weight: bold;
        text-align: right;
        position: absolute;
        z-index: 6;
    }
```

Before we can display the price badge, we need to populate it with the actual price information from the HTML. Inside the center cover's click handler `this` refers to the link element. Since the price is in a `<span>` element within the link, obtaining the text is straightforward:

```
    var price = $(this).find('.price').text();
```

Now we can display the badge when the cover is enlarged:

```
    $priceBadge.css({
        'right': ($('body').width() - 360) / 2,
        'top' : 100
    }).text(price).show();
```

This will fix the price at the top-right corner of the enlarged image:

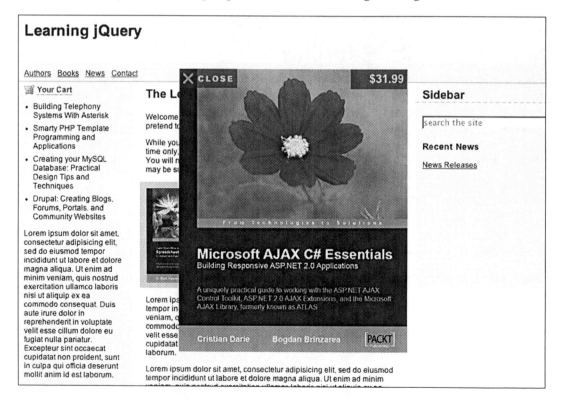

Once we place a $priceBadge.hide(); within the cover's click handler to clean up after ourselves, we're done.

Animating the Cover Enlargement

When the user clicks on the center cover, the enlarged version appears in the center of the page with no flourish. Instead, we can use the built-in animation capabilities of jQuery to smoothly transition between the thumbnail view of the cover and the full-size version.

To do this, we need to know the starting coordinates of the animation; i.e. the position of the center cover on the page. We can calculate the position of the image by adding up the offsetTop and offsetLeft properties of the image and its ancestors in the DOM tree:

```
var element = $(this).find('img').get(0);
var coverLeft = 0;
var coverTop = 0;
var coverWidth = element.width;
var coverHeight = element.height;
while (element.offsetParent) {
  coverLeft += element.offsetLeft;
  coverTop += element.offsetTop;
  element = element.offsetParent;
}
```

The **Dimensions** plug-in for jQuery provides readily accessible values for calculations such as this. For more information on plug-ins please refer to Chapter 10.

The actual animation is performed by setting the enlarged image to the center cover's dimensions and position, then calling .animate() with the full-size dimensions as a destination:

```
$enlargedCover.attr('src', $(this).attr('href')).css({
  'left': coverLeft,
  'top' : coverTop,
  'width': coverWidth,
  'height': coverHeight
}).animate({
  'left': ($('body').width() - coverWidth * 3) / 2,
  'top' : 100,
  'width': coverWidth * 3,
  'height': coverHeight * 3
}, 'normal', function() {
  $enlargedCover.one('click', function() {
```

```
    $closeButton.unbind('click').hide();
    $priceBadge.hide();
    $enlargedCover.fadeOut();
  });

  $closeButton.css({
    'left': ($('body').width() - coverWidth * 3) / 2,
    'top' : 100
  }).click(function() {
    $enlargedCover.click();
  }).show();

  $priceBadge.css({
    'right': ($('body').width() - coverWidth * 3) / 2,
    'top' : 100
  }).text(price).show();
});
```

Now that we have the width and height of the thumbnail captured, we can use
these values to calculate the enlarged version rather than hard-coding this number.
Here we assume that the full-size version will always be three times the size of
the thumbnail. The positioning of the close button and the price badge need to be
deferred until the animation is complete, so we place them in the callback. Now we
have a smooth transition from small to large cover:

Learning jQuery

Authors Books News Contact

Your Cart

- Building Telephony Systems With Asterisk
- Smarty PHP Template Programming and Applications
- Creating your MySQL Database: Practical Design Tips and Techniques
- Drupal: Creating Blogs, Forums, Portals, and Community Websites

Lorem ipsum dolor sit amet, consectetur adipisicing elit, sed do eiusmod tempor incididunt ut labore et dolore magna aliqua. Ut enim ad minim veniam, quis nostrud exercitation ullamco laboris nisi ut aliquip ex ea commodo consequat. Duis aute irure dolor in reprehenderit in voluptate velit esse cillum dolore eu fugiat nulla pariatur. Excepteur sint occaecat cupidatat non proident, sunt in culpa qui officia deserunt mollit anim id est laborum.

The Learning jQuery Fake Bookstore

Welcome to our fake bookstore. Feel free to browse through the site and pretend to buy books. We'll pretend to sell them to you.

While you're here we'd like to present to you our special offer: For a limited time only, you can click on anything you like in this site for free. That's right! You will not be charged one peso. So stop reading, and start clicking. You may be surprised by what you find.

Lorem ipsum dolor sit amet, consectetur adipisicing elit, sed do eiusmod tempor incididunt ut labore et dolore magna aliqua. Ut enim ad minim veniam, quis nostrud exercitation ullamco laboris nisi ut aliquip ex ea commodo consequat. Duis aute irure dolor in reprehenderit in voluptate velit esse cillum dolore eu fugiat nulla pariatur. Excepteur sint occaecat cupidatat non proident, sunt in culpa qui officia deserunt mollit anim id est laborum.

Lorem ipsum dolor sit amet, consectetur adipisicing elit, sed do eiusmod tempor incididunt ut labore et dolore magna aliqua. Ut enim ad minim

Sidebar

search the site

Recent News

News Releases

Learning jQuery

Authors Books News Contact

Your Cart

- Building Telephony Systems With Asterisk
- Smarty PHP Template Programming and Applications
- Creating your MySQL Database: Practical Design Tips and Techniques
- Drupal: Creating Blogs, Forums, Portals, and Community Websites

Lorem ipsum dolor sit amet, consectetur adipisicing elit, sed do eiusmod tempor incididunt ut labore et dolore magna aliqua. Ut enim ad minim veniam, quis nostrud exercitation ullamco laboris nisi ut aliquip ex ea commodo consequat. Duis aute irure dolor in reprehenderit in voluptate velit esse cillum dolore eu fugiat nulla pariatur. Excepteur sint occaecat cupidatat non proident, sunt in culpa qui officia deserunt mollit anim id est laborum.

The Learning jQuery Fake Bookstore

Welcome to our fake bookstore. Feel free to browse through the site and pretend to buy books. We'll pretend to sell them to you.

While you're here v············· r: For a limited time only, you can ········· e. That's right! You will not be cha··········· t clicking. You may be surprised b·····

Lorem ipsum dolor······ ········ do eiusmod tempor incididunt u····· ···· ad minim veniam, quis nostrud exercitation ullamco laboris nisi ut aliquip ex ea commodo consequat. Duis aute irure dolor in reprehenderit in voluptate velit esse cillum dolore eu fugiat nulla pariatur. Excepteur sint occaecat cupidatat non proident, sunt in culpa qui officia deserunt mollit anim id est laborum.

Lorem ipsum dolor sit amet, consectetur adipisicing elit, sed do eiusmod tempor incididunt ut labore et dolore magna aliqua. Ut enim ad minim

Sidebar

search the site

Recent News

News Releases

Learning jQuery

Authors Books News Contact

Your Cart

- Building Telephony Systems With Asterisk
- Smarty PHP Template Programming and Applications
- Creating your MySQL Database: Practical Design Tips and Techniques
- Drupal: Creating Blogs, Forums, Portals, and Community Websites

Lorem ipsum dolor sit amet, consectetur adipisicing elit, sed do eiusmod tempor incididunt ut labore et dolore magna aliqua. Ut enim ad minim veniam, quis nostrud exercitation ullamco laboris nisi ut aliquip ex ea commodo consequat. Duis aute irure dolor in reprehenderit in voluptate velit esse cillum dolore eu fugiat nulla pariatur. Excepteur sint occaecat cupidatat non proident, sunt in culpa qui officia deserunt mollit anim id est laborum.

The Learning jQuery Fake Bookstore

Welcome to o··········· nd pretend to buy

While you're h········· mited time only, you········· right! You will not b········· You may be surpri·····

Lorem ipsum ·········od tempor incidid······· veniam, quis ········· commodo cor········· te velit esse cillum dolore eu fugiat nulla pariatur. Excepteur sint occaecat cupidatat non proident, sunt in culpa qui officia deserunt mollit anim id est laborum.

Lorem ipsum dolor sit amet, consectetur adipisicing elit, sed do eiusmod tempor incididunt ut labore et dolore magna aliqua. Ut enim ad minim

Sidebar

search the site

Recent News

News Releases

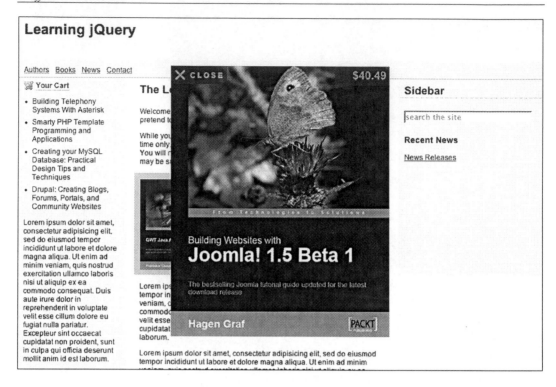

Deferring Animations Until Image Load

Our animation is smooth, but depends on a fast connection to the site. If the enlarged cover takes some time to download, then the first moments of the animation might display the **red X** indicating a broken image. We can make the transition a bit more elegant by waiting until the image has fully loaded before starting the animation:

```
$enlargedCover.attr('src', $(this).attr('href')).css({
  'left': coverLeft,
  'top' : coverTop,
  'width': coverWidth,
  'height': coverHeight
});
var animateEnlarge = function() {
  $enlargedCover.animate({
    'left': ($('body').width() - coverWidth * 3) / 2,
    'top' : 100,
    'width': coverWidth * 3,
    'height': coverHeight * 3
  }, 'normal', function() {
    $enlargedCover.one('click', function() {
```

```
            $closeButton.unbind('click').hide();
            $priceBadge.hide();
            $enlargedCover.fadeOut();
        });

        $closeButton.css({
            'left': ($('body').width() - coverWidth * 3) / 2,
            'top' : 100
        }).click(function() {
            $enlargedCover.click();
        }).show();

        $priceBadge.css({
            'right': ($('body').width() - coverWidth * 3) / 2,
            'top' : 100
        }).text(price).show();
    });
};

if ($enlargedCover[0].complete) {
    animateEnlarge();
}
else {
    $enlargedCover.bind('load', animateEnlarge);
}
```

This is a rare instance in which the load event is more useful to us than jQuery's custom ready event. Since load is triggered on a document, image, or frame when all of its contents have fully loaded, we can observe the event to make sure that all of the image has been loaded into memory. Only then is the handler executed, and the animation is performed.

 We're using the .bind('load') syntax rather than the shorthand .load() method here for clarity since .load() is also an AJAX method; the two syntaxes are interchangeable.

Internet Explorer and Firefox have different interpretations of what to do if the image is already in the browser cache. In this case, Firefox will immediately send the load event to JavaScript, but Internet Explorer will never send the event because no *load* actually occurred. To compensate for this, we use the complete property of the image element. This property is set to true only if the image is fully loaded, so we test this value first and start the animation if the image is ready. If the image is not yet complete, then we wait for a load event to be triggered.

Adding a Loading Indicator

But now we can have an awkward situation on slow network connections when an image takes a few moments to load. Our page appears to do nothing while this download is in progress. As we did when loading the news headlines, we should provide an indication to the user that some activity is occurring by displaying a *loading* indicator in the meantime.

The indicator will be another singleton image that will be displayed when appropriate:

```
var $waitThrobber = $('<img/>')
  .attr('src', 'images/wait.gif')
  .addClass('control')
  .css('z-index', 4)
  .hide();
```

For this image, we're actually using an animated GIF, because the motion will reinforce to the user that the activity is taking place:

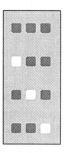

It will just take two lines to put our wait throbber in place, now that we have the element defined. At the very beginning of our click handler for the center image, before we start doing any work, we need to display the indicator:

```
$waitThrobber.appendTo(this).show();
```

And at the beginning of the `animateEnlarge` function, when we know the image has been loaded, we remove it from view:

```
$waitThrobber.hide();
```

This is all it takes to badge the cover being enlarged with the wait throbber. The animation appears overlaying the top left corner of the cover:

The Finished Code

This chapter represents just a small fraction of what can be done on the Web with animated image and text rotators. Taken all together, the code for the headline rotator and image carousel looks like this:

```
$(document).ready(function() {
  //using each as an 'if' and containing stuff inside a private
  //namespace
  $('#news-feed').each(function() {
    var $this = $(this);
    $this.empty();

    var totalHeight = $this.height();
    var fadeHeight = totalHeight / 4;

    for (var i = 0; i < fadeHeight; i+=2) {
      $('<div></div>').css({
        opacity: i / fadeHeight,
        top: totalHeight - fadeHeight + i
      }).addClass('fade-slice').appendTo(this);
    }
    var $newsLoading = $('<img/>')
      .attr({
        'src': '/cookbook/images/loading.gif',
        'alt': 'loading. please wait'}
      )
      .addClass('news-wait');
    $this.ajaxStart(function() {
      $this.append($newsLoading);
    }).ajaxStop(function() {
      $newsLoading.remove();
```

```
});
//retrieve the news feed
$.get('news/feed.php', function(data) {
  $('/rss//item', data).each(function() {
    var title = $('title', this).text();
    var linkText = $('link', this).text();
    var $link = $('<a></a>')
      .attr('href', linkText)
      .text(title);
    $link = $('<h3></h3>').html($link);

    var pubDate = new Date($('pubDate', this).text());
    var pubMonth = pubDate.getMonth() + 1;
    var pubDay = pubDate.getDate();
    var pubYear = pubDate.getFullYear();
    var $pubDiv = $('<div></div>')
      .addClass('publication-date')
      .text(pubMonth + '/' + pubDay + '/' + pubYear);

    var summaryText = $('description', this).text();
    var $summary = $('<div></div>')
      .addClass('summary')
      .html(summaryText);

    $('<div></div>')
      .addClass('headline')
      .append($link)
      .append($pubDiv)
      .append($summary)
      .appendTo('#news-feed');
  });

  //set up the rotator
  var currentHeadline = 0, oldHeadline = 0;
  var hiddenPosition = totalHeight   + 10;
  $('div.headline:eq(' + currentHeadline + ')').css('top','0');
  var headlineCount = $('div.headline').length;
  var headlineTimeout;
  var rotateInProgress = false;

  //rotator function
  var headlineRotate = function() {
   if (!rotateInProgress) {
     rotateInProgress = true;
     headlineTimeout = false;
```

```
              currentHeadline = (oldHeadline + 1) % headlineCount;
              $('div.headline:eq(' + oldHeadline + ')')
              .animate({top: -hiddenPosition}, 'slow', function() {
                $(this).css('top',hiddenPosition);
              });
              $('div.headline:eq(' + currentHeadline + ')')
              .animate({top: 0},'slow', function() {
                rotateInProgress = false;
                if (!headlineTimeout) {
                  headlineTimeout = setTimeout(headlineRotate, 5000);
                }
              });
              oldHeadline = currentHeadline;
            }
          };
          headlineTimeout = setTimeout(headlineRotate,5000);

          // on hover clear the timeout and reset headlineTimeout to 0
          $('#news-feed').hover(function() {
            clearTimeout(headlineTimeout);
            headlineTimeout = false;
          }, function() {
            // Start the rotation soon when the mouse leaves
            if (!headlineTimeout) {
              headlineTimeout = setTimeout(headlineRotate, 250);
            }
          }); //end .hover()
      }); // end $.get()
  }); //end .each() for #news-feed
});


/****************************************
   =IMAGE CAROUSEL
------------------------------------ */
$(document).ready(function() {
  var spacing = 140;

  function createControl(src) {
    return $('<img/>')
      .attr('src', src)
      .addClass('control')
      .css('opacity', 0.6)
      .css('display', 'none');
  }
```

```
var $leftRollover = createControl('images/left.gif');
var $rightRollover = createControl('images/right.gif');
var $enlargeRollover = createControl('images/enlarge.gif');
var $enlargedCover = $('<img/>')
  .addClass('enlarged')
  .hide()
  .appendTo('body');
var $closeButton = createControl('images/close.gif')
  .addClass('enlarged-control')
  .appendTo('body');
var $priceBadge = $('<div/>')
  .addClass('enlarged-price')
  .css('opacity', 0.6)
  .css('display', 'none')
  .appendTo('body');
var $waitThrobber = $('<img/>')
  .attr('src', 'images/wait.gif')
  .addClass('control')
  .css('z-index', 4)
  .hide();

$('#featured-books').css({
  'width': spacing * 3,
  'height': '166px',
  'overflow': 'hidden'
}).find('.covers a').css({
  'float': 'none',
  'position': 'absolute',
  'left': 1000
});

var setUpCovers = function() {
  var $covers = $('#featured-books .covers a');

  $covers.unbind('click').unbind('mouseover').unbind('mouseout');

  // Left image; scroll right (to view images on left) when clicked.
  $covers.eq(0).css('left', 0).click(function(event) {
    $covers.eq(0).animate({'left': spacing}, 'fast');
    $covers.eq(1).animate({'left': spacing * 2}, 'fast');
    $covers.eq(2).animate({'left': spacing * 3}, 'fast');
    $covers.eq($covers.length - 1).css('left', -spacing)
                      .animate({'left': 0}, 'fast', function() {
      $(this).prependTo('#featured-books .covers');
      setUpCovers();
    });
```

```
    event.preventDefault();
}).hover(function() {
  $leftRollover.appendTo(this).show();
}, function() {
  $leftRollover.hide();
});

// Right image; scroll left (
                          to view images on right) when clicked.
$covers.eq(2).css('left', spacing * 2).click(function(event) {
  $covers.eq(0).animate({'left': -spacing}, 'fast', function() {
    $(this).appendTo('#featured-books .covers');
    setUpCovers();
  });
  $covers.eq(1).animate({'left': 0}, 'fast');
  $covers.eq(2).animate({'left': spacing}, 'fast');
  $covers.eq(3).css('left', spacing * 3).animate({
                                  'left': spacing * 2}, 'fast');

  event.preventDefault();
}).hover(function() {
  $rightRollover.appendTo(this).show();
}, function() {
  $rightRollover.hide();
});

// Center image; enlarge cover when clicked.
$covers.eq(1).css('left', spacing).click(function(event) {
  $waitThrobber.appendTo(this).show();

  var price = $(this).find('.price').text();

  var element = $(this).find('img').get(0);
  var coverLeft = 0;
  var coverTop = 0;
  var coverWidth = element.width;
  var coverHeight = element.height;
  while (element.offsetParent) {
    coverLeft += element.offsetLeft;
    coverTop += element.offsetTop;
    element = element.offsetParent;
  }

  $enlargedCover.attr('src', $(this).attr('href')).css({
    'left': coverLeft,
    'top' : coverTop,
    'width': coverWidth,
    'height': coverHeight
```

```
      });
    var animateEnlarge = function() {
      $waitThrobber.hide();
      $enlargedCover.animate({
        'left': ($('body').width() - coverWidth * 3) / 2,
        'top' : 100,
        'width': coverWidth * 3,
        'height': coverHeight * 3
      }, 'normal', function() {
        $enlargedCover.one('click', function() {
          $closeButton.unbind('click').hide();
          $priceBadge.hide();
          $enlargedCover.fadeOut();
        });

        $closeButton.css({
          'left': ($('body').width() - coverWidth * 3) / 2,
          'top' : 100
        }).click(function() {
          $enlargedCover.click();
        }).show();

        $priceBadge.css({
          'right': ($('body').width() - coverWidth * 3) / 2,
          'top' : 100
        }).text(price).show();
      });
    };

    if ($enlargedCover[0].complete) {
      animateEnlarge();
    }
    else {
      $enlargedCover.bind('load', animateEnlarge);
    }

    event.preventDefault();
  }).hover(function() {
    $enlargeRollover.appendTo(this).show();
  }, function() {
    $enlargeRollover.hide();
  });
};

setUpCovers();
});
```

Summary

In this chapter, we have looked into page elements that change over time, either on their own or in response to user intervention. These shufflers and rotators can really set a modern web presence apart from traditionally designed sites. We have covered presenting an XML feed of information on a page as well as rotating items in and out of view on a time delay. Along with displaying a set of images in a navigable carousel-style gallery, we have also discussed enlarging an image for a closer view with a smooth animation and presenting user-interface controls in an unobtrusive way.

These techniques can be combined in many ways to breathe life into otherwise stodgy pages. Animations and effects that would be otherwise tedious to achieve can be effortlessly realized thanks to the power of jQuery.

10
Plug-ins

Like a plug without a socket
I'm just waitin' 'round for you
— Devo,
"Don't You Know"

Throughout this book we have examined many of the ways in which the jQuery library can be used to accomplish a wide variety of tasks. Yet one aspect that has remained relatively unexplored is jQuery's extensibility. As powerful as the library is at its core, its elegant plug-in architecture has allowed developers to extend jQuery, making it an even more feature-rich library.

Although jQuery has been available for less than two years, it already supports over a hundred plug-ins—from small selector helpers to full-scale, user-interface widgets. In this chapter we'll take a brief look at three popular jQuery plug-ins and then create a few of our own.

We've already discussed the power of plug-ins and created a simple one in Chapter 7. Here, we'll look at the way for incorporating pre-existing plug-ins into our web pages and examine how to build our own plug-in in more detail.

How to Use a Plug-in

Using a jQuery plug-in is very straightforward. The first step is to include it in the `<head>` of the document, making sure that it appears after the main jQuery source file:

```
<head>
  <meta http-equiv="Content-Type" content="text/html;
                                       charset=utf-8"/>
  <script src="jquery.js" type="text/javascript"></script>
```

```
      <script src="jquery.plug-in.js" type="text/javascript"></script>
      <script src="custom.js" type="text/javascript"></script>
      <title>Example</title>
   </head>
```

After that, it's just a matter of including a custom JavaScript file in which we use the methods that the plug-in either creates or extends. For example, using the Form plug-in, we can add a single line inside our custom file's `$(document).ready()` method to make a form submit via AJAX:

```
$(document).ready(function() {
  $('#myForm').ajaxForm();
});
```

Many plug-ins have a bit of built-in flexibility as well, providing a number of optional parameters that we can set to modify their behavior. We can customize their operation as much as needed, or simply stick with the defaults.

Popular Plug-Ins

The jQuery website currently provides a long list of available plug-ins at `http://jquery.com/Plugins`, and plans are in the works to add features such as user ratings and comments to help visitors determine which are the most popular ones.

In this chapter we will explore three **official** plug-ins—so designated because of their mature code-base, usefulness, and adherence to a set of coding and documentation standards set by the jQuery project.

Dimensions

The **Dimensions** plug-in, co-authored by *Paul Bakaus* and *Brandon Aaron*, helps to bridge the gap between the CSS box model and developers' need to accurately measure the height and width of elements in a document. It also measures with pixel accuracy the top and left offsets of elements, no matter where they are found on the page.

Height and Width

For measuring height and width, Dimensions provides three sets of methods:

1. `.height()` and `.width()`
2. `.innerHeight()` and `.innerWidth()`
3. `.outerHeight()` and `.outerWidth()`

The .height and .width methods simply use the jQuery core methods of the same names when they are applied to elements. However, Dimensions extends these two methods so that we can apply them to the browser window and the document. Using $(window).width(), for example, will return the number of pixels for the width of the browser, while $(document).width() will return the same for the width of the document alone. If there is a vertical scrollbar, $(window).width() will include it while $(document).width() won't.

The inner and outer methods are very useful for measuring the width and height of elements including padding (inner and outer) and borders (outer). Let's look at an example element called <div class="dim-outer"> with the following CSS rule:

```
.dim-outer {
  height: 200px;
  width: 200px;
  margin: 10px;
  padding: 1em;
  border: 5px solid #e3e3e3;
  overflow: auto;
  font-size: 12px;
}
```

The plain $('div.dim-outer').width() method returns 200, because that is, indeed, the width defined in the CSS. However, it's not a very accurate measurement if we want the width from the inside of the left border to the inside of the right. For that, we can use $('div.dim-outer').innerWidth(), which returns 224. The extra 24 pixels come from the sum of the left and right sides' padding. Since the padding is 1em, and each em is equal to the font-size, which we set at 12px, we get a total of 24 extra pixels. For $('div.dim-outer').outerWidth(), we add the right and left borders (5 + 5) to the element width (+ 200) and the padding (+ 24) to arrive at a total width from outside edge to outside edge of 234.

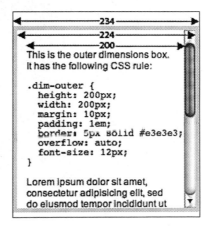

ScrollTop and ScrollLeft

The .scrollTop and .scrollLeft methods return the number of pixels that the user has scrolled the browser or a scrollable element within a document down and to the right, respectively. When used with a numeric argument, they can also move the page to the given scroll position.

Offset

Perhaps the most powerful feature of the Dimensions plug-in is its .offset() method, which allows us to locate the top and left positions of any element anywhere on the page, whether its position is static, relative, or absolute and regardless of window scrollbars or even element scrollbars when overflow is set to auto. With options for factoring margin, border, padding, and scroll into the calculation, .offset() provides great flexibility as well as accuracy. The Dimensions test page can give a sense of how versatile it is:

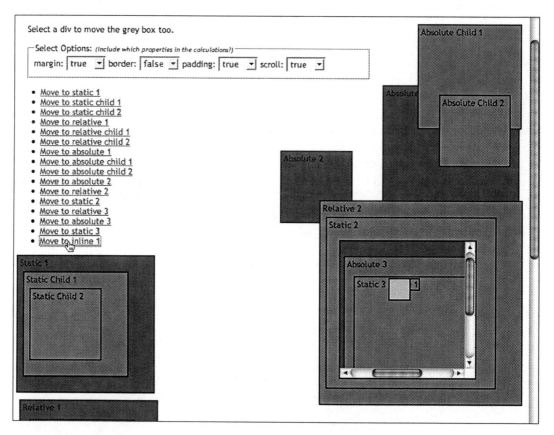

Here, clicking on the **Move to inline 1** link has moved the gray box to exactly the same location as the inline 1 element, with its top and left borders overlapping because the `border` option has been set to `false`. To see more offset permutations, visit the test page at `http://brandon.jquery.com/plugins/dimensions/test/offset.html`.

Form

The **Form** plug-in is a terrific example of a script that makes a difficult, complex task dead simple.

At the heart of the plug-in is the `.ajaxForm` method. As we saw in the *How to Use a Plug-in* section, converting a conventional form into an AJAX form requires one simple line of code:

```
$(document).ready(function() {
  $('#myForm').ajaxForm();
});
```

This example will prepare the form with `id="myForm"` to be submitted without having to refresh the current page. This feature in itself is quite nice, but the real power comes with the map of options that we can pass into the method. For example, the following code calls `.ajaxForm()` with the `target`, `beforeSubmit`, and `success` options:

```
$(document).ready(function() {
  function validateForm() {
    // the form validation code would go here
    // we can return false to abort the submit
  };
  $('#test-form').ajaxForm({
    target: '.log',
    beforeSubmit: validateForm,
    success: function() {
      alert('Thanks for your comment!');
    }
  });
});
```

The `target` option indicates the element(s) — in this case, any element with `class="log"` — that will be updated by the server response.

The `beforeSubmit` option performs tasks before the form is submitted. Here it calls the `validateForm` function. If it returns `false`, the form will not be submitted.

The `success` option performs tasks after the form is successfully submitted. In this example it simply provides an alert message to let the user know that the form has been submitted.

Other options available with `.ajaxForm()` and the similar `.ajaxSubmit()` include:

- `url`: The URL to which the form data will be submitted, if different from the form's `action` attribute.

- `type`: The method used to submit the form — either GET or POST. The default is the form's `method` attribute, or if none is provided, GET.

- `dataType`: The expected data-type of the server response. Possible values are `null`, `xml`, `script`, or `json`. The default value is `null`.

- `resetForm`: Boolean; default is `false`. If set to `true`, all of the form's field values will be reset to their defaults when the submit is successful.

- `clearForm`: Boolean; default is `false`. If set to `true`, all of the form's field values will be cleared when the submit is successful.

The Form plug-in provides a number of other methods to assist in handling forms and their data. For a closer look at these methods, as well as more demos and examples, visit `http://www.malsup.com/jquery/form/`.

Tips & Tricks

Both `.ajaxForm()` and `.ajaxSubmit()` default to using the `action` and `method` values in the form's markup. As long as we use proper markup for the form, the plug-in will work exactly as we expect without any need for tweaking.

Normally when a form is submitted, if the element used to submit the form has a name, its name/value is submitted along with the rest of the form data. The `.ajaxForm()` method is proactive in this regard, adding click handlers to all of the submit elements so it knows which one submitted the form. The `.ajaxSubmit()` method, on the other hand, is reactive and has no way of determining this information. It does not capture the submitting element. The same distinction applies to image input elements as well: `.ajaxForm()` handles them, while `.ajaxSubmit()` ignores them.

The `.ajaxForm()` and `.ajaxSubmit()` methods pass their `options` argument to the `$.ajax()` method that is part of the jQuery core. Therefore, any valid options for `$.ajax()` can be passed in through the form plugin. With this feature in mind, we can make our AJAX form responses even more robust, like so:

```
$(#myForm).ajaxForm({
  timeout: 2000,
  error: function (xml, status, e) {
```

```
    alert(e.message);
  }
});
```

The `.ajaxForm` and `.ajaxSubmit` methods can be passed a function instead of an `options` argument. Because the function is treated as the success handler, we can get the response text back from the server, like so:

```
$(#myForm).ajaxForm(function(responseText) {
  alert(responseText);
});
```

Interface

While the Dimensions and Form Plug-ins do one thing, and do it very well, Interface does a wide variety of things (and does them well). In fact, Interface is not so much a plug-in, but rather a whole suite of plug-ins.

Originally created by *Stefan Petre*, with major contributions by *Paul Bakaus*, Interface helps make the web experience more like that of a desktop application, featuring widgets for dragging, dropping, and sorting items as well as advanced animation effects and rich visual feedback.

Let us briefly examine the **Animate** and **Sortables** plug-ins here.

Animate

Like the Dimension plug-in's `.height` and `.width` methods, the `.animate` method in Interface extends the jQuery core method. While the core `.animate()` has a relatively limited set of options for its parameter, the Interface version opens those options to encompass just about any CSS property and even a class name. Interface's `.animate()` can, for example, animate the change from one class's set of properties to another class's set. Suppose we have the element `<div class="boxbefore">` with the following CSS rule:

```
.boxbefore {
  width: 300px;
  margin: 1em 0;
  padding: 5px;
  overflow: auto;
  background-color: #fff;
  color: #000;
  border: 10px solid #333;
}
```

The style properties give us a 300-pixel-wide box with 5 pixels of padding on each side, a 10-pixel, dark-gray border, and the generic black text on a white background. The overflow property is set to `auto` so that scrollbars will appear if the box is not large enough to display all of the content. However, since no height is prescribed, the box will grow as large as it needs to in order to accomodate the content. With these properties set, our box should look like this:

> This is the box for the animation. It has the following CSS rule:
>
> ```
> .boxbefore {
>   width: 300px;
>   margin: 1em 0;
>   padding: 5px;
>   overflow: auto;
>   background-color: #fff;
>   color: #000;
>   border: 10px solid #333;
> }
> ```
>
> Lorem ipsum dolor sit amet, consectetur adipisicing elit, sed do eiusmod tempor incididunt ut labore et dolore magna aliqua. Ut enim ad minim veniam, quis nostrud exercitation ullamco laboris nisi ut aliquip ex ea commodo consequat. Duis aute irure dolor in reprehenderit in voluptate velit esse cillum dolore eu fugiat nulla pariatur. Excepteur sint occaecat cupidatat non proident, sunt in culpa qui officia deserunt mollit anim id est laborum.

Now let's animate a change from the `boxbefore` class to a new `boxafter` class with the following properties:

```
.boxafter {
  height: 180px;
  width: 500px;
  padding: 15px;
  background-color: #000;
  color: #fff;
  border: 5px solid #ccc;
}
```

With this CSS rule, we are setting the box's height to 180 pixels, increasing its width to 500 pixels, decreasing the border's width while lightening its color, increasing the padding, and inverting the text and background colors. Since we are not defining new overflow and margin properties, they remain the same.

To animate this dramatic change, we simply write the following line:

```
$(document).ready(function() {
  $('div.boxbefore').animate({className:'boxafter'}, 1000);
});
```

A little more than halfway through the animation, our box will look like this:

And by the time the animation stops, the box will have all of the `boxafter` class styles applied to it, along with a vertical scrollbar because the `overflow:auto;` kicks in with the decreased height:

Sortables

The **Sortables** plug-in module for Interface can transform just about any group of elements into a drag-and-drop style list. Here, we have an unordered list with some CSS styles applied to each item:

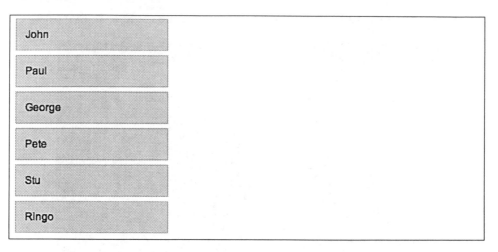

The HTML is pretty straightforward:

```
<ul id="sort-container" class="content">
  <li id="item1" class="sort-item">John</li>
  <li id="item2" class="sort-item">Paul</li>
  <li id="item3" class="sort-item">George</li>
  <li id="item4" class="sort-item">Pete</li>
  <li id="item5" class="sort-item">Stu</li>
  <li id="item6" class="sort-item">Ringo</li>
</ul>
```

Each list item has a unique `id` and a common `class`. Now, to make the list sortable, we simply write the following code:

```
$(document).ready(function() {
  $('#sort-container').Sortable({
    accept : 'sort-item',
    hoverclass : 'hover',
    helperclass : 'helper',
    opacity:    0.5
  });
});
```

This code consists of a single .Sortable method with a map of arguments. The first, accept, is a mandatory argument while the others are optional. In fact, we have left quite a few options out of the script.

As we can see the method makes any item sortable that has class="sort-item". It also applies a class to each item when the mouse cursor hovers over it (hoverclass : 'hover') and identifies the class to use for the helper item (helperclass : 'helper'). In this example, the helper class is nothing more than a dotted red border:

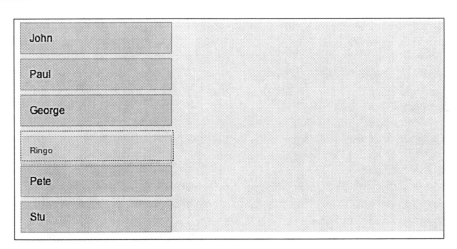

Interface plug-ins such as Sortables help to provide desktop-like functionality to our web applications. For more information about all of the Interface plug-ins, visit http://interface.eyecon.ro/.

Finding Plug-in Documentation

The *jquery.com Plugin Repository* at http://jquery.com/Plugins/ is a great place to start when looking for documentation. Each plug-in listed in the repository has a link to a page from which the plug-in can be downloaded. Additionally, many of the linked pages contain demos, example code, and tutorials to help us get started.

Official jQuery plug-ins also provide ample comments in the source code itself. For many plug-ins, the comment syntax matches the comments of the jquery.js file, providing a description and at least one example of each method. This means that the tools available for viewing jQuery documentation also work with compliant plug-ins.

For example, the `.offset` method of the *Dimensions* plug-in has these comments:

```
/**
 * Returns the location of the element in pixels from the top left
 * corner of the viewport.
 *
 * For accurate readings make sure to use pixel values for margins,
 * borders and padding.
 *
 * @example $("#testdiv").offset()
 * @result { top: 100, left: 100, scrollTop: 10, scrollLeft: 10 }
 *
 * @example $("#testdiv").offset({ scroll: false })
 * @result { top: 90, left: 90 }
 *
 * @example var offset = {}
 * $("#testdiv").offset({ scroll: false }, offset)
 * @result offset = { top: 90, left: 90 }
 *
 * @name offset
 * @param Object options A hash [map] of options describing what
 * should be included in the final calculations of the offset.
 * The options include:
 *      margin: Should the margin of the element be included in the
 *          calculations? True by default.
 *          If set to false the margin of the element is subtracted
 *                                  from the total offset.
 *      border: Should the border of the element be included in the
 *          calculations? True by default.
 *          If set to false the border of the element is subtracted
 *                                  from the total offset.
 *      padding: Should the padding of the element be included in the
 *          calculations? False by default.
 *          If set to true the padding of the element is added to the
 *          total offset.
 *      scroll: Should the scroll offsets of the parent elements be
 *          included in the calculations? True by default. When true,
 *          it adds the total scroll offsets of all parents to the
 *          total offset and also adds two properties to the returned
 *          object, scrollTop and scrollLeft. If set to false the
 *                          scroll offsets of parent elements are ignored.
 *          If scroll offsets are not needed, set to false to get a
 *          performance boost.
 * @param Object returnObject An object to store the return value in,
```

```
 * so as not to break the chain. If passed in, the chain will not be
 * broken and the result will be assigned to this object.
 *
 * @type Object
 * @cat Plugins/Dimensions
 * @author Brandon Aaron (brandon.aaron@gmail.com ||
 *                                        http://brandonaaron.net)
 */
```

Here, we can see that the comments begin with a general description of the method and some brief advice about using pixel values. Following this introductory text is a list of more detailed information, with each list item beginning with an @ symbol. Notice that the name of the method (@name offset) doesn't come until after the examples. There are three examples, arranged in order of increasing complexity.

The method name is followed by parameters that the method can take. These parameters, especially the object options, are described in great detail, noting default values and what we can expect if we apply them.

The last three items provide more information about the method, including the type of data returned, its category, and its author.

If we can't find the answers to all of our questions in the Plugin Repository, the author's website, and the plug-in's comments, we can always turn to the jQuery discussion list. Many of the plug-in authors are frequent contributors to the list and are always willing to help with any problems that new users might face. Instructions for subscribing to the discussion list can be found at http://docs.jquery.com/Discussion.

Developing a Plug-in

The third-party plug-ins available provide a bevy of options for enhancing our coding experience, but sometimes we need to reach a bit farther. When we write code that could be reused by others, or even ourselves, we may want to package it up as a new plug-in. Fortunately, this process is not much more involved than writing the code itself.

Adding New Global Functions

Some of the built-in capabilities of jQuery are provided via what we have been calling **global functions**. As we've seen, these are actually methods of the jQuery object, but practically speaking, they are functions within a jQuery namespace.

A prime example of this technique is the $.ajax function. Everything that $.ajax() does could be accomplished with a regular global function called simply ajax(), but this approach would leave us open for function name conflicts. By placing the function within the jQuery namespace, we only have to worry about conflicts with other jQuery methods.

To add a function to the jQuery namespace, we can just assign the new function as a property of the jQuery object:

```
jQuery.foo = function() {
  alert('This is a test. This is only a test.');
};
```

Now in any code which uses this plug-in, we can write:

```
jQuery.foo();
```

We can also use the $ alias and write:

```
$.foo();
```

This will work just like any other function call, and the alert will be displayed.

Adding Multiple Functions

If our plug-in needs to provide more than one global function, we could declare them independently:

```
jQuery.foo = function() {
  alert('This is a test. This is only a test.');
};
jQuery.bar = function(param) {
  alert('This function takes a parameter, which is "' + param + '".');
};
```

Now both methods are defined; so we can call them in the normal fashion:

```
$.foo();
$.bar('baz');
```

We can clean up the function definitions a bit by using the $.extend() function:

```
jQuery.extend({
  foo: function() {
    alert('This is a test. This is only a test.');
  },
  bar: function(param) {
    alert('This function takes a parameter, which is "' + param +
```

```
'".');
    }
});
```

This produces the same results. We risk a different kind of namespace pollution here, though. Even though we are shielded from most JavaScript function and variable names by using the jQuery namespace, we could still have a conflict with function names defined in other jQuery plug-ins. To avoid this, it is best to encapsulate all of the global functions for a plug-in into an object:

```
jQuery.myPlugin = {
  foo: function() {
    alert('This is a test. This is only a test.');
  },
  bar: function(param) {
    alert('This function takes a parameter, which is "' + param +
'".');
  }
};
```

Though we can still treat these functions as if they were global, they are now technically methods of the global jQuery function, so the way we invoke the functions has to change slightly:

```
$.myPlugin.foo();
$.myPlugin.bar('baz');
```

With this technique (and a sufficiently unique plug-in name), we are fully protected from namespace collisions in our global functions.

What's the Point?

We now have the basics of plug-in development in our bag of tricks. After saving our functions in a file called `jquery.mypluginname.js`, we can include this script and use the functions from other scripts on the page. But how is this different from any other JavaScript file we could create and include?

We already discussed the namespace benefits of gathering our code inside the jQuery object. There is another key advantage of writing our function library as a jQuery extension, however: the functions can use jQuery itself. By labeling the code as a plug-in, we explicitly require that jQuery is always included on the page.

Even though jQuery will be included, we shouldn't assume that the $ shortcut is available. Our plug-ins should always call jQuery methods using `jQuery` or internally define $ themselves, as described later.

These are just organizational benefits, though. To really tap into the power of jQuery plug-ins, we need to learn how to create new methods on individual jQuery object instances.

Adding jQuery Object Methods

Most of jQuery's built-in functionality is provided through its methods, and this is where plug-ins shine as well. It is appropriate to create new methods whenever a function needs to act on part of the DOM.

We have seen that adding global functions requires extending the `jQuery` object with new methods. Adding instance methods is similar, but we instead extend the `jQuery.fn` object:

```
jQuery.fn.xyzzy = function() {
  alert('Nothing happens.');
}
```

 The `jQuery.fn` object is an alias to `jQuery.prototype`, provided for conciseness.

We can then call this new method from our code after using any selector expression:

```
$('div').xyzzy();
```

Our alert is displayed when we invoke the method. We might as well have written a global function, though, as we haven't used the matched DOM nodes in any way. A reasonable method implementation acts on its context.

Object Method Context

Within any plug-in method, the keyword `this` is set to the current jQuery object. Therefore we can call any built-in jQuery method on `this`, or extract its DOM nodes and work on them:

```
jQuery.fn.showAlert = function() {
  alert('You called this method on "' + this[0] + '".');
}
```

But we need to remember that a jQuery selector expression can always match zero, one, or multiple elements. We must allow for any of these scenarios when designing a plug-in method. The easiest way to accomplish this is to always call `.each()` on the method context; this enforces **implicit iteration**, which is important for maintaining consistency between plug-in and built-in methods. Within the `.each()` call, `this` refers to each DOM element in turn:

```
jQuery.fn.showAlert = function() {
  this.each(function() {
    alert('You called this method on "' + this + '".');
  });
}
```

Now our method produces a separate alert for each element that was matched by the preceding selector expression.

Method Chaining

In addition to implicit iteration, jQuery users should be able to rely on **chaining** behavior. This means that we need to return a jQuery object from all plug-in methods, unless the method is clearly intended to retrieve a different piece of information. The returned jQuery object is usually just the one provided as `this`. If we use `.each()` to iterate over `this`, we can just return its result:

```
jQuery.fn.showAlert = function() {
  return this.each(function() {
    alert('You called this method on "' + this + '".');
  });
}
```

With the return statement in place, we can chain our plug-in method with built-in methods:

```
$('div').showAlert().hide('slow');
```

DOM Traversal Methods

In some cases, our method may change which DOM elements are referenced by the jQuery object. For example, suppose we wanted to add a DOM traversal method that found the grandparents of the matched elements:

```
jQuery.fn.grandparent = function() {
  var grandparents = [];
  jQuery.each(this, function(index, value) {
    grandparents.push(value.parentNode.parentNode);
```

```
    });
    grandparents = $.unique(grandparents);
    return this.setArray(grandparents);
};
```

This method creates a new `grandparents` array, populating it by iterating over all of the elements currently referenced by the jQuery object. The built-in `.parentNode` property is used to find the grandparent elements, which are pushed onto the array. This array is stripped of its duplicates with a call to `$.unique()`. Then the jQuery `.setArray` method changes the set of matched elements to the new array. Now we can find and operate on the grandparent of an element:

```
$('.foo').grandparent().addClass('bar');
```

However, this method is **destructive**. The actual jQuery object is modified as a side effect—one that becomes evident if we store the jQuery object in a variable:

```
var $frood = $('.hoopy');
$frood.grandparent().hide();
$frood.show();
```

This code hides the `grandparent` element, then shows it again. The jQuery object stored in `$frood` has changed to refer to the grandparent. If instead we had **non-destructively** coded the method, this confusing case would not have occured:

```
jQuery.fn.grandparent = function() {
  var grandparents = [];
  jQuery.each(this, function(index, value) {
    grandparents.push(value.parentNode.parentNode);
  });
  grandparents = $.unique(grandparents);
      return this.pushStack(grandparents);
};
```

The `.pushStack` method creates a new jQuery object, rather than modifying the old one. This fixes the problem we just encountered. Now, the `$frood.show()` line still refers to the original `$('.hoopy')`. As a side benefit, `.pushStack()` also allows the `.end` method to work with our new method, so we can chain methods together properly:

```
$('.fred').grandparent().addClass('grandma').end()
                                      .addClass('grandson');
```

DOM traversal methods such as .children() were destructive operations in jQuery 1.0, but became non-destructive in 1.1.

Method Parameters

The most important parameter passed to any method is the keyword this, but of course we are free to define additional parameters. To make our plug-in's API as friendly as possible, we place required parameters at the start of the argument list. While optional parameters can be provided in the argument list as well, it is often simpler and more convenient to use a map for optional parameters.

For example, suppose our method can accept a string and a number. We could define the method to accept two arguments:

```
jQuery.fn.myMethod = function(aString, aNumber) {
  alert('The string is "' + aString + '".');
  alert('The number is ' + aNumber + '.');
}
```

If these arguments are optional, though, we have to account for four possibilities:

```
$('div').myMethod('hello', 52);
$('div').myMethod('hello');
$('div').myMethod(52);
$('div').myMethod();
```

We can check to see if the parameters are defined and if they are not defined then provide default values:

```
jQuery.fn.myMethod= function(aString, aNumber) {
  if (aString == undefined) {
    aString = 'goodbye';
  }
  if (aNumber == undefined) {
    aNumber = 97;
  }
  alert('The string is "' + aString + '".');
  alert('The number is ' + aNumber + '.');
}
```

This works in the cases where both parameters are present, just the string is given, or neither is provided. But when the number is supplied but the string is not, the number gets passed in as aString. We thus need to detect the data type of the parameter:

```
jQuery.fn.myMethod= function(aString, aNumber) {
  if (aString == undefined) {
    aString = 'goodbye';
  }
  if (aNumber == undefined) {
    if (aString.constructor == Number) {
      aNumber = aString;
      aString = 'goodbye';
    }
    else {
      aNumber = 97;
    }
  }
  alert('The string is "' + aString + '".');
  alert('The number is ' + aNumber + '.');
}
```

This is manageable with two parameters, but quickly becomes a headache with more. To avoid all this hassle, we can use a map instead:

```
jQuery.fn.myMethod= function(parameters) {
  defaults = {
    aString: 'goodbye',
    aNumber: 97
  };
  jQuery.extend(defaults, parameters);
  alert('The string is "' + defaults.aString + '".');
  alert('The number is ' + defaults.aNumber + '.');
}
```

By using `jQuery.extend()`, we can easily provide default values that are overwritten by whatever parameters are supplied. Our method invocation remains roughly the same, except using a map rather than a plain parameter list:

```
$('div').myMethod({aString: 'hello', aNumber: 52});
$('div').myMethod({aString: 'hello'});
$('div').myMethod({aNumber: 52});
$('div').myMethod();
```

This strategy scales much more nicely than data type detection. As a side benefit, named parameters mean that adding new options is unlikely to break existing code, and scripts that use the plug-in are more self-documenting.

Adding New Shortcut Methods

The jQuery library must maintain a delicate balance between convenience and complexity. Each method that is added to the library can help developers to write certain pieces of code more quickly, but adds to the overall size of the code base and can reduce performance. For this reason, many shortcuts for built-in functionality are relegated to plug-ins, so that we can pick and choose the ones that are useful for each project and omit the irrelevant ones.

When we find ourselves repeating an idiom in our code many times, it may call for the creation of a shortcut method. The core jQuery library contains some of these shortcuts, such as `.click()` as a shortcut for `.bind('click')`. These plug-ins are simple to create, as they just require passing arguments along to a core function and supplying some of our own.

For example, suppose we frequently animate items using a combination of the built-in "slide" and "fade" techniques. Putting these effects together means animating the height and opacity of an element simultaneously. The `.animate()` method makes this easy:

```
.animate({height: 'hide', opacity: 'hide'});
```

We can create a pair of shortcut methods to perform this animation when showing and hiding elements:

```
jQuery.fn.slideFadeOut = function() {
  return this.animate({height: 'hide', opacity: 'hide'});
}
jQuery.fn.slideFadeIn = function() {
  return this.animate({height: 'show', opacity: 'show'});
}
```

Now we can call `$('.myClass').slideFadeOut()` and trigger the animation whenever it is needed. Because, within a plug-in method definition, `this` refers to the current jQuery object, the animation will be performed on all matched elements at once.

For completeness, our new methods should support the same parameters that the built-in shortcuts do. In particular, methods such as `.fadeIn()` can be customized with speeds and callback functions. Since `.animate()` also takes these parameters, allowing this is straightforward. We just accept the parameters and forward them on to `.animate()`:

```
jQuery.fn.slideFadeOut = function(speed, callback) {
  return this.animate({height: 'hide', opacity: 'hide'},
                                    speed, callback);
```

```
}

jQuery.fn.slideFadeIn = function(speed, callback) {
  return this.animate({height: 'show', opacity: 'show'},
                                         speed, callback);
}
```

Now we have custom shortcut methods that function just like their built-in counterparts.

Maintaining Multiple Event Logs

As a JavaScript developer we'll find the need to display log events when various events occur. JavaScript's `alert()` function is often used for demonstration but does not allow the frequent, timely messages we need on occasions. A better alternative is the `console.log()` function available to Firefox and Safari, which allows printing messages to a separate log that does not interrupt the flow of interaction on the page. As this function is not available to Internet Explorer, however, we'll use a custom function to achieve this style of message logging.

 The **Firebug Lite script** (described in Appendix B) provides a very robust cross-platform logging facility. The method we develop here is tailored for general utility, though, Firebug Lite is typically preferable.

A simple way to log messages would be creating a global function that appends messages to a specific element on the page:

```
jQuery.log = function(message) {
  $('<div class="log-message" />').text(message).appendTo('.log');
};
```

We can even get a bit fancier, and have the new message appear with an animation:

```
jQuery.log = function(message) {
  $('<div class="log-message" />')
    .text(message)
    .hide()
    .appendTo('.log')
    .fadeIn();
};
```

Now, we can call `$.log('foo')` to display `foo` in the log box on the page.

We sometimes have multiple examples on a single page, however, it is convenient to be able to keep separate logs for each example. We can accomplish this by using a method rather than a global function:

```
jQuery.fn.log = function(message) {
  return this.each(function() {
    $('<div class="log-message" />')
      .text(message)
      .hide()
      .appendTo(this)
      .fadeIn();
  });
};
```

Now calling `$('.log').log('foo')` has the effect our global function call did previously, but we can change the selector expression to target different log boxes.

Ideally, though, the `.log` method would be intelligent enough to locate the most relevant box to use for the log message without an explicit selector. By exploiting the context passed to the method, we can traverse the DOM to find the log box nearest the selected element:

```
jQuery.fn.log = function(message) {
  return this.each(function() {
    $context = $(this);
    while ($context.length) {
      $log = $context.find('.log');
      if ($log.length) {
        $('<div class="log-message" />').text(message).hide()
                                        .appendTo($log).fadeIn();
        break;
      }
      $context = $context.parent();
    }
  });
};
```

This code looks for a log message box within the matched elements, and if one is not found, walks up the DOM in search of one.

Finally, at times we require the ability to display the contents of an object. Printing out the object itself yields something barely informative like `[object Object]`, so we can detect the argument type and do some of our own pretty-printing in the case that an object is passed in:

```
jQuery.fn.log = function(message) {
  if (typeof(message) == 'object') {
    string = '{';
    $.each(message, function(key, value) {
      string += key + ': ' + value + ', ';
    });
    string += '}';
    message = string;
  }
  return this.each(function() {
    $context = $(this);
    while ($context.length) {
      $log = $context.find('.log');
      if ($log.length) {
        $('<div class="log-message" />').text(message).hide()
                                .appendTo($log).fadeIn();
        break;
      }
      $context = $context.parent();
    }
  });
};
```

Now we have a method that can be used to write out both objects and strings in a place that is relevant to the work being done on the page.

Adding a Selector Expression

Built-in parts of jQuery can be extended, as well. Rather than adding new methods, we can customize existing ones. A common desire, for example, is to expand on the selector expressions provided by jQuery to provide more esoteric options.

The `:nth-child()` pseudo-class as implemented by jQuery allows us to find items that are at a given position within their parent element. Suppose we construct an ordered list of ten items:

```
<ol class="nthchild">
  <li>Item</li>
  <li>Item</li>
  <li>Item</li>
  <li>Item</li>
  <li>Item</li>
  <li>Item</li>
  <li>Item</li>
  <li>Item</li>
```

```
    <li>Item</li>
    <li>Item</li>
  </ol>
```

The expression `$('li:nth-child(4)')` will locate the fourth item in the list. We have seen this ability before. However, the CSS specification this selector is based on is a bit more powerful. In CSS 3, the `:nth-child()` pseudo-class is capable of taking not just integers as arguments, but any expression of the form an+b. If the position of an item is equal to this expression or any integral value of n, the item will be matched. For example, `:nth-child(4n+1)` will match item 1, 5, 9, and so on. We can add this capability to jQuery's selector engine using a plug-in.

The jQuery selector parser first breaks down the selector expression using a set of regular expressions. For each piece of the selector, a function is executed to winnow the possibly matched nodes. This function is found in the `jQuery.expr` map. We can override the built-in behavior of the `:nth-child()` pseudo-class by using `$.extend()`:

```
jQuery.extend(jQuery.expr[':'], {
  'nth-child': 'jQuery.nthchild(a, m)',
});
```

The values of this map are strings containing JavaScript expressions used to filter the elements. In these expressions, a refers to the DOM element being tested, and m is an array holding the components of the selector.

The exact contents of m vary depending on the format of the selector we're implementing, so our first step is to examine the regular expressions in `jQuery.parse` inside `jquery.js`. Looking at the matches done there, we can see that for pseudo-classes of the form `:x(y(z))`, the components in m will be:

```
m[0]  ==  ':x(y(z))'
m[1]  ==  ':'
m[2]  ==  'x'
m[3]  ==  'y(z)'
m[4]  ==  '(z)'
```

Our code for the `:nth-child()` pseudo-class calls a function called `nthchild()` within the jQuery namespace, which is where we'll do the heavy lifting (using this opportunity to rename a and m to the more understandable `element` and `components` respectively):

```
jQuery.nthchild = function(element, components) {
  var index = $(element).parent().children().index(element) + 1;

  var numbers = components[3].match(/((\d+)n)?\+?(\d+)?/);
```

```
if (numbers[2] == undefined) {
  return index == numbers[3];
}
if (numbers[3] == undefined) {
  numbers[3] = 0;
}

return (index - numbers[3]) % numbers[2] == 0;
}
```

First this function finds the index of the current node from among its siblings. This operation could be made faster by using pure DOM traversal functions, but by using jQuery methods here we can make the code more readable. We add 1 to the result since CSS specifies the `:nth-child()` pseudo-class as one-based rather than zero-based.

Once we have found the index, we break the mathematical expression down into its parts. An expression such as `4n+1` will be split apart so that `numbers[2]` is 4 and `numbers[3]` is 1. We add some special cases to deal with expressions like `4n` and `1`.

Finally, we do a little algebraic manipulation to find that if $an + b = i$, then $(i - b) / a = n$. This reveals a calculation we can perform to determine if a given index passes the test. If the element should be a part of the result set, we return `true`; otherwise, we return `false`.

With our new plug-in installed, we can now use jQuery selectors such as `$('li:nth-child(3n+2)')` and easily find every third item in the list, starting with item #2.

Creating an Easing Style

When we call an animation method, we are specifying a start and end point for each attribute we are animating. We also can tell the method how quickly to travel from point A to point B. We have not, however, been providing any indication of the manner in which we travel from A to B. The animation is not necessarily at a constant rate, and in fact by default is not.

Consider an animation of an element from left to right, fading its opacity on the way:

```
$('.sprite').animate({'left': 791, 'opacity': 0.1}, 5000);
```

If we watch the animation progress and capture the element's position at even time intervals, we get an idea of its speed during the journey:

We can see from this demonstration that the animation starts off slowly, speeds up for the bulk of the animation duration, and slows down again at the end. The practice of performing an animation at a non-constant rate is called **easing**. This default easing style, called **swing**, feels more natural and less abrupt than a purely constant rate of motion would.

We can change the easing style used by a jQuery animation by providing an extra parameter to the `.animate()` method. This parameter identifies which easing function should be used. The only function built into jQuery is the default one we just saw; to use others, we have to get them from a plug-in or write our own.

Adding new easing functions is similar to adding new selector expressions. We extend the global jQuery object to add properties to its `easing` attribute. Each property corresponds to a single easing function.

For example, suppose we wanted to implement a truly linear easing style, causing animations to progress at a constant rate from start to finish. We can accomplish this with a single-line easing function:

```
jQuery.extend({
  'easing': {
    'linear': function(fraction, elapsed, attrStart, attrDelta,
                                                    duration) {
      return fraction * attrDelta + attrStart;
    }
  }
});
```

Easing Function Parameters

All easing functions take five parameters:

- `fraction`: The current position of the animation, as measured in time between 0 (the beginning of the animation) and 1 (the end of the animation)
- `elapsed`: The number of milliseconds that have passed since the beginning of the animation (seldom used)
- `attrStart`: The beginning value of the CSS attribute that is being animated
- `attrDelta`: The difference between the start and end values of the CSS attribute that is being animated

- `duration`: The total number of milliseconds that will pass during the animation (seldom used)

Easing functions are expected to use these five parameters to produce a number indicating what the value of the parameter being animated should be at any given time. For example, suppose we are using our linear easing function to animate the height of an element from 20 pixels to 30 pixels:

fraction	elapsed	attrStart	attrDelta	duration	function value
0	0	20	10	100	20
.25	25	20	10	100	22.5
.5	50	20	10	100	25
.75	75	20	10	100	27.5
1	100	20	10	100	30

In this simple case, we can just multiply the `attrDelta` value by `fraction` to come up with the incremental distance the parameter has traveled so far. Note that the value of `elapsed` goes from 0 to `duration`, `fraction` is always equal to `elapsed` / `duration`, and the function value travels from `attrStart` to `attrStart + attrDelta`.

We can now repeat our animation using the new easing style:

```
$('.sprite').animate({'left': 791, 'opacity': 0.1}, 5000, 'linear');
```

With this easing function, our time-lapse capture of the animation reveals a different picture:

The animation is now progressing at a constant rate.

Multi-Part Easing Styles

For a somewhat more interesting animation, we can craft an easing function that follows different curves through separate parts of the journey:

```
jQuery.extend({
  'easing': {
    'back-n-forth': function(fraction, elapsed, attrStart, attrDelta,
                                                             duration) {
      if (fraction < 0.33)
        return fraction * (1.0 / 0.33) * attrDelta + attrStart;
      if (fraction < 0.66)
        return (-fraction + 0.66) * (1.0 / 0.33) * attrDelta +
                                                     attrStart;
      return (fraction - 0.66) * (1.0 / 0.34) * attrDelta + attrStart;
    }
  }
});
```

This function breaks the animation down into three equal chunks, each of which follows a linear motion. We can test the easing style in the same manner as before:

```
$('.sprite').animate({'left': 791, 'opacity': 0.1}, 5000,
                                             'back-n-forth');
```

The effect of this is that the animation will appear to proceed forward, backward, and forward once again:

Building more complex easing styles is now primarily a matter of finding the mathematical expression (or expressions) to generate the curve we want to follow, and then codifying this expression in JavaScript.

Many easing functions are already available through existing plug-ins, such as Interface.

How to Be a Good Citizen

There are a few rules to follow in writing plug-ins in order to play well with other code. We have covered some of these in passing already, but they are collected again here for convenience.

Naming Conventions

All plug-in files must be named `jQuery.myPlugin.js` where `myPlugin` is the name of the plug-in. Within the file, all global functions should be grouped into an object called `jQuery.myPlugin`, unless there is only one, in which case it may be a function just called `jQuery.myPlugin()`.

Method names are more flexible, but should be kept as unique as possible. If only one method is defined, it should be called `jQuery.fn.myPlugin()`. If more than one is defined, attempt to prefix each method name with the plug-in name to prevent confusion. Avoid short, ambiguous method names such as `.load()` or `.get()` that may be confused with methods defined in other plug-ins.

Use of the $ Alias

jQuery plug-ins may not assume that the `$` alias is available. Instead, the full `jQuery` name must be written out each time.

In longer plug-ins, many developers find that the lack of the `$` shortcut makes code more difficult to read. To combat this, the shortcut can be locally defined for the scope of the plug-in by defining and executing a function. The syntax for defining and executing a function at once looks like this:

```
(function($) {
  // Code goes here
})(jQuery);
```

The wrapping function takes a single parameter, to which we pass the global `jQuery` object. The parameter is named `$`, so within the function we can use the `$` alias with no conflicts.

Method Interfaces

All jQuery methods get called within the context of a jQuery object, so `this` refers to an object that may wrap one or more DOM elements. All methods must behave correctly regardless of the number of elements actually matched. In general, methods should call `this.each()` to iterate over the matched elements, operating on each one in turn.

Methods should return the jQuery object to preserve chaining. If the set of matched objects is modified, a new object should be created by calling `.pushStack()` and this object should be returned instead. If something other than a jQuery object is returned, this must be prominently documented.

Method definitions *must* end in a semicolon character so that code compressors can properly parse the files.

Documentation Style

In-file documentation should be prepended to each function or method definition in **ScriptDoc** format. This format is documented at `http://www.scriptdoc.org/`.

Summary

In this final chapter, we have seen how the functionality that is provided by the jQuery core need not limit the library's capabilities. Plug-ins that are readily available extend the menu of features substantially, and we can easily create our own that push the boundaries further.

We have examined the Dimensions plug-in, for measuring and manipulating sizes of elements. The Form plug-in is useful for interacting with HTML forms. We have also studied the Interface plug-in, for enabling a variety of user-interface widgets.

We have also learned how to create plug-ins with various features, including global functions that use the jQuery library, new methods of the jQuery object for acting on DOM elements, enhanced selector expressions for finding DOM elements in new ways, and easing functions that alter the rates of animations.

With these tools at our disposal, we can shape jQuery—and our own JavaScript code—into whatever form we desire.

Online Resources

I can't remember what I used to know
Somebody help me now and let me go
— Devo,
"Deep Sleep"

The following online resources represent a starting point for learning more about jQuery, JavaScript, and web development in general, beyond what is covered in this book. There are far too many sources of quality information on the web for this appendix to approach anything resembling an exhaustive list. Furthermore, while other print publications can also provide valuable information, they are not noted here.

jQuery Documentation

jQuery Wiki

The documentation on jquery.com is in the form of a wiki, which means that the content is editable by the public. The site includes the full jQuery API, tutorials, getting started guides, a plug-in repository, and more:

```
http://docs.jquery.com/
```

jQuery API

On jQuery.com, the API is available in two locations — the documentation section and the paginated API browser.

The documentation section of jQuery.com includes not only jQuery methods, but also all of the jQuery selector expressions:

```
http://docs.jquery.com/Selectors
http://docs.jquery.com/
http://jquery.com/api
```

jQuery API Browser

Jörn Zaeferrer has put together a convenient tree-view browser of the jQuery API with a search feature and alphabetical or categorical sorting:

```
http://jquery.bassistance.de/api-browser/
```

Visual jQuery

This API browser designed by *Yehuda Katz* is both beautiful and convenient. It also provides quick viewing of methods for a number of jQuery plug-ins:

```
http://www.visualjquery.com/
```

Web Developer Blog

Sam Collet keeps a master list of jQuery documentation, including downloadable versions and cheat sheets, on his blog:

```
http://webdevel.blogspot.com/2007/01/jquery-documentation.html
```

JavaScript Reference

Mozilla Developer Center

This site has a comprehensive JavaScript reference, a guide to programming with JavaScript, links to helpful tools, and more:

```
http://developer.mozilla.org/en/docs/JavaScript/
```

Dev.Opera

While focused primarily on its own browser platform, *Opera's* site for web developers includes a number of useful articles on JavaScript:

```
http://dev.opera.com/articles/
```

Quirksmode

Peter-Paul Koch's Quirksmode site is a terrific resource for understanding differences in the way browsers implement various JavaScript functions, as well as many CSS properties:

```
http://www.quirksmode.org/
```

JavaScript Toolbox

Matt Kruse's JavaScript Toolbox offers a large assortment of homespun JavaScript libraries, as well as sound advice on JavaScript best practices and a collection of vetted JavaScript resources elsewhere on the Web:

```
http://www.javascripttoolbox.com/
```

JavaScript Code Compressors

Packer

This JavaScript compressor/obfuscator by *Dean Edwards* is used to compress the jQuery source code. It's available as a web-based tool or as a free download. The resulting code is very efficient in file size, at a cost of a small increase in execution time:

```
http://dean.edwards.name/packer/
http://dean.edwards.name/download/#packer
```

JSMin

Created by *Douglas Crockford*, *JSMin* is a filter that removes comments and unnecessary white space from JavaScript files. It typically reduces file size by half, resulting in faster downloads:

```
http://www.crockford.com/javascript/jsmin.html
```

Pretty Printer

This tool *prettifies* JavaScript that has been compressed, restoring line breaks and indentation where possible. It provides a number of options for tailoring the results:

```
http://www.prettyprinter.de/
```

(X)HTML Reference

W3C Hypertext Markup Language Home Page

The *World Wide Web Consortium* (*W3C*) sets the standard for (X)HTML, and the HTML home page is a great launching point for its specifications and guidelines:

```
http://www.w3.org/MarkUp/
```

CSS Reference

W3C Cascading Style Sheets Home Page

The W3C's CSS home page provides links to tutorials, specifications, test suites, and other resources:

```
http://www.w3.org/Style/CSS/
```

Mezzoblue CSS Cribsheet

Dave Shea provides this helpful *CSS cribsheet* in an attempt to make the design process easier, and provides a quick reference to check when you run into trouble:

```
http://mezzoblue.com/css/cribsheet/
```

Position Is Everything

This site includes a catalog of CSS browser bugs along with explanations of how to overcome them:

```
http://www.positioniseverything.net/
```

XPath Reference

W3C XML Path Language Version 1.0 Specification

Although jQuery's XPath support is limited, the W3C's *XPath Specification* may still be useful for those wanting to learn more about the variety of possible XPath selectors:

```
http://www.w3.org/TR/xpath
```

TopXML XPath Reference

The *TopXML* site provides helpful charts of axes, node tests, and functions for those wanting to learn more about XPath:

```
http://www.topxml.com/xsl/XPathRef.asp
```

MSDN XPath Reference

The *Microsoft Developer Network* website has information on XPath syntax and functions:

```
http://msdn2.microsoft.com/en-us/library/ms256115.aspx
```

Useful Blogs

The jQuery Blog

John Resig and other contributors to the official jQuery blog posts announcements about new versions and other initiatives among the project team, as well as occasional tutorials and editorial pieces.

```
http://jquery.com/blog/
```

Learning jQuery

Karl Swedberg, Jonathan Chaffer, Brandon Aaron, et al. are running a blog for jQuery tutorials, examples, and announcements:

```
http://www.learningjquery.com/
```

Jack Slocum's Blog

Jack Slocum, the author of the popular *EXT suite* of JavaScript components, writes about his work and JavaScript programming in general:

```
http://www.jackslocum.com/blog/
```

Web Standards with Imagination

Dustin Diaz's blog features articles on web design and development, with an emphasis on JavaScript:

```
http://www.dustindiaz.com/
```

Snook

Jonathan Snook's general programming/web-development blog:

```
http://snook.ca/
```

I Can't

Three sites by *Christian Heilmann* provide blog entries, sample code, and lengthy articles related to JavaScript and web development:

```
http://icant.co.uk/
http://www.wait-till-i.com/
http://www.onlinetools.org/
```

DOM Scripting

Jeremy Keith's blog picks up where the popular DOM scripting book leaves off—a fantastic resource for unobtrusive JavaScript:

```
http://domscripting.com/blog/
```

As Days Pass By

Stuart Langridge experiments with advanced use of the browser DOM:

```
http://www.kryogenix.org/code/browser/
```

A List Apart

A List Apart explores the design, development, and meaning of web content, with a special focus on web standards and best practices:

```
http://www.alistapart.com/
```

Particletree

Chris Campbell, Kevin Hale, and Ryan Campbell started a blog that provides valuable information on many aspects of web development:

```
http://particletree.com/
```

The Strange Zen of JavaScript

Scott Andrew LePera's weblog about JavaScript quirks, caveats, odd hacks, curiosities and collected wisdom. Focused on practical uses for web application development:

```
http://jszen.blogspot.com/
```

Web Development Frameworks Using jQuery

As developers of open-source projects become aware of jQuery, many are incorporating the JavaScript library into their own systems. The following is a brief list of some of the early adopters:

- Drupal: `http://drupal.org/`
- Joomla Extensions: `http://extensions.joomla.org/`
- Pommo: `http://pommo.org/`
- SPIP: `http://www.spip.net/`
- Textpattern: `http://textpattern./`
- Trac: `http://trac.edgewall.org/`
- WordPress: `http://wordpress.org/`

For a more complete list, visit the *Sites Using jQuery* page at:

```
http://docs.jquery.com/Sites_Using_jQuery
```

B
Development Tools

When a problem comes along
You must whip it
> *— Devo,*
> *"Whip It"*

Documentation can help in troubleshooting issues with our JavaScript applications, but there is no replacement for a good set of software development tools. Fortunately, there are many software packages available for inspecting and debugging JavaScript code, and most of them are available for free.

Tools for Firefox

Mozilla Firefox is the browser of choice for the lion's share of web developers, and therefore has some of the most extensive and well-respected development tools.

Firebug

The *Firebug* extension for Firefox is indispensable for jQuery development:

```
http://www.getfirebug.com/
```

Some of the features of Firebug are :

- An excellent DOM inspector for finding names and selectors for pieces of the document
- CSS manipulation tools for finding out why a page looks a certain way and changing it
- An interactive JavaScript console
- A JavaScript debugger that can watch variables and trace code execution

Web Developer Toolbar

This not only overlaps Firebug in the area of DOM inspection, but also contains tools for common tasks like cookie manipulation, form inspection, and page resizing. You can also use this toolbar to quickly and easily disable JavaScript for a site to ensure that functionality degrades gracefully when the user's browser is less capable:

```
http://chrispederick.com/work/web-developer/
```

Venkman

Venkman is the official JavaScript debugger for the Mozilla project. It provides a troubleshooting environment that is reminiscent of the GDB system for debugging programs that are written in other languages.

```
http://www.mozilla.org/projects/venkman/
```

Regular Expressions Tester

Regular expressions for matching strings in JavaScript can be tricky to craft. This extension for Firefox allows easy experimentation with regular expressions using an interface for entering search text:

```
http://sebastianzartner.ath.cx/new/downloads/RExT/
```

Tools for Internet Explorer

Sites often behave differently in IE than in other web browsers, so having debugging tools for this platform is important.

Microsoft Internet Explorer Developer Toolbar

The *Developer Toolbar* primarily provides a view of the DOM tree for a web page. Elements can be located visually, and modified on the fly with new CSS rules. It also provides other miscellaneous development aids, such as a ruler for measuring page elements:

```
http://www.microsoft.com/downloads/details.
aspx?FamilyID=e59c3964-672d-4511-bb3e-2d5e1db91038
```

Microsoft Visual Web Developer

Microsoft's Visual Studio package can be used to inspect and debug JavaScript code:

```
http://msdn.microsoft.com/vstudio/express/vwd/
```

To run the debugger interactively in the free version (Visual Web Developer Express), follow the process outlined here:

```
http://www.berniecode.com/blog/2007/03/08/
how-to-debug-javascript-with-visual-web-developer-express/
```

DebugBar

The *DebugBar* provides a DOM inspector as well as a JavaScript console for debugging:

```
http://www.debugbar.com/
```

Drip

Memory leaks in JavaScript code can cause performance and stability issues for Internet Explorer. *Drip* helps to detect and isolate these memory issues:

```
http://Sourceforge.net/projects/ieleak/
```

To learn more about a common cause of Internet Explorer memory leaks, see Appendix C, *JavaScript Closures*.

Tools for Safari

Safari remains the new kid on the block as a development platform, but there are still tools available for situations in which code behaves differently in this browser than elsewhere.

Web Inspector

Nightly builds of Safari include the ability to inspect individual page elements and collect information especially about the CSS rules that apply to each one.

```
http://trac.webkit.org/projects/webkit/wiki/Web%20Inspector
```

Drosera

Drosera is the JavaScript debugger for Safari and other WebKit-driven applications. It enables breakpoints, variable watching, and an interactive console.

```
http://trac.webkit.org/projects/webkit/wiki/Drosera
```

Other Tools

Firebug Lite

Though the Firebug extension itself is limited to the Firefox web browser, some of the features can be replicated by including the *Firebug Lite* script on the web page. This package simulates the Firebug console, including allowing calls to `console.log()` to work in all browsers and not raise JavaScript errors:

```
http://www.getfirebug.com/lite.html
```

TextMate jQuery Bundle

This extension for the popular Mac OS X text editor *TextMate* provides syntax highlighting for jQuery methods and selectors, code completion for methods, and a quick API reference from within your code. The bundle is also compatible with the *E* text editor for Windows:

```
http://www.learningjquery.com/2006/09/textmate-bundle-for-jquery
```

Charles

When developing AJAX-intensive applications, it can be useful to see exactly what data is being sent between the browser and the server. The *Charles* web debugging proxy displays all HTTP traffic between two points, including normal web requests, HTTPS traffic, Flash remoting, and AJAX responses:

```
http://www.xk72.com/charles/
```

Aptana

This Java-based web development IDE is free and cross-platform. Along with both standard and advanced code editing features, it incorporates a full copy of the jQuery API documentation.

```
http://www.aptana.com/
```

C
JavaScript Closures

Let's close our eyes together
Now can you see how good it's going to be?
— Devo,
"Pink Jazz Trancers"

Throughout this book, we have seen many jQuery methods that take functions as parameters. Our examples have thus created, called, and passed around functions time and again. While usually we can do this with only a cursory understanding of the inner JavaScript mechanics at work, at times side effects of our actions can seem strange if we do not have knowledge of the language features. In this appendix, we will study one of the more esoteric (yet prevalent) types of functions, called **closures**.

Inner Functions

JavaScript is fortunate to number itself among the programming languages that support **inner function declarations**. Many traditional programming languages, such as C, collect all functions in a single top-level scope. Languages with inner functions, on the other hand, allow us to gather small utility functions where they are needed, avoiding namespace pollution.

An inner function is simply a function that is defined inside of another function. For example:

```
function outerFun() {
  function innerFun() {
    alert('hello');
  }
}
```

The `innerFun()` is an inner function, contained within the scope of `outerFun()`. This means that a call to `innerFun()` is valid within `outerFun()`, but not outside of it. The following code results in a JavaScript error:

```
function outerFun() {
  function innerFun() {
    alert('hello');
  }
}
innerFun();
```

We can trigger the alert, though, by calling `innerFun()` from within `outerFun()`:

```
function outerFun() {
  function innerFun() {
    alert('hello');
  }
  innerFun();
}
outerFun();
```

This technique is especially handy for small, single-purpose functions. For example, algorithms that are recursive but have a non-recursive API wrapper are often best expressed with an inner function as a helper.

The Great Escape

The plot thickens when **function references** come into play. Some languages, such as Pascal, do allow the use of inner functions for the purpose of code hiding, and those functions are forever entombed within their parent functions. JavaScript, on the other hand, allows us to pass functions around just as if they were any other kind of data. This means inner functions can escape their captors.

The escape route can wind in many different directions. For example, suppose the function is assigned to a global variable:

```
var globVar;

function outerFun() {
  function innerFun() {
    alert('hello');
  }
  globVar = innerFun;
}
outerFun();
globVar();
```

The call to `outerFun()` after the function definition modifies the global variable `globVar`. It is now a reference to `innerFun()`. This means that the later call to `globVar()` operates just as an inner call to `innerFun()` would, and the alert is displayed. Note that a call to `innerFun()` from outside of `outerFun()` still results in an error! Though the function has escaped by way of the reference stored in the global variable, the function *name* is still trapped inside the scope of `outerFun()`.

A function reference can also find its way out of a parent function through a return value:

```
function outerFun() {
  function innerFun() {
    alert('hello');
  }
  return innerFun ;
}
var globVar = outerFun();
globVar();
```

Here, there is no global variable modified inside `outerFun()`. Instead, `outerFun()` returns a reference to `innerFun()`. The call to `outerFun()` results in this reference, which can be stored and called itself in turn, triggering the alert again.

The fact that inner functions can be invoked through a reference even after the function has gone out of scope means that JavaScript needs to keep referenced functions available as long as they could possibly be called. Each variable that refers to the function is tracked by the JavaScript runtime, and once the last has gone away the JavaScript garbage collector comes along and frees up that bit of memory.

Variable Scoping

Inner functions can of course have their own variables, which are restricted in scope to the function itself:

```
function outerFun() {
  function innerFun() {
    var innerVar = 0;
    innerVar++;
    alert(innerVar);
  }
  return innerFun;
}
```

Each time the function is called, through a reference or otherwise, a new variable innerVar is created, incremented, and displayed:

```
var globVar = outerFun();
globVar(); // Alerts "1"
globVar(); // Alerts "1"
var innerVar2 = outerFun();
innerVar2(); // Alerts "1"
innerVar2(); // Alerts "1"
```

Inner functions can reference global variables, in the same way as any other function can:

```
var globVar = 0;
function outerFun() {
  function innerFun() {
    globVar++;
    alert(globVar);
  }
  return innerFun;
}
```

Now our function will consistently increment the variable with each call:

```
var globVar = outerFun();
globVar(); // Alerts "1"
globVar(); // Alerts "2"
var globVar2 = outerFun();
globVar2(); // Alerts "3"
globVar2(); // Alerts "4"
```

But what if the variable is local to the parent function? Since the inner function inherits its parent's scope, this variable can be referenced too:

```
function outerFun() {
  var outerVar = 0;
  function innerFun() {
    outerVar++;
    alert(outerVar);
  }
  return innerFun;
}
```

Now our function calls have more interesting behavior:

```
var globVar = outerFun();
globVar(); // Alerts "1"
globVar(); // Alerts "2"
```

```
var globVar2 = outerFun();
globVar2(); // Alerts "1"
globVar2(); // Alerts "2"
```

We get a mix of the two earlier effects. The calls to innerFun() through each reference increment innerVar independently. Note that the second call to outerFun() is not resetting the value of innerVar, but rather creating a new instance of innerVar, bound to the scope of the second function call. The upshot of this is that after the above calls, another call to globVar() will alert 3, and a subsequent call to globVar2() will also alert 3. The two counters are completely separate.

When a reference to an inner function finds its way outside of the scope in which the function was defined, this creates a **closure** on that function. We call variables that are not local to the inner function **free variables**, and the environment of the outer function call **closes** them. Essentially, the fact that the function refers to a local variable in the outer function grants the variable a stay of execution. The memory is not released when the function completes, as it is still needed by the closure.

Interactions between Closures

When more than one inner function exists, closures can have effects that are not as easy to anticipate. Suppose we pair our incrementing function with another function, this time incrementing by two:

```
function outerFun() {
  var outerVar = 0;
  function innerFun() {
    outerVar++;
    alert(outerVar);
  }
  function innerFun2() {
    outerVar = outerVar + 2;
    alert(globVar);
  }
  return {'innerFun': innerFun, 'outerFun2': outerFun2};
}
```

We return references to both functions, using a map to do so (this illustrates another way in which reference to an inner function can escape its parent). Both functions can be called through the references:

```
var globVar = outerFun();
globVar.innerFun(); // Alerts "1"
globVar.innerFun2(); // Alerts "3"
globVar.innerFun(); // Alerts "4"
```

```
var globVar2 = outerFun();
globVar2.innerFun(); // Alerts "1"
globVar2.innerFun2(); // Alerts "3"
globVar2.innerFun(); // Alerts "4"
```

The two inner functions refer to the same local variable, so they share the same closing environment. When `innerFun()` increments `outerVar` by 1, this sets the new starting value of `outerVar` when `innerFun2()` is called. Once again, though, we see that a subsequent call to `outerFun()` creates new instances of these closures with a new closing environment to match. Fans of object-oriented programming will note that we have in essence created a new object, with the free variables acting as instance variables and the closures acting as instance methods. The variables are also private, as they cannot be directly referenced outside of their enclosing scope, enabling true object-oriented data privacy.

Closures in jQuery

The methods we have seen throughout the jQuery library often take at least one function as a parameter. For convenience, we often use anonymous functions so that we can define the function behavior right when it is needed. This means that functions are rarely in the top-level namespace; they are usually inner functions, which means they can quite easily become closures.

Arguments to $(document).ready()

Nearly all of the code we write using jQuery ends up getting placed inside a function as an argument to `$(document).ready()`. We do this to guarantee that the DOM has loaded before the code is run, which is usually a requirement for interesting jQuery code. When a function is created and passed to `.ready()`, a reference to the function is stored as part of the global jQuery object. This reference is then called at a later time, when the DOM is ready.

We usually place the `$(document).ready()` construct at the top level of the code structure, so this function is not really a closure. However, since our code is usually written inside this function, everything else is an inner function:

```
$(document).ready(function() {
  var readyVar = 0;
  function outerFun() {
    function innerFun() {
      readyVar++;
      alert(readyVar);
    }
```

```
      return innerFun;
   }
   var readyVar2 = outerFun();
   readyVar2();
});
```

This looks like our global variable example from before, except now it is wrapped in a $(document).ready() call as so much of our code always is. This means that readyVar is not a global variable, but a local variable to the anonymous function. The variable readyVar2 gets a reference to a closure with readyVar in its environment.

The fact that most jQuery code is inside a function body is useful, because this can protect against some namespace collisions. For example, it is this feature that allows us to use jQuery.noConflict() to free up the $ shortcut for other libraries, while still being able to define the shortcut locally for use within $(document).ready().

Event Handlers

The $(document).ready() construct usually wraps the rest of our code, including the assignment of event handlers. Since handlers are functions, they become inner functions and since those inner functions are stored and called later, they become closures. A simple click handler can illustrate this:

```
$(document).ready(function() {
   var readyVar = 0;
   $('.trigger').click(function() {
     readyVar++;
     alert(readyVar);
   });
});
```

Because the variable readyVar is declared inside of the .ready() handler, it is only available to the jQuery code inside this block and not to outside code. It can be referenced by the code in the .click() handler, however, which increments and displays the variable. Because a closure is created, the same instance of readyVar is referenced each time the button is clicked. This means that the alerts display a continuously incrementing set of values, not just 1 each time.

Event handlers can share their closing environments, just like other functions can:

```
$(document).ready(function() {
   var readyVar = 0;
   $('.add').click(function() {
     readyVar++;
     alert(readyVar);
```

```
  });
  $('.subtract').click(function() {
    readyVar--;
    alert(readyVar);
  });
});
```

Since both of the functions reference the same variable, the incrementing and decrementing operations of the two buttons affect the same value rather than being independent.

These examples have used anonymous functions, as has been our custom in jQuery code. This makes no difference in the construction of closures. For example, we can write an anonymous function to report the index of an item within a jQuery object:

```
$(document).ready(function() {
  $('li').each(function(index) {
    $(this).click(function() {
      alert(index);
    });
  });
});
```

Because the innermost function is defined within the .each() callback, this code actually creates as many functions as there are list items. Each of these functions is attached as a click handler to one of the items. The functions have index in their closing environment, since it is a parameter to the .each() callback. This behaves the same way as the same code with the click handler written as a named function:

```
$(document).ready(function() {
  $('li').each(function(index) {
    function clickHandler() {
      alert(index);
    }

    $(this).click(clickHandler);
  });
});
```

The version with the anonymous function is just a bit shorter. The position of this named function is still relevant, however:

```
$(document).ready(function() {
  function clickHandler() {
    alert(index);
  }
```

```
$('li').each(function(index) {
    $(this).click(clickHandler);
  });
});
```

This version will trigger a JavaScript error whenever a list item is clicked, because `index` is not found in the closing environment of `clickHandler()`. It remains a free variable, and so is undefined in this context.

Memory Leak Hazards

JavaScript manages its memory using a technique known as **garbage collection**. This is in contrast to low-level languages like C, which require programmers to explicitly reserve blocks of memory and free them when they are no longer being used. Other languages such as Objective-C assist the programmer by implementing a reference counting system, which allows the user to note how many pieces of the program are using a particular piece of memory so it can be cleaned up when no longer used. JavaScript is a high-level language, on the other hand, and generally takes care of this bookkeeping behind the scenes.

Whenever a new memory-resident item such as an object or function comes into being in JavaScript code, a chunk of memory is set aside for this item. As the object gets passed around to functions and assigned to variables, more pieces of code begin to *point* to the object. JavaScript keeps track of these pointers, and when the last one is gone, the memory taken by the object is released. Consider a chain of pointers:

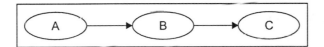

Here object A has a property that points to B, and B has a property that points to C. Even if object A here is the only one that is a variable in the current scope, all three objects must remain in memory because of the pointers to them. When A goes out of scope, however (such as at the end of the function it was declared in), then it can be released by the garbage collector. Now B has nothing pointing to it, so can be released, and finally C can be released as well.

More complicated arrangements of references can be harder to deal with:

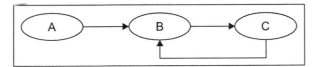

Now we've added a property to object C that refers back to B. In this case, when A is released, B still has a pointer to it from C. This **reference loop** needs to be handled specially by JavaScript, which must notice that the entire loop is isolated from the variables that are in scope.

Accidental Reference Loops

Closures can cause reference loops to be inadvertently created. Since functions are objects that must be kept in memory, any variables they have in their closing environment are also kept in memory:

```
function outerFun() {
  var outerVar = {};
  function innerFun() {
    alert(outerVar);
  };
  outerVar.innerFun = innerFun;
  return innerFun;
};
```

Here an object called `innerFun` is created, and referenced from within the inner function `innerFun()`. Then a property of `outerVar` that points to `innerFun()` is created, and `innerFun()` is returned. This creates a closure on `innerFun()` that refers to `innerFun`, which in turn refers back to `innerFun()`. But the loop can be more insidious than this:

```
function outerFun() {
  var outerVar = {};
  function innerFun() {
    alert('hello');
  };
  outerVar.innerFun = innerFun;
  return innerFun;
};
```

Here we've changed `innerFun()` so that it no longer refers to `outerVar`. However, this does not break the loop. Even though `outerVar` is never referred to from `innerFun()`, it is still in `innerFun()`'s closing environment. All variables in the scope of `outerFun()` are implicitly referred to by `innerFun()` due to the closure. So, closures make it easy to accidentally create these loops.

The Internet Explorer Memory Leak Problem

All of this is generally not an issue because JavaScript is able to detect these loops and clean them up when they become orphaned. Internet Explorer, however, has difficulty handling one particular class of reference loops. When a loop contains both DOM elements and regular JavaScript objects, IE cannot release either one because they are handled by different memory managers. These loops are never freed until the browser is closed, which can eat up a great deal of memory over time. A common cause of such a loop is a simple event handler:

```
$(document).ready(function() {
  var div = document.getElementById('foo');
  div.onclick = function() {
    alert('hello');
  }
});
```

When the click handler is assigned, this creates a closure with div in the closing environment. But div now contains a reference back to the closure, and the resulting loop can't be released by Internet Explorer even when we navigate away from the page.

The Good News

Now let's write the same code, but using normal jQuery constructs:

```
$(document).ready(function() {
  var $div = $('#foo');
  $div.click(function() {
    alert('hello');
  });
});
```

Even though a closure is still created causing the same kind of loop as before, we do not get an IE memory leak from this code. Fortunately, jQuery is aware of the potential for leaks, and manually releases all of the event handlers that it assigns. As long as we faithfully adhere to using jQuery event binding methods for our handlers, we need not fear leaks caused by this particular common idiom.

This doesn't mean we're completely out of the woods; we must continue to take care when we're performing other tasks with DOM elements. Attaching JavaScript objects to DOM elements can still cause memory leaks in Internet Explorer; jQuery just helps make this situation far less prevalent.

Conclusion

JavaScript closures are a powerful language feature. They are often quite useful in hiding variables from other code, so that we don't tread on variable names being used elsewhere. Due to jQuery's frequent reliance on functions as method arguments, they can also be inadvertently created quite often. Understanding them allows us to write more efficient and concise code, and with a bit of care and the use of jQuery's built-in safeguards we can avoid the memory-related pitfalls they can introduce.

Index

downloading 8
effects 57
events 33
features 6
first document, creating 8
forms 193
hide() function 61
HTML document, setting up 8-10
inline CSS modification 57
lambda functions 13
licence 8
page load tasks 33
pagination 152
plug-ins 299
row striping 162
selectors 17
show() function 61
strategies 7, 8
tables, manipulating 135
uses 6
XPath selectors 22
jQuery code
anonymous functions 13
executing 12, 13
lambda functions 13
new class, injecting 12
text, finding 12
writing 11
jQuery documentation
jQuery API 331
jQuery API browser 332
jQuery wiki 331
visual jQuery 332
web developer blog 332
JSON 109

K

keyboard, navigating
about 222-224
arrow keys, handling 224, 225
suggestion list, removing 226
suggestions, inserting in the field 225

L

live search
versus auto-completion 227

M

memory leak hazards
about 349
accidental reference loop 350
garbage collection 349
Internet Explorer memory leak problem 351
reference loop 350
multiple effects
animated show(), building 65
CSS, positioning with 67
custom animation, creating 66
custom animation, improving 69, 70

N

numeric calculations
about 234
curreny, formatting 235, 236
curreny, parsing 235-238
decimal places 236, 237
other calculations 238
values, rounding 239

O

online resources
(X)HTML reference 333
blogs 334
CSS reference 333
JavaScript compressors 333
JavaScript reference 332
jQuery documentation 331
web development frameworks, jQuery used 336
XPath reference 334

P

page load tasks
code execution timing 33, 34
multiple scripts on one page 34, 35
performing 33
shortcuts 35
pager
buttons, enabling 155-157
displaying 154

final code 159
JavaScript sorting 137
paging with sorting 158
server-side sorting 136
table data 136
style switcher
about 36
buttons, enabling 38
consolidating 42, 43
event handler context 40-42
styling
alternate rows 24
category cell 28
header row 28
links 22
list-item levels 20
swing, easing style 325

T

table
advanced row striping 162
collapsing 180
data, sorting 136
expanding 180
filtering 182
highlighting 172
JavaScript sorting 137
pagination 152
row highlighting 172
row striping 162
server-side sorting 136
sorting 136
tooltips 174
Thickbox 279
tools. *See* **development tools**
tooltips 174

V

validation, forms
about 203
immediate feedback 203
required fields, immediate feedback
204-207
required formats, immediate feedback 207,
208
testing 209-211

variable scoping
about 343
free variables 345

W

web development frameworks 336

X

(X)HTML reference
W3C HTML home page 333
XML document
loading 115-117
XPath reference
MSDN XPath reference 334
TopXML XPath reference 334
W3C XPath specification 334
XPath selectors
about 22
attribute selectors 22
links, styling 22
XPath support 117

Packt Open Source Project Royalties

When we sell a book written on an Open Source project, we pay a royalty directly to that project. Therefore by purchasing Learning jQuery, Packt will have given some of the money received to the jQuery project.

In the long term, we see ourselves and you—customers and readers of our books—as part of the Open Source ecosystem, providing sustainable revenue for the projects we publish on. Our aim at Packt is to establish publishing royalties as an essential part of the service and support a business model that sustains Open Source.

If you're working with an Open Source project that you would like us to publish on, and subsequently pay royalties to, please get in touch with us.

Writing for Packt

We welcome all inquiries from people who are interested in authoring. Book proposals should be sent to authors@packtpub.com. If your book idea is still at an early stage and you would like to discuss it first before writing a formal book proposal, contact us; one of our commissioning editors will get in touch with you.

We're not just looking for published authors; if you have strong technical skills but no writing experience, our experienced editors can help you develop a writing career, or simply get some additional reward for your expertise.

About Packt Publishing

Packt, pronounced 'packed', published its first book "Mastering phpMyAdmin for Effective MySQL Management" in April 2004 and subsequently continued to specialize in publishing highly focused books on specific technologies and solutions.

Our books and publications share the experiences of your fellow IT professionals in adapting and customizing today's systems, applications, and frameworks. Our solution based books give you the knowledge and power to customize the software and technologies you're using to get the job done. Packt books are more specific and less general than the IT books you have seen in the past. Our unique business model allows us to bring you more focused information, giving you more of what you need to know, and less of what you don't.

Packt is a modern, yet unique publishing company, which focuses on producing quality, cutting-edge books for communities of developers, administrators, and newbies alike. For more information, please visit our website: www.PacktPub.com.

PUBLISHING

Building Responsive Web Applications
AJAX and PHP

AJAX and PHP: Building Responsive Web Applications

ISBN: 1-904811-82-5   Paperback: 275 pages

Enhance the user experience of your PHP website using AJAX with this practical tutorial featuring detailed case studies

1. Build a solid foundation for your next generation of web applications

2. Use better JavaScript code to enable powerful web features

3. Leverage the power of PHP and MySQL to create powerful back-end functionality and make it work in harmony with the smart AJAX client

PHP Web 2.0 Mashup Projects

Create practical mashups in PHP grabbing and mixing data from Google Maps, Flickr, Amazon, YouTube, MSN Search, Yahoo!, Last.fm, and 411Sync.com

Shu-Wai Chow

PHP Web 2.0 Mashup Projects

ISBN: 978-1-847190-88-8   Paperback: 250 pages

Create practical mashups in PHP grabbing and mixing data from Google Maps, Flickr, Amazon, YouTube, MSN Search, Yahoo!, Last.fm, and 411Sync.com

1. Expand your website and applications using mashups

2. Gain a thorough understanding of mashup fundamentals

3. Clear, detailed walk-through of the key PHP mashup building technologies

4. Five fully implemented example mashups with full code

Please check **www.PacktPub.com** for information on our titles

Google Web Toolkit GWT Java AJAX Programming

ISBN: 978-1-847191-00-7　　　Paperback: 240 pages

A step-by-step to Google Web Toolkit for creating Ajax applications fast

1. **Create rich Ajax applications** in the style of Gmail, Google Maps, and Google Calendar

2. **Interface with Web APIs** create GWT applications that consume web services

3. **Completely practical** with hands on examples and complete tutorials right from the first chapter

Building Websites with Joomla! v1.0

ISBN: 1-904811-94-9　　　Paperback: 250 pages

A step by step tutorial to getting your Joomla! CMS website up fast

1. Walk through each step in a friendly and accessible way

2. Customize and extend your Joomla! site

3. Get your Joomla! website up fast

4. Also available covering Joomla v1.5 Beta

Please check **www.PacktPub.com** for information on our titles

Printed in the United States
108164LV00005B/47-52/A

9 781847 192509